LIVES ELSEWHERE

LIVES ELSEWHERE
Migration and Psychic Malaise

Natale Losi

with contributions by

Franceline James

Saskia von Overbeck Ottino

translated by

Brett Shapiro

The International Series of Psychosocial Perspectives on Trauma, Displaced People, and Political Violence

SERIES EDITOR: Renos K. Papadopoulos

KARNAC

LONDON NEW YORK

First published in 2006 by
H. Karnac (Books) Ltd.
6 Pembroke Buildings, London NW10 6RE

Italian edition: *Vite altrove. Migrazione e disagio psichico*, published by Feltrinelli, Milan, 2000.

British Library Cataloguing in Publication Data

A C.I.P. for this book is available from the British Library

ISBN: 1-85575-465-7

Edited, designed, and produced by Communication Crafts

Printed in Great Britain by Hobbs the Printers Ltd, Totton, Hampshire

www.karnacbooks.com

To my ancestors, to Carol who reminds me of them,
and to Luigino who went to join their house

CONTENTS

PART II

ACKNOWLEDGEMENTS

I would like to thank the people who, in various ways, have helped me with this book. First, I owe a particular debt of gratitude to the members of the ethnopsychotherapy group in Geneva, and its director Franceline James, author of one of the contributions: nearly everything that I know of ethnopsychiatry and the pleasant aspects of my migration are due to them. I cannot name them individually, but I hold each one of them in my heart. I would like to add special thanks to the Editor of this series, Renos K. Papadopoulos, for the invaluable preciousness of his friendship. It would have been difficult to finish this book without Carol, who was able to maintain an appropriate distance to support my concentration and serenity and contribute the warmth necessary for writing. My friends of Ikaria have done the rest. And even if they are now part of an invisible universe, I would like to thank my ancestors, without whom neither my children nor I would exist. This book is dedicated especially to them.

Geneva, January 1999

Rome, March 2006

ABOUT THE AUTHOR AND CONTRIBUTORS

Natale Losi, a family psychotherapist, medical anthropologist, and sociologist, has extensive professional experience in African countries (Mali, Ethiopia) as well as in various conflict and post-conflict societies (Albania, Bosnia, Kosovo, Palestine, Serbia). He is currently the Head of the Psychosocial and Cultural Integration Unit at the Regional Mediterranean Mission of the International Organization for Migration, based in Rome. Through its clinical and academic experience he has developed the ethno-systemic-narrative model, as described in this book and in other recent titles, including *Psychosocial and Trauma Response in War-Torn Societies: The Case of Kosovo* (2000); *Archives of Memory: Supporting Traumatized Communities through Narration and Remembrance* (2001); and "L'uovo bianco della gallina Bianca, ovvero la terapia delle coppie miste nell'approccio etno-sistemico-narrativo", in *Famiglie immigrante e psicoterapia transculturale* (ed. M. Andolfi, 2004).

Franceline James, a psychiatrist and psychotherapist, is in charge of ethnopsychiatric consultation at the University Hospital in Geneva, Switzerland.

Saskia von Overbeck Ottino is a medical doctor specializing in psychiatry and psychotherapy for children, adolescents, and adults and is also a psychoanalyst. She has been working in the ethnopsychiatric field since 1990 and leads two ethnopsychiatric consultations in Geneva and Montreux. She is in charge of the Centre of Psychological Care for Immigrant Families, of the Association Appartenances in Geneva.

SERIES EDITOR'S FOREWORD

This is a most fitting book to launch Karnac's latest book series, The International Series of Psychosocial Perspectives on Trauma, Displaced People, and Political Violence.

Lives Elsewhere: Migration and Psychic Malaise offers English-speaking readers one of the best examples of continental European approaches to working psychologically with refugees and migrants. Unfortunately, the relevant literature in English, by and large, hardly acknowledges these continental perspectives, tending to remain close to Anglo–North American traditions. Yet, as readers will discover, there is a great deal of richness in these neglected approaches.

This particular book is mainly based on the "ethnopsychiatric" approach, which extends traditional psychiatric, psychological, and psychotherapeutic horizons by connecting them with theories and methods borrowed from anthropology and sociology. Moreover, as Natale Losi clarifies in the Introduction, this book introduces an additional innovation to ethnopsychiatry which he calls "ethno-systemic-narrative". This is a most apt description because this book, in effect, combines ethnopsychiatric elements with insights from systemic approaches as well as from the theory and practice of narrative psychotherapies. This unique blend interrelates the inner and outer worlds, the intrapsychic, the interpersonal, and the wider socio-political realms, appreciating the importance of rites and rituals as well as the power of narrative accounts. An additional strength of this book is the inclusion of case studies that demonstrate clearly how one can use this approach in practice.

A purist may consider the book as somewhat dated, insofar as it does not include much up-to-date literature in the field. However, the approach itself as well as the themes and methods of practice that it addresses and introduces are by no means dated; they cannot possibly be dated. These are typical issues that all practitioners working with this group of people are grappling with, and this book offers a wealth of material that can instruct and inspire all readers.

Natale Losi is the head of the Psychosocial and Cultural Integration Unit of the International Organization for Migration, and he is both an anthropologist and a systemic family therapist. His considerable experience as a practitioner and theoretician, and as an organiser and manager of projects with refugees and traumatized people, enables him to bring to the book his sensitivity and expertise in ways that make the book accessible not only to the specialist reader but also to practitioners of psychotherapy in general (regardless of the groups they work with), as well as to social scientists and other professionals and interested persons who are addressing issues of forced migration.

Renos K. Papadopoulos
Series Editor

PREFACE

Lives Elsewhere was first published in Italian—the language in which I wrote the book—in 2000, six years ago. The manuscript had been submitted to the Italian publisher, Feltrinelli, about two years before that; the first publication in English therefore comes almost eight years after the book was originally written. Much has changed during those eight years, in the world at large and for me as well, even if I limit myself to considering only my professional psychotherapeutic practice. My work has increasingly taken place in war-affected areas: Kosovo, Serbia, Palestine. And the "ethno-systemic-narrative" approach that I propose has been tried and validated in all of these situations—in the field, where the wars have been or are still being fought, but also at "home", in our own countries, which are far from war zones. In addition to the news brought to us by newspapers and television, there are the people themselves, in flesh and blood, refugees escaping from their homelands.

The ethno-systemic-narrative approach, originally elaborated through my work with migrants, has recently had to address the effects (the invisible wounds) of war. Unfortunately, these wounds take a long time to heal. I am not so naïve as to propose this approach as a panacea for all ills. However, in order to understand how effective this way of thinking about therapy may be, I have used this approach in war zones, through my work with patients and their families and communities. I have also used this approach in the countries of exile, many of them wealthy countries that are fearful of welcoming the thousands of refugees who arrive on their shores. In ancient Greek, *therapéia* means "service, cure", which is primarily understood as services rendered to the gods, as worship, and to men through medical treatment. In both meanings, the therapist does not act exclusively within a narrow space and within an isolated and dual relationship with a patient. The therapist avoids reducing the wounds inflicted by life to mere personal and pathological matters, whether these wounds are inflicted by migration or by war. The therapist makes them public, choral, endowed with a sense that can be understood by the patient without having to resort to symptoms and stories that induce illness. The first step towards healing is often the awareness of not being the only one to have experienced such suffering.

In this book, I attempt to provide a theoretical base and clinical examples for the application of an approach that knows how to offer therapeutic alternatives to the reigning medicalization of illness and suffering. Those who migrate, whether by force or by choice, cannot be placed in the position of being a victim or of being ill, even if they have undergone periods of serious psychic and existential malaise. In ethno-systemic-narrative thought, the migrant is the modern hero. As in fairy tales, this hero can experience failure and have need of allies in order to reach his or her goals. From my perspective, the therapist is precisely this ally.

Natale Losi
Rome, April 2006

LIVES ELSEWHERE

Introduction

Easter 1998 was cold. Or rather it felt cold in the South of Italy on our long-awaited holiday. After emigrating to the damp cold of Switzerland, we were returning to our imaginary homeland, where in our dreams the sun always shone. We had packed for warm sunny weather. Fortunately, at the last minute I had also packed a wool jumper for my son Alvise, who usually wears just a shirt. One particularly cold evening, Alvise reluctantly put on the sweater: "a swot's sweater". From that evening on, the "swot's sweater" became part of our family vocabulary.

On holiday I had also brought along a textbook on family therapy, and as I turned its pages, it occurred to me that this was a "swot's book". At that moment, I decided that the present book, which I had been thinking about for some time and had already outlined, would not be a book "by a swot", nor "for swots". I wanted to write a simple and clear account of complex material based on ethnopsychotherapy and migrations—or, if one prefers, on the mental health of immigrants. Now that the book is finished, I realize how difficult and ambitious such a project is. The only way to be simple and clear seemed to be to avoid writing a "definitive" text dealing with such intractable material and, instead, merely to try to clarify some key questions. But which questions, among the many possibilities?

The book moved between two principal poles: migrations and psychological malaise. I began from the more accessible pole of migrations, to deal successively with the more complex pole of psychological malaise in our culture and in others. I sought to combine the two poles and to provide some key concepts for the reading of this combination.

The first part of this book is divided into three chapters. In the first chapter, I seek to show how the traumas attached to emigration reproduce possible psychological conflicts that the individual had experienced before migrating. I analyse some specific characteristics of these traumas and propose the use of image and metaphor to help the migrant assimilate through acting like a hero in folk tales, interpreting this as a transformation of rites of passage practised in traditional cultures. Following on from this interpretation, I propose to interpret the ethnopsychotherapeutic work as a way to retell and reweave the parts of a trauma that migration tends to fragment and scatter.

In the second chapter I describe the ways of thinking that underlie the visions of the world, of sickness and of mental health, that are different from the dominant Western culture. Since a considerable part of the immigrant population (and not only them) base their actions on these ways of thinking, they can indicate various therapeutic paths of treatment with immigrant patients (and not only them). In particular, I analyse and discuss the characteristics of the ways of thinking colouring the culture "subordinate" to "ours"[1] in a diachronic perspective and "others" in synchronic perspective. I seek to emphasize the central importance of the concept of syncretism, in its function as a binding force between a way of thinking that is purely rational and linear and other ways of thinking that may be circular or refer to multiple universes.

In the third chapter, I focus on the work of Tobie Nathan, an inevitable point of reference—whether positively or negatively—in any discussion of ethnopsychotherapy in Europe, and I then show the concrete application of different psychotherapeutic approaches to the needs and problems of migrants. A dynamic process is emerging from this, less rigid than Nathan's views, but full of respect for his original approach.[2] If asked to name my approach, I would suggest the "ethno-systemic-narrative" model.

The case of Armand, reported in the second part of the book, describes, as I have already mentioned, a kind of approach that from the point of view of the setting's structure, is close to Nathan's methodology and his therapeutic outlook, even if the key interpretative concepts are ethno-systemic-narrative and his are ethnopsychiatric.

Some recurrent examples from art, migration, and daily life

In an article published in the Italian daily *l'Unita* years ago, Annamaria Guadagni criticized the main character of the film *Palombella rossa*, Michele (i.e. the director Nanni Moretti), for creating a dichotomy between past and present.

Past and present, the times in which we are often or continually torn or confused when planning for the future, often take the form of mirage and homesickness for immigrants. Guadagni, turning to Michele, criticizes this rigid juxtaposition between past and present: "Well, yes, it makes us suffer too much, this thing we don't want to name. Why not say it: homesickness is getting you down . . . it is an important feeling, accept it, don't waste it."[3]

In Guadagni's interpretation, Moretti makes a symbolic migration: in time, in his mind, in his psyche. And he is scolded for rejecting both the present and the past: a form of "either/or" strands him between two shores, two cultures, two ways of thinking, and living the transition as a dichotomy or a schism. We can look at the experience of migrants in these terms, as well as the experience of therapists. When faced with the difficulty of interpreting the experience and the malaise, the latter often opt for a dichotomy: they either use academic Western language or reject it.

In this book, I try to show how both options are unproductive. Nothing should be considered invalid and tossed into the rubbish bin. There are also nuances in therapies, just as there are in the skin colour of immigrants and everyone else, in our voices, in language, in art, in music. Many people today speak of a multi-ethnic world, a creole society. We need to be capable of responding to this complexity and accepting it. To see everything in a two-dimensional way is bound to stifle any growth and deny one's own memory. But to mature and become open to the subtleties in ourselves that mirror and integrate the complexity of this creole society, we need to learn how to use instruments that are somewhat more subtle and refined. In this research, nostalgia emerges as both a feeling and an indispensable tool for therapeutic work.

Guadagni also writes: "In every Indo-European language there are precise links between the substantive *noos*, which signifies mind, thought, and the verb *nostos,* which means return. The thesis is that returning home represents returning to light from darkness. It is a returning to consciousness, which explains the closing of the semantic circle with respect to the ancient derivation of *noos* and *nostos* from the verb *nèomai,* which means to return home."

The migrant is basically no different from us, especially those of us who ask ourselves about the significance of experiences and feelings such as nostalgia, a going back towards our origins: "to belong to oneself and be oneself, it doesn't seem very wrong to be nostalgic. In Western culture this is evident in references to Ulysses and Ithaca; in fact Odysseus embodies this duplicity, man's ingenuity and his desire to return home." Claudio Magris (1991) also writes about this, in *Ithaca and Beyond:* the place of return and of flight in a journey through the great themes of our culture. And our culture is that of heroes who follow a straightforward odyssey, without end and without return, "in a continual questioning of and experimentation with the world, which makes them continually become different and other than who they are."

At the end of *Psychoanalysis of Migration and Exile,* Leon and Rebecca Grinberg write in their epilogue, "It is clear that there is no return, one is always going away" (Grinberg & Grinberg, 1990, p. 227).

In these pages, I try to show how the experience of being an immigrant can stimulate a positive attitude—and not self-pity or commiseration, which tend to be pathological—whenever the figure of the hero from Indo-European folk tales and legends is superimposed. This does not mean, as some might assume through simplification, that I am proposing to treat immigrants by using fables, but that the latter can serve as a guide to the therapist in his or her effort to stimulate in the patient an active and conscious position in confronting his or her own afflictions. In chapter one there is a discussion of the possible therapeutic functions of the metaphoric use of fables when working with migrants. The following are the main justifications for using them:

1. The experience of migration is and has a "life" in itself. It therefore reproduces, within one or more of its phases, the same critical points that characterize the course of an individual life. If within one or more of these phases there is a transition that was not or could not have been fully elaborated through the resources furnished by one's personal history or culture, a "disorder" is produced.
2. The rites of passage in so called traditional cultures, which articulate the principal critical points in life (birth, childhood/adolescence/marriage, parenthood, death), reproduce the same structures as the migration experience (detachment/departure, arrival, integration, return).
3. Within their structure, fables reproduce the rites of passage foreseen by the traditional cultures of many migrants. Consequently, they also reproduce the phases of the migration experience.
4. The migration experience creates a fragility in migrants because they no longer find themselves surrounded by the basic elements of their environment and history that had protected them up until their departure. Even the sense of cultural belonging becomes uncertain.
5. Within a structural framework that symbolically assimilates migration, rites of passage, and fables, attributing the role of hero to the life of the migrant can help the therapist to strengthen the ability of the patient to take an active position.

The migrant experiments with the superimposition of myth and reality; of symbols and concrete material conditions; of remembered time and migration in his or her inner world; of spaces for migrating and places in the external world. By placing the metaphor of internal voyage side by side with real migration, I am trying to help the migrant create a link between the inner world and the outer world.

It has been noted that for many migrants the experience of return is lodged in myth more than in an actual plan. However, when the subject of return is introduced into psychotherapy, even through the mediation of fables, it takes on an entirely different meaning. In fact, in the therapeutic setting, the basic issue of the migrant is that of being between two worlds. Within a family of migrants, the malaise is usually developed by those who remain at the intersection of different worlds and lack the tools for completing this work of *passeur* or ferryman, of a bridge between two worlds, cultures, generations, places, often between village and city. In therapies with migrants, it is the therapist or therapeutic group that must assume responsibility as *passeur*, lightening a burden that patients often find unbearable, becoming for them the good village in their memory.

Literary metaphors locate this sense of being between two worlds in a codified order that has settled over time, which the professional medical-psychological world—too often separated from other types of human knowledge and reality—finds difficult to grasp. For example, legends and folk tales are not only myths or stories for children, but a codified tool that enables a paragon to be established and builds a new order in a world that had lost it. What traditional cultures have transmitted through the wisdom of their healers and played out in rites of passage survives only as fable in our society.

The experiences of migration are—like much of life—complex, contradictory, and diverse, and perhaps this is why a literary genre like the fable or folk tale can register this complexity better than attempts at simplification used by many pseudo-scientists.

The impossibility—and the necessity—of a synthesis

Transitions and conflicts in life are not restricted to today's migrants; the best of Western literature has been describing them admirably since time immemorial.

In "Mephistopheles' Embarrassment", Claudio Magris (1991) tells us that Italo Svevo, in one of his last written works (interrupted by his death), "imagines that the old man who is the protagonist of these short stories is about to go to bed, where his elderly wife is already in a sluggish and heavy sleep."

The old man imagines that Mephistopheles could come at midnight, to offer him something in exchange for his soul. He realizes that he wouldn't know what to request; certainly not youth, which is senseless and cruel, although old age is intolerable; nor immortality, since life is unbearable, "even though this knowledge of 'unbearability' would not ease the anxiety about death." Thus it is clear to him that he has nothing to ask of Mephistopheles, who in turn no longer has anything to offer him. And with this image of the poor devil duped, the old man starts to laugh as he gets into bed, waking his wife who growls, "Lucky you, you still want to laugh at this hour."

Magris uses the parable to show us individual consciousness in a complex society, confused by a daily life that pulsates with passions and tensions. "To the unitary model of a form of reasoning able to comprehend contradictions, discontinuities, diversities and the negative, filtering everything through the light of an essential principle or at least a determined spiritual direction, the explosion of myriad unities or multiple subunities enters the scene, an anarchy of atoms, each claiming its own unharnessed independence and simultaneously venturing forth in all possible directions, without choosing or discarding any."

In this description of a literary individual, the figure of the immigrant seems to finds its place emblematically, given the absence of a central value or a homogeneous culture as point of reference. This emblematic positioning concerns not only the immigrant but also our relationship to the immigrant as therapists and citizens. Thus the experience of our encounter with this individual, this "other", is lived as a reflection of our existential experience and the inadequacy of theories and nosographies to understand disturbances and behaviours that our manuals did not foresee.

Theories reflect what happens to individuals. Magris also recalls that Musil defines his (and our) times as an epoch "in which being is merely a delirium of many and the relationship between people consists of dissociation". He remarks, "The eclipse of the foundation, and all unified thought, is undeniable, and undeniable are those liberating aspects with respect to the systems that have attempted to force life onto a single one-way track. Nevertheless it remains to be seen whether this eclipse is joyful" (Magris, 1991, pp. 5–9).

These literary references lead Magris to speak of uprootedness. Uprootedneses and nostalgia, therefore, are the basic themes of our time. But perhaps in this new century (and millennium) we can leave these themes behind, together with the tendency towards withdrawal and individualistic crises. Thanks to our encounter with the "other" and the "others," we can now move forward, searching together for a truer unity, a centre, a relationship that is both existential and theoretical, towards a more satisfactory response.

If the model of Western rationality has now failed in its universal pretexts, it is time to recognize the existence of other forms that reason has assumed in the course of history in other civilizations.

These are the themes that I take up in the second chapter, referring to the interpretations of illness and treatment in traditional cultures—"ours" (i.e. subjugated in the Western world) and "others". In chapter three, I describe the practical application of these concepts in clinical work with immigrants, discussing in particular Nathan's approach, aware of the ambiguities in which this particular relationship between doctor and patient is discussed. A meeting/clash is played out between different cultures, therapeutic training and qualifications, socialization, and integration in the respective societies to which they belong, and thousands of other conditions of implicit or explicit disparity. The ambiguous nature of this relationship is reflected in the theories formulated on "primitive" thought by Claude Lévi-Strauss and Mary Douglas. Lévi-Strauss elaborates a structuralist hypothesis to explain both the essential requirement for effective therapy in traditional treatment (that the healer, the patient, and the community should belong to the same culture), as well as the mode of communication/contact and exchange between different subsystems (from the symbolic to the material: soul/body). It assumes that the subjects engaged in treatment share his or her own culture and subscribe to his or her own beliefs. On the other hand, Douglas attributes to the "primitive" a point of view that is different from what it first appears to be. The English anthropologist maintains that "primitives" in some way "pretend" when, for example, they claim to believe in a series of events caused by supernatural forces. The pretence would arise out of the necessity to reinforce a sense community and society upheld by politically fragile structures.

Frequently the therapist—the ethnotherapist who works with immigrants coming from "other" cultures—finds him/herself inside this very ambiguity. Which of the two theories to follow, then? Perhaps there are others? What does the patient think and actually feel? Which vision of the world emerges when the patient is interpreting his or her own malaise? In fact, the patient belongs to two worlds, and his or her disorientation and nostalgia pull the patient irremediably into this ambiguity. Psychology, and, in general, scientific studies of man (such as medicine), should be aware that we are babbling and that the presence of people around us who are "different" makes our babbling more emphatic. Perhaps in past times, when it was easier to consider our culture as dominant and total, as a single point of reference, we would not have given sufficient attention to the ways of thinking and to the cultures of "others".

To conclude

In such a hurried and distracted world—one that is increasingly marked by relocations, trips, escapes, returns, confusions, meldings—who can understand, even in the context of treatment, the multiple functions of theory, literature, and fable?

For my birthday I was sent an excerpt from Kafka's short story *Ulysses and the Sirens,* which has had something to do with both writing and this book.

> "In fact, when Ulysses arrived, the powerful singers were not singing, believing either that only silence could overwhelm such an adversary, or forgetting to sing at the sight of the blissfulness emanating from Ulysses' visage. He, on the other hand, we might say, did not hear their silence, believing that they were singing and imagining that only he had been protected from hearing them. He caught sight of them turning their heads, breathing deeply, noticed their eyes were full of tears, their lips parted, and believed that everything was part

> of the melodies that, unheard, were lost all around him. But his expression remained fixed on the distance. The sirens disappeared in the face of his resolve, and just when he was closest to them, he knew nothing more of them."

Aware of how hard it is to put thoughts into words and how reductive words can be, I offer these pages to the reader in the hope that he or she will be able to hold on to the complexity of a theme that might seem oversimplified at times.

Notes

1. By "ours" (here and throughout the volume) I mean the contemporary culture of Western Europe, and of Italy in particular.

2. I would like to emphasize, that while both Nathan and I trained as anthropologists and psychotherapists (although Nathan's psychotherapeutic training is psychoanalytic and mine is family systemic), I began to work with immigrants from an ethnopsychotherapeutic perspective much more recently, in 1994. In other words, the group to which I belong in Geneva has adopted the type of therapeutic setting devised by Nathan. But, through my clinical experience I have reached the conclusion that some of Nathan's views, especially in his most recent works (see chapter three), are due on the one hand to his communication strategy—which I might define as "mass-media provocation"—and on the other to his tendency to see things as a folklorist from that single dimension of traditional cultures. In my view, this is the least convincing aspect of Nathan's thinking and perhaps is due to his limited experience of first-hand fieldwork in traditional societies.

3. This is also a recurrent theme in our conversations during ethnopsychotherapy sessions. By "our sessions" I mean, here and elsewhere, those held within the work of the Geneva group.

PART I

CHAPTER ONE

The structure of migration trauma in ethno-systemic-narrative practice: initiation rites and fables

> *Harmony between European nations has been achieved despite and precisely because they have allowed the weakest members to be excluded and persecuted.*
>
> Hannah Arendt, "Nous autres réfugiés" (1987)

Immigrants are a widely diversified social group; consequently it is difficult to make general or generalizing statements about them and improper to use a term to designate them globally, except out of linguistic necessity. Moreover, migration processes have a life of their own, independent of both our schematizations and national politics. They are a living body, not a passive object to be handled with no expectation of an intelligent response. The failure to recognize this peculiarity has led to rigidly imposed actions whose processes and social movements are completely contradictory to those intended by the institutions that implement them. This is the case with French migration politics of the second half of the 1970s; the block on granting visitors' permits led to the interruption of the periodic and seasonal migrations from the

Maghreb and French-speaking black Africa, transforming them into permanent, and partially clandestine, migrations.

To approach an understanding of the dynamics of migration, it is important to consider not only the causes that unleash migration but also the socio-demographic, cultural, and psychological characteristics of those who emigrate. The elusive nature of the phenomenon, however, is reflected in the variability of certain key concepts necessary for defining the socio-anthropological characteristics and conditions, such as family, poverty, kinship ties, and rights.

At first sight, economic motives appear to be the principal ones, followed by violent events such as war, famine, and persecution, which provoke temporary migrations, sometimes destined to become permanent. However, it has been observed that in similar circumstances while some individuals from certain areas/communities/villages will emigrate, others or significantly fewer will not.

This phenomenon can be more fully explained by referring to a culture of emigration, which enables certain groups within a population to relocate to other countries using networks established through relatives, neighbours, and friendships. This culture also embraces the imitation and myth of the possibility of "making one's fortune" in the new country. In other words, in addition to the economic (structural) component, it is important to take the cultural dimension into account in any analysis of migration, including the importance that could be attached to the implicit requests for migration in the Western media.[1]

A second characteristic of these migration processes is the typical evolution of their social composition. Some scholars have identified four phases in the so-called "chain of migration" (see in particular, Reyneri, 1979; Sayad, 1990):

- first phase: young single male workers; short-term stay;
- second phase: workers who are not so young, and those who are highly qualified; longer stay;
- third phase: presence of women, adolescents, and children, a greater need for social assistance; establishment of permanent residence;

- fourth phase: immigration reflects the population of origin in its complexity; ethnic structures develop.

The phases proposed here obviously represent a schematic point of reference, which adheres only partially to a considerably more complex reality. In the last several years in particular, the immigration phenomenon has become more turbulent. "When development is particularly rapid," Jacques Decornoy (1996a) remarks, "it has correspondingly destabilizing social effects and increases the urge to migrate." And, citing Teitelbaum (1993), he continues, "The modernization of the rural communities, which increases agricultural productivity, contributes . . . to the disintegration of the social fabric and traditional economic relationships and consequently favours the exodus of populations from the country towards the city. But rapid urbanization brings saturation of the job market and unequal income distribution. The urban environment stimulates aspirations and disseminates information about international emigration and the possibilities of taking part among those who only have access to low-wage labour and live on the fringes of the national economy." Therefore, it is important to look at these processes globally, in particular the interconnections between local, national, and international ones.

Other authors have articulated the phases of the migration process differently. Booth (1992), for example, gives greater weight to the process than to the demographic or cultural characteristics of the individuals caught up in them. This leads him to emphasize how the process of migration had already started in the country of origin, with the creation and development of a new category of potential migrants. They pass through a period of uncertainty and transition in their new status, undergoing ordeals more or less formally set by the leaders of the community. In other cases the decision-making process is less formal. It does not involve the participation of other family members and/or the community and is therefore defined roughly as an individual choice.[2]

Alternatively, Sluzki (1979) has proposed seeing the migration process as a sequence of phases that expresses what happens to the immigrant during the experience of migration, independent of the fact that it may be voluntary or forced. In his view, the migration process would follow these steps:

1. the preparatory phase;
2. the departure (act of migration);
3. the period of "overcompensation";
4. the period of "decompensation";
5. the period in which transgenerational issues emerge.

Apart from the differences in their depth and articulation, these analyses share the limitation of a certain levelling-off of attention given to the individual experiences of migration and a detachment from the previous experiences and future expectations of migrants. For example, in a fragmented vision, the function of "return" as a part of the collective imagination of migrants tends to be left in the shadows.

In my therapeutic experience, it is clear that in each phase or group of phases of the migration process, migrants had corresponding psychological issues. What is more, the phases of migration merely retrace the preceding life experiences of these individuals, which are the framework on which their personalities have been constructed.

The preparatory phase, for example, seems to be characterized by alternating highs and lows, with periods of euphoria that are suddenly followed by prolonged moments of low activity and a sense of "heaviness."

The departure, in turn, is influenced by conflicting feelings that emerge depending on the specific situation. In the "euphoric" period of *overcompensation,* many migrants seem to be (or wish to be) unaware of the stresses of their departure, while in the *decompensation* phase a rather stormy process begins, which is characterized by changes in the role of the family, conflicts, and an increase in somatic and psychiatric symptoms. From Sluzki's point of view, if there should be a protracted delay in the family's adaptation to the new situation, the consequences will inevitably emerge in the second generation.

Some writers have criticized Sluzki's model, since he bases his interpretation essentially on psychological reactions to the departure, without taking into account the variables introduced by the social and political organization of the society of arrival. In particular, Sundquist (1994) has emphasized that exile is an experience influenced by circumstances linked to the society of origin as well as the society offering asylum. On his part, Åhlund (quoted in Sundquist, 1994, p. 28) has insisted on migration as a process of continual change, which begins in the social context of the country of origin and continues in the new country—in particular, the parameters of space and time—for generations and generations. This uninterrupted process could be subdivided into three phases:

1. intensified *socialization* reinforcing the awareness of one's own cultural identity;
2. *de-socialization,* with the dissolution of traditional values and assimilation of new ones;
3. *re-socialization,* or assimilation of new values and a new cultural identity.

According to Åhlund, the unfolding of this process is to a large degree determined by the interaction of two different dynamics: forces that work "from behind", in the form of a cultural inheritance; and forces that work "from ahead" and represent the present time, the "here-and-now." Always following her point of view, belonging to the class of migrants would be highly relevant in influencing the process of change, even for entire generations. In my opinion, Åhlund does well to focus on two dimensions—psycho-cultural and social-structural—that are usually prevalent in determining immigrants' state of well-being or malaise. In fact, although different social politics are adopted towards immigrants in different countries, immigrants more than anyone else invariably belong to the least privileged sector of the population. This means that in all phases of the migration chain, they tend to have more difficult and strenuous working and living conditions, suffer the greatest levels of unemployment and employment instability, and experience greater discrimination and prejudice than the local population.

However, within this general picture very different situations arise. For example, in Italy the percentage of unemployed people is lower among immigrants than among the local population. Immigrants show greater willingness to change their place of residence or work and more readily accept jobs that are strenuous and sometimes unprotected—in other words, paradoxically, in opposition to their contractual weakness in the job market. It might be more elegant or more neutral to call this their flexibility.

Another writer, Hertz (1981), identifies a sequence of phases in the migration experience that are characterized by stress. He lists:

1. a pre-migratory phase, characterized by high expectations of a positive nature;
2. a coping stage, which is subdivided into three consecutive phases:
   a. impact
   b. rebound
   c. settlement.

According to this scheme, the impact phase would be characterized by a succession of brief periods of euphoria followed by relaxation, a sense of accomplishment, and satisfaction. The rebound second phase would quickly follow, with feelings of disappointment and discontent, anger, withdrawal or depression; finally there is the most realistic and positive phase, of settling, accompanied by a more or less strong sense of belonging.

In my experience, and that of many colleagues, the phase that Hertz defines as *rebound* is the most important for understanding the effects of migration on the psyche;[3] withdrawal, in particular, is the most pronounced indication. In this period, in the observations and records of many patients but also of those, like me, who have experienced emigration directly, marginal and "normal" episodes become sources of disproportionate anxiety and nervousness. Meetings or social occasions that would be experienced as relaxing and pleasant in one's own country can be experienced as stressful, often for linguistic reasons. For some immigrants, if these situations are anxiety-producing, they give rise to feelings and disturbances of a psychological origin, which often affect their motor skills. "It is as if my eyes and ears had stopped working", they sometimes say.

Another aspect of the condition of withdrawal, based on our clinical experience, is the tendency to babble exhibited by some patients. This is a form of useless loquacity in which nothing of importance is actually communicated. The use of incomprehensible discourse—or, at least, what seems to be that for the therapist and the local interlocutors—could be interpreted as a defence against possible questions that would compel the patient to enter into contact with an external world experienced as threatening. Paradoxically, this expedient also serves to lessen the burden of solitude.[4] It has also been observed that some patients enhance this verbal behaviour using clown-like mime and body language.

In other words, withdrawal can be interpreted as a choice of isolation from a new context—that is, a mechanism of self-protection in response to difficulties imposed by a foreign language and by a flow of countless new stimuli that can represent other factors of stress.[5] Therefore, withdrawal can have a beneficial and physiological effect, serving as a coping mechanism, if it is temporary. Should the rebound phase persist and stabilize into a destructive behaviour, the immigrant risks becoming caught up in a vicious circle of regression, which might be erroneously interpreted as chronic psychosis, and precipitated into a destructiveness with no escape. In these cases, isolation does not come only because the immigrant is considered a "foreigner" or "stranger", but also derives from the family and the people around him or her, in addition to the individual's own particular qualities, his or her deepest being.

In my experience, and as also confirmed in the literature, this happens most frequently in the cases of immigrants who are forced to leave and who, in their own country or in their travels to the host country, have been subjected to violence, torture, or mistreatment for a long time. They may even have been caught up in or responsible for episodes of this sort in order to save their own lives.[6] Their behaviour becomes progressively more limited, elementary, almost stereotyped, egocentric, and hypotonic. If the situation becomes chronic, the negative emotions from which the subject is trying to escape—which we could call feeling like a social intruder— paradoxically intensify. Thus the circuit risks closing and the level of rebound becoming fixed or crystallized. During this phase, in which the dimension of withdrawal and isolation predominates, attitudes of anger and outbursts of rage, hostility, and aggressiveness can suddenly appear without apparent justification. Since these individuals experience difficulties communicating with an external world that they feel is treacherous, they turn against the people nearest to them, often family members, friends, or colleagues at work.

Observing that aggressiveness is often connected with thoughts and behaviours of a totalitarian nature, Eitinger (1981) provides an explanation in terms of a weakening of the individual's perception of his or her own identity, which the immigrant tends to reconstruct using more primitive models and totalitarian behaviours to connect with or draw attention away from experiences in the external world. For example, an exaggerated chauvinism can be observed, especially in the workplace, or an uncalled-for externalizing of values, habits, discussions, experienced as characteristics of the old cultural traditions (see Stanfield & Dennis, 1993).

It has been rightly observed that this mechanism of reverting to a past that is more imaginary than real accounts for the high percentage of immigrants (higher than the percentage within the population from which they came) who become literally captured by the most extreme, fundamentalist, and bizarre religious sects. This is a form of compensatory behaviour that immigrants develop in an attempt to combat a sense of deprivation, inferiority, and loss of real values from their original background (see Eitinger, 1981). Diffidence and suspicion are other extremely common feelings in the rebound phase, connected to the experiences that preceded the migration as well as the difficulties in understanding and coming to terms with all the novelty encountered in the place of arrival.

In this book, the detailed (and I hope thorough) description of migratory conditions is aimed at showing the possible connections with specific psychological vulnerabilities of migrants. Therefore, I believe that it would be helpful to focus on the essential charac teristics of a specific group of migrants, the so-called forced migrants—that is, refugees, those requesting asylum.[7] I shall also call them "the exiled", a term that strikes me as the most comprehensive of those available, as well as the most appropriate for describing a common condition of the internal world of immigrants and refugees—in particular, because it is difficult to make a clear distinction between "voluntary" and "forced" migrants (just as it is difficult to distinguish precisely between the inner world and the outer world), and, above all, because the experience of exile is present, in varying degrees, in migrants.

In working with the exiled, psychiatry and politics are clearly linked. In the emblematic case of Bosnia, Michel Grappe maintains that the international impunity granted to the so-called ethnic cleansing has caused, and will continue to cause, psychic damage to the refugees who were its victims, reinforcing the psychological disturbances of their parents and children (Grappe, 1993). These affirmations weigh on our personal and professional consciences like boulders. Even though we try to concern ourselves with specifically psychological matters, we would like to keep them impermeable to law and politics.

According to a report focusing on the former Yugoslavia written by the emergency section of the European Union, of the more than four million people who fled or were evacuated, as estimated by the United Nations in April 1995, more than 700,000 individuals suffered from severe psychic trauma in Bosnia-Herzegovina and Croatia alone (see Anger, 1995).

Deploring the fact that no one thought to provide a remedy for the suffering or psychic damage of these people, the author of the report stressed that this lack of an adequate intervention would doubtless have repercussions on the two generations to follow. It would show in the increase in alcoholism, the use of drugs, and the increase in the suicide rate and, more generally, mental disorders.[8] The report indicated a certain number of factors that cause psychosocial stress, which, although elucidated in the Yugoslavia case study, are certainly applicable more widely. The factors are:

1. economic deprivation;
2. break-up of the social order, separation of families, disappearance of some family members;
3. modification of social roles and their devaluing;
4. psychic and psychological violence;
5. ethnic persecution;
6. loss of home, country, family members, friends;
7. danger and abuse undergone in the course of flight;
8. type of welcome on arrival after the flight;
9. the living conditions and sense of inclusion at the collective centres and in private houses;
10. uncertainty about the future.

I shall briefly analyse some of these elements.[9] Often we consider the conditions of refugees as a short-term situation that begins at the moment of flight. However, flight is accompanied by a constellation of multiple losses and is more often than not preceded by traumatic events: bombings, shootings, massacres, capture, imprisonment, separation, torture, death. On the other hand, flight in itself is a traumatic event, nearly always experienced in conditions of uncertainty, precariousness, and risk. Refugees—especially those who have not voluntarily fled or escaped as a precaution but have been actively hunted, threatened, or persecuted—are, for the most part, unable to talk about it for years. After fleeing, they often find themselves trapped by some law that is both judicial and existential and in itself generates traumas. In exchange for survival, they descend into a situation outside the world, of continual transit, which repeats the exclusion and violence they have already lived through in a less drastic way—a sort of limbo for the living dead.

To be exiled means, therefore, both to have lived through tragic events, which take the form of many ties severed, and to relive these tragic events continually, not only in the realm of fantasy or nightmare which often accompanies exile for a long period of time, but also in actual daily life. We shall analyse all of these components, as they constitute material that is specific and essential to understand in psychotherapeutic work.

Of all the breaks connected to flight, the dispersion and cutting-off of family members seems to produce the most prolonged traumatic effect. Dispersion often implies a conflictual experience. On the one hand, reuniting with dear ones left behind in the country of origin is the most frequent request; on the other, when this actually happens in the country of immigration, the family members go through a period of depressive mourning. They are aware that there is no longer anyone waiting for them in their homeland, and perhaps all of their possessions will be lost, if this has not already happened, and their hope of return becomes ever dimmer.

Members of the same family often take flight at different times. The first to leave are usually the young or adolescent sons, who are old enough to manage the journey on their own; they leave the country at the instigation of their parents when they become aware of a dangerous situation. Their legal status is the most generic: they are students or so-called economic immigrants (i.e. motivated by employment). Thus, within the same family there can be extremely different experiences and places of arrival that are distant, even on different continents.

The dispersion of families, which is often intergenerational, is one of the causes of suffering most frequently lamented by the exiled. From the point of view of psychological work, the different legal and social conditions in which family members are found are of scarce importance. Does it make sense to think that a son who has left before the most savage episodes of a war suffers less than a father or a brother who flees later and has acquired the right to asylum?

The exiled frequently experience the drama of the disappearance of one or more members of the family. When this occurs in a situation of refuge, the problem amplifies because the social and family context has vanished, taking with it those expressions of mourning appropriate to the traditions of the migrants' own culture and faith. "While in normal conditions mourning departs from a common knowledge base . . . mourning by refugees for a missing family member must be conducted under the added burden of a deformed and imposed knowledge. . . . There are no points of certainty, law and social order are completely lacking or are deficient, and the social dimension is ambiguous; without the confirmation of someone sufficiently important, the narcissistic contract falls apart and, in the end, funeral rites are dismantled and destroyed" (Braun de Dunayevich & Pelento, 1989).

An accumulation of material and symbolic breaks and losses takes place, from country, land, home, culture, work—in other words, from their *residence*, "the entire social fabric in which they were born and have managed to find their distinct place in the world"(Arendt, 1982, p. 276). The loss of residence simultaneously brings the loss of the links created through practical and symbolic activities; added to this loss is the extreme difficulty of establishing another residence, "because there is no place in the world where emigrants can go without finding themselves under the severest restrictions" (p. 276).

The lack of all these *enveloppes psychiques*[10] is accompanied inevitably by changes and loss of social roles, especially in terms of work. It is probable that this aspect, at least for those who are exiled from so-called developing countries, is especially hard on the men. But the shifts in the reciprocity/complementarity of male/female roles contain the most dramatic "breaks" (both psychic and familial). It has been written that "all of these different levels of loss transform individuals in the world into individuals outside the world" (Chauvenet, 1996, p. 37).

For one who is in exile, yet another wound comes out of the profound sense of injustice and the resentment at not being understood or accepted. The request for justice is not only individual but also collective and does not necessarily harbour a sense of revenge. As Kaës (1989) keenly emphasizes, it means, above all, the opposition to the act of erasing memory and denying the possibility of transmitting it: "What is concealed as if it had not taken place has no place or takes on the meaning of influencing the course of individual and collective histories."

Following these multiple breaks, we often observe conditions in the exiled of self-abandonment, self-neglect, and disillusionment—disillusionment often connected with surprise, a sense of guilt and inadequacy for not having understood a situation that has led to the cruelty of exile. Chauvenet (1996, p. 41) analyses this specific condition, likening it to the one Ferenczi has defined as "psychic compassion": "This [psychic compassion] must have been preceded by a sense of security which switched to a sense of disappointment following the events; first they had too much faith in themselves and their surroundings; afterwards, too little or none at all. They had overestimated their own resources and lived under the mad illusion that such a thing could never happen; 'not to me'" (Ferenczi, 1968, p. 140).

Disillusionment therefore follows incredulity or coexists with it. In the Bosnian case, for example, many people still speak of the astonishment they felt when they had learned that neighbours belonging to another ethnic group had been warned of an attack on their city or village and had escaped in time.

Again in the case of Bosnia, many refugees, as well as people who had never left their town, describe a depressive condition that is widespread in their particular, and more or less restricted, context, a context to which they may no longer feel that they belong. This condition can be associated with a sort of extended sense of social guilt or, as Held (1988) observes, an introjection of repulsion for the aggressor. "This last mechanism gradually develops its self-destructive power through the fundamental impossibility of any reconciliation with the object. . . . This reaction, which can be defined as negative melancholy, leads the victim to undervalue himself or herself in the hope of containing his or her own executioner" (p. 1422).

So it is possible to consider abandonment as a form of defence and of self-help for many exiled people enduring conditions of great suffering. It is also a transactional space that creates a bridge between the previous time and the present. Within the therapeutic situation or in the community of arrival, this space can help the individual to become welcome in a container-group that can serve as a new protective layer in which values and feelings are shared. On the other hand, the feeling of abandonment can be an obstacle to mourning, especially in traditional cultures that do not give it an individual character but require the presence and the support of the community.

The condition of the exiled has also been likened to that of prisoners, because of the restrictions of all types of rights and the impossibility of actively participating in social life. In addition to the loss of freedom, refugee families, who are often guests in an affluent consumer society, are mostly limited to the consumption of essentials. In many refugee camps visited in Italy and elsewhere, the promiscuity, lack of intimacy, and obsessive control of comings and goings point out the affinity with totalitarian institutions.[11] As I have already said, this experience has the effect of repeating the refugees' experiences that had led to their original flight. This is a common psychic experience for refugees and is also shared by many immigrants.

Using sociological and anthropological literature as a point of departure, Julia Braun de Dunayevich and Maria-Lucila Pelento have identified three fundamental social elements that enable a person to gain full access to his or her culture: funeral rites and practices, the prohibition of incest, and the prohibition of cannibalism (Braun de Dunayevich & Pelento, 1989, p. 92). Of these basic and structuring social rites, the ritual of the funeral and the associated care given to the corpse is the one denied most frequently to those who are in exile. This is due to a number of factors, including the lack of a community to bestow a sense of ritual, the splintering of the family, economic reasons, the rules and norms of the country of arrival, and other countless material impediments (e.g. the absence of a cemetery for those of a certain religion).

In research conducted on former Yugoslavia, an episode illuminating this theory is recounted, which I shall summarize. An elderly Bosnian woman had lost thirteen family members, massacred under her very eyes. The most dramatic aspect for her was the impossibility of doing something for her dead family, who were left on the street for a week. She took refuge in Croatia with her only remaining granddaughter, and several days later the young girl was struck and killed by a car. The woman remembers with grief the infamy and inhumanity of the situation in which she found herself, without enough money to buy a coffin. The little girl was put in a plastic rubbish bag. The poor woman ended her story by speaking of the effect of reparation and consolation she had received from a local family who had invited her to put the little girl's body temporarily in their cellar until it could be returned home. Thanks to them, she was able to begin re-establishing her sense of belonging to the world of human beings (see Chauvenet, Despret, & Lemaire, 1996, pp. 45–83).

For all intents and purposes, the impossibility of conducting funeral rites prevents the separation of the world of the dead from that of the living, the organization of a culturally shared period of time together with one's group to acknowledge the passage from a world that is visible to one that is invisible. In many popular cultures it is said that when the dead cannot be buried, they return to visit the living. In 1928, Hertz had already written, "Give death its due if you don't want it lingering inside the group".

Using psychological terminology, we could say that survivors come to terms with the dead through the enactment of traumas. Often this is the only way to remain in contact with the dead who have not been adequately buried.[12] We shall see later, both in chapter three and in the description of the case of Armand in chapter six, other patterns and motives for acting out these traumas.

Therefore, only through rituals that are shared socially and culturally is it possible to separate the dead from the living and the past from the present, and to rebuild the basis for succession and affiliation. A condition that impedes the active fulfilment of these rites—as often is the case objectively for the exiled, refugees, or immigrants—favours the invasion of what is real by the most utter horror, precisely in those spaces where social life is most richly symbolized. This means the confusion of the dead with the living, temporal chaos, the impossibility of a collective and individual belonging to ancestors and all those who have preceded us to the land of the dead. It is not by chance that, in Amharic, "illness" (*beshita*) literally means "not having put things in order with the ancestors".

One of the most frequently used terms in connection with immigrants is "uprooting". In the specialized literature on the mental health of migrants, the experience of uprooting is linked with the category of trauma. Naturally the experience of migration can be lived in more or less traumatic ways. The so-called voluntary immigrants undergo a trauma that is quite different from those unable to return to their own country for various reasons, often political, and who emigrated because of violence or natural disasters or were victims of war, had been confined in concentration camps, or had experienced other types of persecution.

Considering that the idea of uprooting is normally associated with the loss of values, habits, and customs that are cultural and material in nature and provided a protective layer or context within which one was supported and secure throughout the former migratory experience, an in-depth analysis of the literature on migrants can enable the various facets of this experience to be identified.

There is general agreement that linguistic difficulties and the consequent gap in communication are at the core of the experience of being uprooted. According to many, the greatest stress for immigrants occurs in the area of linguistic communication. Women, usually confined to domestic work and child care, seem particularly to feel this difficulty. Within immigrant families, they are often the ones who are the least integrated into the new surroundings, and frequently this social isolation replicates the one within the family, in which the role of wives and mothers becomes devalued to the point of enclosing them in a sort of existential vacuum, which has rightly been called the result of a process of "multiple negativity" (Morokvasic, 1981).

Together with language, the cultural gap can certainly represent a strong stress factor for some immigrant groups. This is the case, for example, with many immigrants who move from a small village in their country into a large Western city and suddenly experience the differences between a family context that is protective and the impersonality of urban outskirts, where values, habits, customs, ways of behaving and doing things, and family relationships are often completely new and, in many cases, are in conflict with the immigrants' previous experiences. Some authors have been emphasizing this crisis for some time, a true collapse of values brought on by the conflict between traditions and the impact of new social expectations. One consequence is that many migrants have difficulty orienting themselves in a big city and keep themselves in a kind of isolation within their own neighbourhood. Second-generation immigrants experience another barrier, particularly during adolescence: the generation gap with their parents, which is much more accentuated than the "normal" one. (Erik Erikson had already described this process in 1968, in *Identity and Uprootedness.*) These family dynamics prove to be an additional stress factor for immigrants.

Prejudice is another problem that immigrants experience daily. In addition to skin colour, even a trace of foreign accent can create an occasion for prejudice. These are the points of departure for the clear line of demarcation between the local population and the immigrants, between "them" and "us". In this sense, the immigrants are seen more as a group than as individuals. Littlewood and Lipsedge (1982) emphasize how ethnic identity constitutes one of the most profound representations of the concept of self, and they point out that racial prejudice towards immigrants can have extremely negative repercussions, including a high incidence of medical and psychiatric misdiagnoses.

Another significant stress factor for immigrants is the anxiety and insecurity connected to the continual search for work (and to the precariousness of the work itself). There is an extremely high rate of workplace accidents.

Furthermore, immigrants who have left their families behind in the country of origin are concerned for their well-being in the face of all the objective hardships of life, and they also fear the disintegration of the family, a fear that is more or less realistic.

It was once aptly noted that the experiences of many immigrants function as a sort of microscope that tends to over-magnify their personality traits, their way of reacting to difficulties, and their feelings of fear, anxiety, inadequacy, and loneliness. This same magnification is also true for their positive experiences and feelings. A typical example of this "exaggeration" can be found in the words of one of the immigrants we have followed: "When I arrived I was full of hope, but very quickly my expectations were shattered. The world suddenly became different. We are completely rootless, we have lost our point of reference in the world. I feel like I've fallen from a cloud."

Often immigrants—and not only those who seek psychological help—feel strongly influenced by the climate of the place of immigration. Like other characteristics of their own country, the weather is also idealized. They also miss their own food greatly, as well as the different elements surrounding food: its preparation and the place and time that the meals are eaten. Compared to where they come from, it is very different to live in the outskirts of a central or northern Europe city, where darkness falls early in autumn and winter, the shops close between five and six o'clock in the afternoon, and most food is sold in supermarkets, with an impersonal relationship between customers and personnel.

All these factors weaken the immigrants' ability to face an experience that is already in itself harsh and stressful. It is as if a vicious circle has taken hold, in which the reduced capacity for reaction and the accumulation of stress give rise to regression and disintegration of the personality. Extreme poverty seems to be the basic condition that causes migration. In reality, other coincidences must be taking place in order to arrive at such a choice. These coincidences concern the internal situation of departure as well as the external and, in particular, the attraction that the society of arrival can exert for various reasons. Delia Frigessi (1993) rightly says, "The speed with which immigration transforms itself has put not a few theories that had been taken for granted in crisis" (p. 43). In particular, Frigessi emphasizes the passage from the theory of push–pull, to the hypotheses of socio-economic and cultural distance (not to mention logistical) to those on the importance of the migratory tradition, specifying how the present theory that associates migration with mental illness is particularly insidious, defined by the author as "the pathological model of immigration".

Taking the complex and dynamic nature of the phenomena into account, it is nevertheless possible to state that while in traditional societies with a strong cultural identity shared by a group, the decision to migrate—like all other decisions—is settled, or in any case influenced, by the community in the societies that are most marked (I would like to say wounded) by the processes of modernization, many decisions to migrate are also individual ones. In other words, if in the former the choice to migrate is made in harmony with the culture, in the latter it represents a clear break.

There are also camouflaged decisions to migrate. They are more frequent than one would believe and can have psychopathological consequences that are hard to understand without making reference to the categories and knowledge accumulated in ethnopsychiatry and psychiatric anthropology. (For an application of this approach, see Losi, 1996.)

Obviously, belonging to one or the other of these migratory choices brings with it, in every phase of migration, phenomenologies and migratory experiences that are completely different. Zin-Doung[13] maintains, for example, that the emigration of a significant number of women from her country is due more to the desire to escape unbearable personal conditions of private violence—often sexual and within the family—than to indigence. The same variability can be found in the group of migrants defined synthetically as the exiled. We can therefore conclude that the modalities of choice for migration are essentially tied to culture, personal and social relationships, and the individual or collective experiences of the migrant him/herself.

Since the late 1960s, a distinction has been introduced in sociological literature on migration between two principal categories of non-voluntary migrants: the impelled and the forced. In the former, the migrant has a certain margin of choice in deciding whether to leave or not, while in the latter there is no choice. Nevertheless, the border between the two categories is not always clear. Migrants belonging to the first category have also been called "anticipatory refugees"; those in the second category, "acute refugees". While the former feel in danger and leave in their own time, the latter leave home suddenly.

This distinction not only has a theoretical value, but also has specific consequences on the level of internal psychological experience, as well as the external level of acknowledgement of, and relationships with, those who have remained. Above all, the experience of someone who was able to make a choice after careful consideration is completely different from that of someone who had to choose in haste. In research that I conducted on Yugoslavian refugees housed in the refugee camps in Italy, it emerged that about a quarter of the refugees, had they been able to go backwards in time, would have done all they could to stay in their home country. It should be noted that at the time of the survey (summer–autumn 1994), the war in Bosnia was in one of its cruellest phases. The survey results indicate the need of attachment to something that is irremediably lost and, in reality, no longer exists. In fact, among the refugees who tried to return, not even a third were content to have done so, 40% thought they had made a mistake, and 8% were already thinking of leaving again (Losi, 1995). For these refugees, thinking twice was therefore a concrete modality for not being in the world, of living in limbo, of colluding with the "behind-the-scene forces"; the same "forces" that participate in the construction of the two shores, in time and in space, experienced in the course of exile—shores that are no longer an acceptable or accepting cover, or that no longer exist.

To be a refugee or a migrant, which is certainly influenced by the modalities of and motives for the departure in some way, therefore means dragging behind a very long, perhaps endless, "double". "The lacerations of someone who chooses the condition of the journey are terribly ambiguous: to someone who voluntarily leaves Zagreb, Belgrade, Sarajevo—each situation with its own peculiarities—not only his or her own town appears in a dream, but Yugoslavia when it was entire. . . . Yugo-nostalgia is no longer a sentiment with political colours. The memories of the vanished country are confused with those of a country during a time of peace" (Janigro, 1994, p. 8).

Therefore, easy interpretations are not acceptable—that is, those interpretations that attribute the causes for departure and the suffering of the migratory experience, even in the case of refugees and exiles, to a single dimension, with a schematic separation of refugees' experiences into two distinct and uncommunicating worlds: a *there* that is bad and unbearable and a *here* that is good and redeeming. If we were to accept this simplification, we would no longer be able to understand the perverse effect of repetition that is often provoked by our framework of reception.

Furthermore, on the level of understanding ethnic disturbances, this approach would not help at all, since it flattens the complexity of the motivations for departure, obscuring the understanding of the "double" that every immigrant carries, a "double" that is devalued by us, convinced as we are of the unity of our culture and the attraction it holds in comparison with "others". But if that is the case, I do not see how we can explain what this migrant says: "according to the criteria of the industrialized European world, we are poor peasants, but when I embrace my grandfather I feel rich, as if I were a note in the very heartbeat of the universe" (Tayeb Salih, 1992, p. 74).

The description of the condition of the exiled could continue at length, accompanied by many other examples. However, for the purposes of this work, what has been described so far is sufficient to enable me to show a fundamental connection in the following chapters. The capacity and sensitivity of the therapist to share with the patient the suffering of "living in limbo" enable certain helpful movements of "influence" acted out by the therapist (or the therapeutic group) to emerge during the sessions.

Inner world and outer world

The figure of the immigrant has been repeatedly delineated using categories of inclusion and exclusion and has been associated, above all, with the concept of "the stranger", who, in Simmel's definition, is the ambivalent person *par excellence,* living within society as a producer of wealth, but outside it as a non-citizen: "He is at the same time near and far, excluded and included. He comes from outside, but now he is an integrating part of the group. Within the community, he occupies a marginal but positive position, which consists of strengthening the internal role, encouraging social change, and taking on an economic function that is rejected by the other members of society or is not suitable for them" (Simmel, quoted in Tabboni, 1984, p. 13).

The ambivalence of the stranger-immigrant is not only sociological but, to a great extent, cultural and psychological. In fact he or she needs to make "a superhuman effort to bear up without succumbing to devastating feelings such as grief for losses endured. At the same time he or she needs to sustain yet another superhuman effort to respond appropriately to the needs of the moment" (Calvo, 1977). It is possible that the ambivalence of the migrant is due in part to a psychic swinging of boundaries, perceived as confusion by the new interlocutors. During and after the first phase of emigration, an anxiety can arise that is persecutory, confusing and depressing. According to Léon and Rebeca Grinberg, "The anxiety of confusion arises out of difficulties in distinguishing between feelings about the two primary sources of interest and conflict: the country and people abandoned and the new environment recently reached. . . . Emigration can revive the triangular oedipal situation in which the two countries symbolically represent the parents as sources of ambivalence and conflicts of loyalty. Sometimes they can represent the parents as separated, experienced as if one of the two had made a pact of allegiance to the detriment of the other" (Grinberg & Grinberg, 1990, p. 94).

Psychological malaise of the immigrant can also be triggered by unresolved conflicts in the past or by the impact of the culture shock of emigration. More than one author differentiates between a pathological development of emigration, with crises of unresolved identity, depression, and chronic failure to adapt socially, and a so-called healthy development characterized by vicissitudes of identity derived from culture shock (the distinction can be found in, for example, Garza-Guerrero, 1974). The "healthy" development would be essentially connected to the function of "self-limiting crises" produced by the culture shock: ample description of this phenomenon has been provided above. (Various types of coping mechanism used in different cultures form part of this: see Ticho, 1971, in addition to numerous more recent interpretations, e.g. van der Veer, 1992.)

A metaphorical model and its use in therapy

In order to provide an adequate description of the complex and subtle multiplicity of the migration phenomenon, I believe it is useful and productive to rely on metaphors like the journey and, especially, the fable, rather than rigid sociological categories. "Leaving is a bit like dying", according to an old adage. The fear of becoming lost, or of irretrievably losing at least a part of one's own life and identity, is at the root of why many people would rather die than leave, whereas others (a minority) leave with such a heavy burden that can only be expressed, sooner or later, through psychological suffering and malaise.

In the Indo-European folk tales that he has analysed, Propp (1958) indicates several constants, which he calls functions, common to all popular folk tales. There are thirty-one, and their articulations enable the form taken by all of the fables to be described.[14]

Distancing of the hero
Prohibition
Infraction
Investigation
Denunciation
Entrapment
Connivance
Damage (or loss)
Mediation
Consensus of the hero
Departure of the hero
The hero put to the test by the gift-giver
Reaction of the hero
Provision of the magical means
Transfer of the hero
Struggle between hero and antagonist
The hero marked
Victory over the antagonist
Removal of the disaster or initial loss
Return of the hero
His persecution
The hero rescues himself
The hero arrives home incognito
Claims of the false hero
The hero is given a difficult task

Accomplishment of the task
Recognition of the hero
Unmasking of the false hero and the antagonist
Transfiguration of the hero
Punishment of the antagonist
Marriage of the hero

One function concerns the hero, the protagonist of the tale, who is forced to embark on a journey and overcome a series of tests and, in the end, to show his innocence, protect his family, vanquish the enemies of the community, and so forth. (As in fables, in popular aetiology and traditional cultures these enemies can be both earthly and supernatural figures.) In our cultural roots, there is a link between the person who emigrates and that of the hero, both of whose ultimate objective is to return home after having faced a number of obstacles and mortal dangers

However, the fable represents the point of view of a narrator who belongs to the same community of origin as the hero and is placed at the conclusion of the migratory adventure. The hero/migrant is actually only recognized as such at the end of the tale, after he has overcome the many challenges that await him. Then he is recognized by both his own people as well as those he has met during his journey. Analysing the components of the fable from the point of view of the people he encounters along his way, the hero/migrant will often be seen as an undesirable, a danger, someone to fight. Most of the people he meets on his journey will be obstacles to him, which he will have to overcome by demonstrating his own good faith and capacities, and eventually succeeding in being seen in a good light.[15]

One of the difficulties that the hero/migrant might face in the course of his journey is that of falling ill, often due to a curse, sorcery, or witchcraft. Overcoming such a challenge often requires the help of a friendly person, usually a wise person who knows the secret of healing. If, therefore, from the point of view of the original community, the migrant can be compared metaphorically to a deviant or a hero—and according to which his departure will decided individually or collectively—the community with which he will gradually come into contact will not always offer a warm welcome.

An anthropological reading of fables places the experience of return in the myth—that is, in the imagination of the migrant. However, the use of the thoughts of return in psychotherapy with migrants, even through the mediation of fables, carries a meaning that is completely different from myth. We shall see this in another part of this book (particularly in chapter three; in addition, for the application of this approach, see my version of the case of Armand in chapter six).

In the fable, the tension of being between two worlds, which is common to the hero and the migrant, is located in a fixed order; in fact, it is not only myth, nor children's story, but a codified tool that makes comparisons possible, a new order in a world that has lost its order.[16] In the folk tale, the variety and complexity of migratory motivations are also recorded, which bear on the departure, the course of the journey, and its possible developments. The economic push (to "seek one's fortune") is never the only reason—there are always others.

I have made reference to Propp's *Morphology of the Folktale* (1958), which has provided me with the valuable metaphor of the folk tale for analysing the conditions of migrants: in fact, in the course of developing my hypotheses, two of his other books have also been relevant, *Fairy Tale Transformations* (1971) and *The Historical Roots of Fairy Tales* (1986). In the latter, Propp sets forth a convincing case, arguing that there has been a passage from initiation rites in what he terms primitive society to the ancient form of magical folk tales. In this case, the tales would be an evolved form of initiation rites.[17] If Propp's hypothesis were not only credible but "true", folk tales would narrate what actually took place once upon a time and what still takes place in many societies and cultures.

Gianni Rodari has also written about this:

> When boys reached a certain age, they would be separated from the family and taken into the woods . . . where the medicine men of the tribe, clad in a way to make them terrifying . . . (which makes us think of magicians and witches) . . . would make them undergo ordeals that were difficult and sometimes deadly (all heroes of folk tales meet them in the course of their journey . . . the boys would listen to the tales of the tribal myths and be given weapons (magical gifts which, in fairy tales, are

> handed out by supernatural donors to the heroes in danger) . . . and finally they were allowed to return home, often with another name (the heroes of fairy tales often return home incognito) . . . and they were mature enough to marry. . . . [Rodari, 1979, p. 72]

I am convinced that, just as the structure of initiation rites is repeated in the folk tale, in therapy with migrants coming from other cultures (but not only them) it is important to take up and reconnect the parts of the ritual that have been broken into pieces. Throughout the centuries, folk tales have begun to live when ancient rituals have disappeared, leaving only a metaphorical story in their place. Migrants face a similar process. Although they have not had centuries at their disposal to metabolize the enormous changes weighing on their shoulders, it is important to reconstruct an order within which they can find themselves again and which they can accept, independently of the fact that the order is identical to their original myth. We can call this specific therapeutic approach the *principle of influence*: a possible technique of treatment that, in the specific case of migrants (but which could also be effective for anyone who is facing an important change—adolescents, couples in crisis, etc.), gives sense to his or her experiences that are psychologically painful and full of conflicts. In some way, with different instruments, all therapies function in this way (e.g., see Stern, 1987).

From this perspective, the work of exchange between patient and therapist could be none other than a continuation of the relationship that in the past, but even now in some cultures, took place between the community and special individuals, such as *griots* and healers, medicine men and shamans. (In subsequent pages, I discuss this process further, particularly the analogy between diverse "professional" figures in the traditional societies and in our societies, respectively.) In fact, as Propp affirms, throughout the centuries *griots* have progressively betrayed the memory of ritual, transforming it into folk tale and modifying it slowly but surely to meet the needs of the latter, introducing variants to accommodate social changes (including migrations) undergone in times past. In a certain sense, folk tales have been created because of the *fall* of the sacred dimension to the secular and profane. In the same way, successive falls have resulted in their relegation to the world of childhood, further reducing themselves from ritual and cultural objects to toys and hobbies of disinterested consumption. First Propp and then Rodari and Calvino (although for different reasons) have agreed that ritualized representations of myth and social structures lie at the root of folk tales.[18]

In *Fairy Tale Transformations* (1971), Propp also emphasizes how, surrounding the original magic nucleus, fairy tales have gathered together other myths that are not sacred, introducing characters from the real world, especially peasants, side by side with the magic characters. What is more, studying the evolution of Russian fairy tales in particular, Propp cites four types of transformation.[19]

- *through reduction:* from a scene with many elements characterizing a scene to one with fewer elements or only one;
- *through amplification:* the reverse procedure;
- *through substitution:* instead of the element most characteristic of a scene, another one appears (e.g., instead of a dark woods, a stormy sea);
- *through intensification:* instead of characterizing a single scene, the elements extend into other scenes if not to the entire story.

Despite these changes, the principal dynamic of the ritual/folk tale remains intact. In other words, one can emphasize that the structure or form is much more important than the content, and this is crucial for understanding the meaning of our therapeutic rituals.

The thirty-one functions listed above are not present in all fairy tales or folk tales (or stories of migrants). The sequence is not obligatory: there can be some leaps, accumulations of functions, syntheses, but they do not go against the general line. As Rodari (1979) emphasizes, "A folk tale can begin with the first function, the seventh or the twelfth, but, if it is sufficiently ancient, it almost never leaps backwards, to recover forgotten steps."

Propp also points out that it is possible to identify three constants in the functions listed above:

1. they are *stable*, independent of the doer and his methods of execution;

2. their *number* is limited;
3. their *sequence* is always identical.

If, as I suggest, the underlying structure of the experience of migration can be read through the folk tale, then the order of the experience that caused the trauma can be reproduced in a session, and it can then be recomposed through the support and presence of the group (supplying the magic weapon/the struggle between hero and antagonist). Therefore, the functions are useful and illuminating because "we can use them to construct infinite stories" for reconstructing and re-inventing infinite experiences with patients who have lost a sense of ordered structure, an experience that can be narrated and passed on to the next generation. We need only be aware that every function represents not only itself, but also an entire slice of the folk-tale world and—going backwards—from the ritualized world of the patient's original culture, seething with echoes that are perhaps mere fantasies but are essential for the reconstruction of the patient's psychic protective layer. In other words, every function is rich with convocations of the patient's personal world. To offer an example, further on we shall see several functions that recur most often in the therapeutic context: that of *prohibition*, that of *deception* (combinations of entrapment, connivance, and damage or loss), and that of *redemption* (combinations of reaction, struggle, and victory over the antagonist).

The function of *prohibition* recalls the world of childhood above all and, by extension, some characteristics of the world the migrant has left behind, through his or her own decision or because of the exile. In this new, difficult, and limiting experience of the country of immigration, he or she relives the primary prohibitions of childhood, when, in his or her relationship with the world, "only the mother's yes and no helped distinguish between good and bad, what was accepted and what was forbidden". In other words, the prohibition is the relationship/conflict with authority, or authoritarianism, that migrants experienced in the country they left behind and now in the place where they are actually living; through the differences and their similar structures, the two environments bring back painful experiences. At the same time, and more positively, the prohibition also means the discovery of the order of things, of the rules of the game ("it's done this way, not that"). It is the encounter with the boundaries that reality and society impose on his or her liberty and is therefore one of the instruments of his or her re-socialization and of the possibility of engaging in the task of re-attributing meaning to the inner disorder.

Folklore registers all these possibilities, as well as the eventuality that the hero/migrant, in the course of the migration experience (from the departure/arrival until the return) undergoes a true and proper deception (comparable, as mentioned above, to the functions of entrapment, connivance, damage). (For the use of this concept in the explanation of many psychiatric syndromes, see Selvini Palazzoli, Cirillo, Selvini, & Sorrentino, 1988.) It is neither surprising nor rare to encounter migrants who are "deceived" in various ways and in different phases of their migration. Aside from the newspaper stories of immigrants duped with false promises—episodes generally taken up by those who are concerned with criminality or crime news reporting—it is extremely common among migrants to encourage the departure of family and friends by describing the destination in a way that has little to do with the actual place. This happens during a migrant's return for holidays or through letters and telephone calls. In this way, the individual who was first in the migration process tries, unconsciously, to reconstruct and surround him/herself by the village of origin, including family and community. This process has been described by patients more than once, and part of the therapeutic process consists precisely in reinterpreting and recognizing, with the patient, the existence and significance of, or motivations for, this deception. Even the involuntary call to emigration on the part of the mass media can fit into this category.

In fact, there is a common dimension that synthesizes the different concatenations of causes that form the prelude to the departure: *redemption* (a combination, as we have seen, of the functions of reaction, struggle, and victory over the antagonist). Shifting from the folk tale to reality, this dimension consists of both economic push factors—compelling some to improve a situation that seems destitute—as well as non-structural reasons (relationship-based, cultural, psychological) that together drive some, and not others, to migrate.

The category of *redemption* offers a wider point of view of migration. On the one hand, more complex motivations can be considered that respond to questions at an individual or group level, such as: "In circumstances of equal economic difficulty, why do some individuals and/or families emigrate and others not?" "In regions or communities sharing the same economic difficulties, why is there emigration from some communities or regions and not from others?" In this sense the motivation of "redemption" is less generic than that of "migratory culture", on the one hand, and reveals an effective instrument for discriminating between a migrant culture and one that is not, on the other.

Furthermore, the category of redemption leaves open, at least ideally, the necessity/possibility of return. Otherwise to whom—aside from oneself, even if this is the principal process that needs to be understood—does one show oneself as being redeemed? In other words, it permits migrants/patients to legitimize their own double, their investigation, and their recognition. Only after such recognition will it be possible to put things in order again and create a stable and definitive situation, whether it be a return, integration into a new reality, or a further migration.

Therefore, the structure of folk tales, in addition to reproducing those rites of initiation that are still practised in societies and cultures only tangentially touched by modernization (see the case of Armand), are also repeated in human experience. Using fantasy to undertake missions, duels, and difficult ordeals and to experience painful and frustrating periods (even if they are inevitable) enables the patient (as it may all of us) to find a place in the world of humans. It seems to me that the function of folk tales, brought into the therapeutic context, is to help us to see the light within ourselves. As Rodari rightly affirms, folk tales "are there, ready, tried and tested, easy to use; it would seem to me utterly wasteful to discard them". This is true for all of us, not just the migrant members of "other" cultures; nevertheless, in those traditional cultures that have only recently experienced the *fall* from ritual to folk tale, they have a particularly important function.[20]

Given that, as I have tried to illustrate, migratory experiences are complex, contradictory, and diverse (as all of life tends to be), the folk-tale genre probably reveals these complexities better than many theoretical simplifications. Even if a long process of trial, verification, and translation of this metaphoric model into an operational therapeutic model is still before us, the first steps have been taken, and I am convinced that a new and productive path has been outlined.

Notes

1. Cf. J. Decornoy (1996b), who, quoting G. Simon (1995), notes that (in his opinion) we are "speaking about a phenomenon without precedent and at its very inception, whose most important consequence is not so much the impetus behind migration in its physical sense . . . as much as the cultural and psychological uprooting, both individual and collective, that arises with the emergence of social categories bombarded by global mono-colour messages." While not undervaluing this hypothesis, I believe it is substantially alarmist when set against data derived from clinical and anthropological work. Changes in cultural processes and, still more, in visions of the world, health, illness, and cures are in reality very slow and only *seem* as if they can be assimilated into the mutations that affect social structural organization. Adhesion to this or that "modernistic" conviction implies, on the therapeutic level, recourse to different approaches. I revisit this theme more fully in chapters two and three.

2. The insistence on this initial phase of the migratory process and the necessity of studying it is motivated by the fact that, as we progressively deepen our understanding, many psychological/psychiatric problems of immigrants are more easily acknowledged if we concentrate our attentions on this phase and on the often transgenerational premises that precede it.

3. Also in our experience with our group in Geneva, many patients find themselves in this migratory phase, though there are numerous others distributed in other precedent or successive phases. In general, the common denominator that all immigrants undergoing therapy seem to share is the fact of being assailed by numerous, contemporaneous difficulties and situations that cannot be articulated with the cultural and psychological instruments at their disposition. An illuminating case is that of a Kurdish couple, K (husband and wife), who have resided in Geneva for numerous years. Their problem—a "rupture" that is expressed in the wife through insupportable physical pain diffused throughout her entire body and seemingly without organic causes—appears to be related to the combination of two events: her husband losing his job and she having an abortion; the couple later decided on a hysterectomy (although being only in their early 30s, they already had four children).

4. Dimitris, a friend of mine, emigrated to Athens from his village on an Aegean island and wisely returned after not too lengthy a period. He told me that when he returned to his tiny rented apartment in Athens in the evening after work, he began speaking to himself just to hear the sound of a voice.

5. As already mentioned in note 3 in reference to couple K, it is necessary that numerous events coincide to bring on a rupture, in some cases evident in physical symptoms, in many others expressed through autistic-like withdrawal. Referring to the authors mentioned previously, I believe that the categories proposed by Åhlund (forces "from behind" and "forces from ahead") furnish

a coherent scheme with which to classify psychological problems (quoted in Sundquist, 1994, p. 28). From this perspective, stress factors may be situated in the category "ahead"—that is, in the arrival stage—while the "behind" is more suitable to cultural dimensions and/or previously unelaborated psychic conflicts that are reproduced or reawakened as a result of the migratory experience. Obviously these considerations justify the reasons for and the meaning of determined types of setting or therapeutic arrangements. I enter more deeply into this matter in chapter three and during my discussion in chapter six of the case of Armand.

6. One of our Khmer patients who is still undergoing treatment, whom I will call Mr L, is around 30 years of age and arrived to us completely mute. After numerous difficult sittings, he now communicates with us through drawings. One of these drawings clearly refers to the killing of his parents. A probable hypothesis—not historically, though not entirely unfounded given the atrocities committed by the Khmer Rouge—is that he had been obliged to participate in this killing in order to save his own life. Mr L has lived in Geneva for many years, and prior to his coming to us, he had never given signs of mental disturbance. His complete withdrawal happened years after that event, but we are still not able to ascertain if it is mixed up with some other specific fact to which he was subjected during the migratory experience. (For a deeper analysis of these themes, see Hiegel & Hiegel-Landrac, 1996b.)

7. We could add other, more sophisticated, sociological and legal categories that do not seem essential to the aims of this book. (For further details, see Losi, 1995.)

8. Cited in the introduction to Chauvenet, Despret, and Lemaire (1996, p. 14), which in turn makes reference to Anger's 1995 report.

9. For further details of these aspects of the situation in the former Yugoslavia, see Losi (1995) and Chauvenet, Despret, & Lemaire (1996), in particular chaps. 2 and 3.

10. The best translation of this definition, frequently seen in ethnopsychiatry (particularly in Nathan, as we will see) is "psychic wrapping" [translator's note: in Italian, "*involucro psichico*"].

11. From this point of view, the famous "social strategies" described by E. Goffman (1968) may be utilized to describe and interpret the conditions of people in refugee camps.

12. These examples and these hypotheses throw light on the function and the interpretation of physical pain in general. A non-immigrant father who came to me for psychological support during a difficult period following separation from his wife and children, one of them very young, once said something that seems pertinent. Speaking of his personal mourning, he told me that he had finally understood the meaning of his profound pain—which at times even became physical—in terms of the forced separation from his young child: "In this way I have a constant link with him; he is still with me even if it hurts."

13. Zin-Doung is the pseudonym of a woman deeply involved in the women's liberation movement in her country, whom I purposely do not name. I report here a synthesis of her positions expressed during a global meeting on health. The entire discourse is unpublished.

14. It may be useful here to recall that there has been much debate apropos Propp's hypothesis on the roots of fables. In particular, Claude Lévi-Strauss maintains that the myth–rite–fable relationship is to be understood as dialectical, while according to Propp there is a rigid chronological relationship between primitive/anterior and derived/posterior. For a deeper examination of this debate, see Clara Strada Janovic's introduction to Propp's *Edipo alla luce del folklore* (1975). Another series of interesting reflections and interpretations dealing specifically with African fables can be found in the introduction to the collection *Fiabe africane* edited by Paul Radin (1955). Radin underlines some important characteristics of fables in general (and of the African fable in particular) that may be utilized to prompt psychotherapeutic considerations. I refer above all to the hypothesis according to which the transformation of the fable from myth/ritual has followed, much more than a linear process of social change, the "artistic" interventions of particularly able and creative *griots*. Another aspect underlined by Radin concerning African fables refers to their "continentalism" on the one hand, and their extreme realism on the other. Radin writes: "Contrary to the idea that the rest of the world has, autochthonic Africa does not think that man was once imbued with divine particles that he successively lost. . . . Man, for example, does not ascend to the heavens in order to communicate with the gods; rather, the gods descend to earth, from where they have been obliged to transfer for various reasons, taking up residence in the heavens. Indigenous African gods, one might say, must lose their terrestrial components, their earthly ties, before becoming real gods" (Radin, 1955, p. xvi).

15. If the similarity proposed between heroes and immigrants is acceptable (admitting the necessary distinctions), it follows that a simplification of the debate on migratory policies to mere issues of integration/assimilation is, at the very least, unsatisfactory: it might be the case to speak also of contribution/exchange.

16. The function of giving back a ritual mediating order that re-proposes a culture's founding myths is extremely well described by Lévi-Strauss (1998a, chaps. IX–XI).

17. I willingly recognize that the greater part of the merit for the hypothesis that I am about to propose goes to my son Michele and to his kindergarten teacher, Tina. Though they may be unaware of the fact, thanks to them many years ago I read a wonderful book by Gianni Rodari, *La grammatica della fantasia* (1979). I found chapter 22, "Le carte di Propp" particularly illuminating. In this chapter Rodari gives a marvellous description of an aspect of his work in the nursery schools of Reggio Emilia. At the time of reading about this experience, I thought that it might be replicable in other environments and probably with other functions.

18. I refer to Calvino: "This was not a hallucination, or a kind of professional illness. It was, rather, confirmation of something that I knew even when I began . . . the single conviction that pushed me to journey into the world of fables; namely, that I believe fables are true" (Calvino, 1971, p. xviii). Calvino demonstrates that he knows well the debate concerning the historical roots and ethnological of fables, as well as the interpretations of Propp (see, in particular, p. xxxv, n. 2).

19. Well before Propp (it is again Rodari who underlines the fact), in describing work on the imagination, St Augustine used more or less the same terms: "in some way *lay out, multiply, extend, order, recompose* the images." Further ahead, we will note that the same transformation typical of the fable occurs in other areas of human production. For example, the precise articulation of functions described by St Augustine and by Propp was adopted at a "meta" level by cybernetics, with its two base communicative typologies; analogue and digital.

20. In reality, as the case of Armand testifies, in many cultures the *fall*, the passage, has not yet happened, and therapeutic work consists also in constructing this symbolic bridge. Whatever procedure adds value to the therapeutic function must, in my opinion, be fully accepted in our work, independently of the different positions expressed by folklorists, ethnologists, and scholars of the fable.

CHAPTER TWO

Ethnopsychiatry, visions of the world, and medical paradigms

In Italy and in other Western countries, ethnopsychiatry was defined in the past as that part of popular medicine[1] concerned with interpreting and treating nervous and psychological disturbances and what was considered abnormal behaviour (Di Nola, 1981, p. 9). In ethnopsychiatry so defined, such disturbances were perceived and interpreted from the point of view of subjugated or marginal cultures, outside the nosological categories of erudite psychiatry and its diagnostic and therapeutic system.

In this approach, which was subsequently put aside and forgotten, the analyses of psychological malaise in subjugated classes took into account not only the ethnolinguistic dimension but the structural and social dimension, which meant speaking of an opposition between subjugated classes and ruling classes. With the arrival and progressive expansion of industrial and post-industrial society, and therefore the cultural hegemony of the paradigm of modernization, ethnopsychiatry has ceased to look within its own culture in transformation, choosing instead to orient itself towards geographically "other" cultures. In this way, it confines itself once and for all, almost as if within "our" society *otherness* had suddenly vanished, leaving a field that is modernized and homogenous.

Today the coincidence of multiple social and cultural processes (such as the uncontainable processes of internal, international, and intercontinental migration and the consequent establishment of "creolized" societies and the crisis of the biotechnological medical model) should provoke us to reconsider ethnopsychiatry as a reflection on our culture and the social conditions of marginalized groups.[2]

From this perspective, ethnopsychiatry and ethnopsychotherapy, with the various approaches for treating psychological and psychiatric disturbances of immigrants that are currently being tried out in Western societies, can be linked to three major issues:

1. the relationship between therapeutic systems previously developed as part of "our" subjugated cultures, and the systems brought by immigrants coming from traditional cultures;
2. the conceptions of the world, health, and sickness as a part of "other" traditional cultures, by those countries from which the immigrants have come;
3. the placing of ethnopsychiatry in the present debate on the relationship between popular medicine, parallel (or "diverse", "sweet", "alternative", etc.) medicine, and official medicine.

In discussing these three issues in this chapter, I shall try to demonstrate more concretely the anthropological and sociological meaning of the term "creolization" of society and how the latter is reflected in the interpretation and treatment of illness and mental suffering. This will enable me to construct, together with the reader, a frame of reference that will then permit us to explore the clinical experiences of ethnopsychotherapy. Our constant reference will be, in contrast, the Western (European and American) psychiatric model, based on three fundamental assumptions:

- an egocentric vision of the self;
- body–mind dualism;
- the conception of culture as an epiphenomenon.

The first carries an interpretation of the self as a closed and autonomous entity. Psychological normality and abnormality, to the extent they are within the self, obscure the origins and social experience of the "mental illness".

The second assumption maintains that problems, illnesses, and mental disorders can originate either in the brain or in the mind, but in reality they originate predominantly in the brain, which is a physical organ. This leads to a division of psychopathology into two categories of disorder: organic and psychological. Nevertheless, the majority of human beings experience these sufferings in an integrated body–mind modality. In fact, many cultures give great importance to the spiritual dimension. Western psychiatrists often exchange this "other" vision with an "incapacity" to distinguish between mind–body–spirit, which is understood as a lack of psychological outlook or introspective capacity. In the second section of this chapter, we shall see that this widespread interpretation has no acceptable basis.

The third assumption implies that culture is a collection of "beliefs" superimposed on biological "reality". This view leads to devaluing, even disparaging, the beliefs, which are interpreted as ignorance or even dangerous superstitions. The conceptions and experiences of illness, as well as the methods of treatment practised in "other" or subjugated cultural groups, are judged to be obstacles to the diagnosis, the treatment, and the success of Western therapies.

Now we shall take a look at how the subjugated constructions of the world—including, obviously, the analysis of madness—have their own dimension, quite distant from the epistemological direction of Western technological society. We shall proceed from two perspectives: first, the diachronic perspective (taking into consideration "our" rural world), followed by a synchronic dimension (taking into consideration the immigrant populations currently from "other" cultures).

The first area: ethnopsychiatry and "our" subjugated cultures

As a study and therapy of mental and psychological disturbances of subjugated cultures, ethnopsychiatry shows, at least in the Italian experience, points of contact and differentiation with "erudite" psychotherapeutic and psychiatric practice. On the therapeutic level, in fact, the psychiatrist and psychotherapist take the origins and social conditions of the patient into account, but the interpretation of the clinical picture is then inserted into an "erudite" model, in which the vision of the "other" world where the case was formed is gradually lost. This transposition is often deceptive and mystifying and does not allow an effective understanding of the "subjugated" disturbance/disorder.

Even if certain approaches in family therapy that favour the presence of members of three generations of the patient's family (a three-generational approach), potentially recognize the importance of the interpretations of malaise from the point of view of the grandparents' generation,[3] the intervention is usually confined to the communicative intrafamilial logic; thus, what is lacking is any deeper understanding of the different generation's cultural models and their necessary syncretism.

Therefore the "erudite" approaches continue to apply the notion of "mental illness/madness" to the subjugated real human based on a presumed universality of the categories used. To resolve this inadequacy, it is essential to move in the direction of rediscovering categories that are "other", appropriate for one or more subjugated visions of the world, and that make it possible to place the psychological disorder in interpretative frameworks that are different from those used by official psychiatry. The common denominator between these categories and interpretative schemes includes the body, the interpersonal relationships that have been important, and the founding myth of the culture of belonging, with its ramifications, religious or otherwise.[4]

Archaic thought organizes the universe around the general principle of analogy, which constructs a system of correspondence among all of the elements of the world. The prevailing modern line of thought reduces the diverse elements that constitute reality into categories: animal, vegetable, mineral, living, inanimate. It introduces a clean classification and rejects any link between diverse elements that is not scientific. In reference to this schematized relationship between archaic and contemporary thought,[5] Di Nola (1981) holds as arguable Gramsci's hypothesis that the cultural model of the subjugated world, in contrast with dominant culture, is characterized by confusion, dis-fragmentation, and irrationality. On the contrary, if the subjugated cultural model is analysed in depth, it has its own coherence, with contradictions that certainly are not lacking in the dominant culture. In this perspective, when the pathological alterations of the personality and the same schizophrenic disintegration emerge in the subjugated universe, they need to be examined according to the categories of the world to which they belong. In particular, according to Di Nola, we cannot exclude traditional world views from the principle of global integration.

A clinical case narrated by Di Nola (1981, p. 14) is connected to an experience the same writer had between the late 1950s and early 1960s in the province of Naples. It concerned a young woman suffering from, according to psychoanalytic nosography, a "compulsive neurosis" or, in the classic psychiatric diagnosis of the time, "delirium and paranoia". These diagnoses would confine her to an insane asylum, where she would die. The story of the woman, whom we shall call Rosaria, is as follows: she was lower-class and was excluded within/by her own family. She survived through prostitution and was then rejected by her family and went into an anxiety crisis, which she resolved through a neurotic ritual that is decipherable only by referring to her vision of the world. Every day she crossed the town using a sequence of compulsive gestures and behaviour that consisted of taking seven steps, kneeling down, and kissing the ground. When she arrived at her father's house, she was systematically rejected. The paternal house was a sort of Catholic sanctuary in which lighted candles made the air unbreathable.

We have seen the diagnoses and the end of Rosaria: Di Nola asks how things would have been if she had encountered a therapist able to understand the "density of subjugated ethnopsychiatry"—capable, that is, of a humanized consideration of the world that Rosaria carried on her shoulders. Perhaps the therapist could have understood that Rosaria's rituals belonged to a vision that was "other" and on the basis of which her behaviour could be explained and resolved: the recurrence of the number seven (the seven sorrows of the Virgin Mary and the seven sufferings of Jesus); kneeling as a penitential act; the sense of sin apparently resolved by returning to her father. These were probable ways to arrive at an ethnopsychiatric understanding of her sufferings. Rosaria's disturbance was reduced to the diagnostic canons of classical psychiatry of the time. This brought catastrophe, impeding any ethnopsychiatric diagnostic effort and, consequently, a treatment that was appropriate to the patient's culture.

The case of Rosaria is an example from which at least two conclusions can be drawn. The first is methodological; the second is clinical-therapeutic. On the methodological level, when madness in subjugated classes is studied, it is important to place it within its global culture—that is, the organic blend of religious, mystical, magical, supernatural, economic, labour, and class components that are usually excised in the scientific study of the dominant classes' conditions of malaise and disturbance. If, as it seems clear, there no longer exists a single psychiatry but many, the principal methodological approach should be that of respecting the rules of the patient's cultural group for an understanding of the disturbance. Therefore, an "anthropological excavation" of the disturbed personality is indispensable.

We cannot, nor should we, conceal from ourselves that, wherever the excavation is done, the information gathered could produce in the psychotherapist of erudite training a conspicuous resistance, brought about by the difficulty of accepting—or the refusal to accept—a "pre-scientific" vision of the world, which would be hard to understand or share.

In the best of cases, the cognitive process of the therapist would bring the components of the clinical framework, which were observed and understood according to categories from within the patient's subjugated culture, back to the diagnostic-therapeutic system of erudite science. Since such an approach entails great effort, it is usually treated merely as an example of what is called "ingenuous realism".[6] In fact, when considering the possibility of a study of popular cultures from an internal point of view, it must be clear that every illness, physical or psychological, comes from a universe of influences that could be defined as supernatural or transcendent and refer to a "world of myth and power that causes upsets in the physiological economy which are also explicit in psychological upsets" (Di Nola, 1981, pp. 16–17). These influences should guide the diagnosis and therapy of a correct "subjugated ethnopsychiatry". The same illnesses attributed by scientific thinking to a microbe or another well-defined linear cause become the consequences of a psychological nucleus correlated with "possession, demonization or sorcery" in the "subjugated" diagnoses.[7]

According to the subjugated world views, the soul is always the source of evil. Illness seems to descend from a vague misty space in the psyche (the soul), taken as the source of blame, sin, transgression. Every illness—even those that scientific medicine calls organic—originate in the psychological sphere and with its "existential exposure to the assaults of external violence, manifested in saints or demons".[8]

In the popular perception on the diagnostic level, if all evil is due to being possessed, on the therapeutic level "nervous" deviance and psychosis call for *sui generis* interventions that dismantle all of the diagnostic categories of official medicine. Official medicine always attempts to establish a linear relationship between the cause of the disturbance and the illness, while in popular cultures the situation is more complicated.

Table 2.1 (adapted from Di Nola, 1981, pp. 18) summarizes the symptomologies, diagnoses, and treatments prescribed in "our" subjugated ethnopsychiatry as they relate to the two main typologies of causes: the first, scientifically proven ones; the second, concerning the "worlds of power".

Table 2.1

Cause	*Symptomatology*	*Diagnosis*	*Cure*
Scientifically verifiable fact or data			Recourse to "erudite" diagnosis and therapy accompanied by parallel recourse (in almost all cases) to the world of "beneficial powers"
Supernatural, or otherworldly Influence	Assorted pictures/ descriptions of a "different world"	Result of personal guilt or sin; exposure to powerful negative actions (spell, evil eye, curse, hex, etc.)	Recourse to the non-demoniacal world or the world of beneficial powers (saints, madonnas, healers, etc.)

In Table 2.2, on the other hand, I have attempted to update the nosological categories of submerged ethnopsychiatry and their relative symptoms (Di Nola, 1981, pp. 20–23).

As Di Nola shows, it is above all in this latter series of clinical illustrations that a net distance can be seen between subjugated ethnopsychiatric categories and the analysis offered by "erudite" psychiatry.

Table 2.1

Subjugated ethnopsychiatric category	*Symptoms*
Signs of diminished vital force and constructive aggression towards reality	Weight loss, abstinence, anorexia, insomnia, tiredness, daytime lethargy, eyes excessively open, impotence (*impotentia coeundi, impotentia generandi*), frequent amnesia, para- and catatonic comportment, paleness, temporary blackouts, excessive agitations, semiologic agitations, agoraphobia, affective anaesthesia, anxiety, aphasia, autism, claustrophobia, confusion, sense of self-blame, etc.
Absence or destruction of personality and of one's psychic structures	Authentic madness, as defined by classic aetiology; violent episodes provoked by paranoia or schizophrenia; crises of alcohol withdrawal; forms of visionary delirium; total disordering of logical and linguistic codes; neurotic habits following anxiety-producing or -anguishing episodes; sexual exhibitionism caused by an illness known in the classic tradition as "priapism"; excessive psychoneuropathological agitation, depressed and neurotic aggression, semiology of antisocial reactions, mental turbulence, Basedow syndrome, coprolalia, epidemic encephalitis, critical forms of carious aetiologies, *bouffées* delirious, demonopathy, melancholia, psychomotor agitations, etc.
Series of behaviours with different diagnoses and aetiology in official psychiatry, here incorporated for common symptomatology: motor responses, loss of consciousness, *bouffées* emerging in physiological symptomatology.	Generically described "evil" depending on invasion and connected to San Donato or other powers; including forms of epilepsy and epilepsis. The "shift" (i.e., the loss of consciousness), joined together at the popular level in organic symptomatology, depends on a great variety of possible aetiologies (hysteria, alcoholism, some forms of acute psychosis, etc.).

Limiting my discussion to the above tables, I wish to underline the two aims of our analysis: first, and above all, to remind ethnopsychiatric diagnostics and therapeutic practice, to a large degree already thoroughly and successfully elaborated, of the enormous number of subjugated cultures and societies; second, to underline the ways in which the logic behind this cataloguing is quite different from that seen in Western medical manuals. I refer specifically to the DSM-IV and the ICD-10. In particular, diagnostics of subjugated cultures and societies are marked by two main characteristics: the use of broad, flexible categories; and specific reference to one's own culture without attempting to incorporate others.

These characteristics mean that:

- the existence of detailed manuals does not substitute for the fundamental necessity of extensive learning and training of caregivers;
- health administration and insurance systems necessitate certain types of cataloguing and labelling (more than anything else, the DSM-IV responds to these needs), but these must not be confused with therapeutic practice.

To avoid confusion, therefore, it is important to underline the fact that all the symptomatologies reported in the above tables refer separately to agitated behaviours. Some of them would mean different things if observed in a ritual, collective context. Ritualized madness, inconceivable within the criteria established by dominant cultures, has, like magic, a cultural-therapeutic function. "After studies conducted by E. de Martino, we cannot avoid the conclusion that both madness and magic appear as expedient ways of reacting to the threat of historical non-being. . . . When all seems in vain because the world's systems of economic stability enter into crisis or because the world has been *de-cultured* by forced emigration, for example, one is launched into a topsy-turvy reality that cannot be understood; madness and magic stem the threat of absolute disorientation and loss, soliciting in the individual and the community a delirious and imaginary reconstruction that represents an apparent collapse into non-history or into an alternative history" (Di Nola, 1981, pp. 24–25).

Di Nola's affirmations can be added to the observations and hypotheses detailed in the first chapter of this book dealing with migratory populations. Before moving on to a discussion of a second area, it is necessary to clarify two further issues. The first concerns similar thought patterns in "our" native subjugated cultures and subjugated cultures that are present among us but belong to the "other". There are, of course, certain differences between these two groups: for example, the degree of adhesion to founding myths that determine visions of the world and, above all, the way in which care is offered and received (training and the intergenerational continuity of healers).

The second issue that requires clarification concerns the different meanings ascribed to "mad" behaviour, depending on whether this behaviour is evident exclusively in the individual or is collective and/or part of a ritual. This difference is a common element in what we have called, respectively, diachronic subjugated cultures (our rural world) and synchronic subjugated cultures (immigrants from "other" cultures currently among us). This point will help us to understand the meaning of several therapeutic approaches that are to be analysed here.

One final note: while the themes dealt with in this first part of the chapter concern local, at most national, realities (the "subjugation" referred to is the subjugation of rural realities in an increasingly urbanized world), the section that follows deals with critical phenomena at the global level. It will be necessary to adopt suitable instruments for this analysis. Today, considering the so-called globalization of the world, translational migrants are in a situation identical to that of "our" rural subjugated cultures in the age of industrialization and modernization.

The second area: ethnopsychiatry and subjugated cultures of "the others"

The social and cultural dimension of health and illness, together with the medical practices used in today's "creolized" societies, can be better understood if we are aware of the historical and anthropological aspects of both "our" popular traditions (i.e. of agrarian societies that preceded us and whose cultural patrimony has been too quickly considered lost) and of traditions belonging to cultures currently considered "other". These latter, which include at least four-fifths of the world population, are essentially societies that are poor, rural, or nomadic and in which traditional cures are practised and administered by healers and therapists trained through an extremely rich and timeless transfer of knowledge from parent to child.

Two extremely common and deeply rooted prejudices that must be overcome are summarized thus: first, diseases—regardless of the various names ascribed to them—are the same everywhere; second, subjugated cultures possess simplistic and/or primitive models of illness and its causes.

Combating the first of these prejudices—the error of the "naïve realist" mentioned earlier—Gilles Bibeau, in a 1981 study on depression in Africa, suggests an analytical methodology for the observation and interpretation of "other" visions of health and sickness. Departing from three distinctive "points" where significant data concerning culture flourish (Bibeau, 1981, p. 97), the researcher will be able to make reliable "inferences." These "points" are:

- the way in which people describe, interpret, and classify objects, events and realities that are part of their daily life;
- the way in which they react and behave, since behaviour constitutes an open explanation of internalized knowledge;
- the comprehension of causality, this being the most accessible element of the cognitive system.

Using this three-point model, Bibeau shows how the Angbandi people of Zaire (since 1998, the Democratic Republic of the Congo) utilize five principles when referring to illness: localization, similarity, representation, aetiology, and therapy. "The same psychological disorder may bear two, three, four, even five different names, depending on whether it has been examined from the point of view of its principal symptom, its secondary symptom, its cause(s), its pathological foundations or, finally, its tendency to provoke in the patient behavior similar to that of an animal" (Bibeau, 1981, pp. 102–103).

Remembering that the names attributed to psychological disorders are modified depending on the social context in which they are used (they change, for example, from a casual conversation among non-experts, to a visit with a ritual healer or with a herbalist), Bibeau hastens to demonstrate that any given mental disorder is a "tangle of names . . . standing at an intersection that can be approached from many different directions. The understanding of a disorder depends on the circularity located inside this complex of names, each of which delineates a particular aspect of the illness. The real face of an illness is reproduced when all the names attributed to it are represented and organized" (Bibeau, 1981, p. 103).

Today, an ever-increasing number of people coming from cultures in which illness is understood in the manner described by Bibeau live in the rich, modern, post-industrial societies of the West. As a result, we are forced to coin new terms like multi-ethnic or creolized societies. Whether they or we are aware of it or not, immigrants are the protagonists of profound change and radical redefinition that also extend to the cure of psychological malaise. Even in our own case, the scholarly treatment of these themes is not undertaken simply to satisfy academic curiosity, but is an attempt to retrace and reinterpret new therapeutic instruments that have often been marginalized, undervalued, and classified as "magic" so as to understand their concrete, healing mechanisms.

The subjugated cultures that we deal with now, coming principally from the African continent, have for some time been a "sample" of synchronic otherness. In general, they are characterized by styles of life, learning, and interpersonal relationships typical of oral cultures.

Concerning orality and its importance for all aspects of culture and society, the esteemed intellectual and writer, Amadou Hampâté Bâ,[9] says, "Many dear readers of this manuscript were surprised that the memory of a man over the age of eighty could contain so many things, and above all, could be recalled in such detail. The memories . . . of people belonging to oral traditions who cannot refer to writing is prodigiously faithful and precise. From childhood, we are accustomed to observe, to watch, to listen so carefully that everything is inscribed in our memories as if on virgin wax." And referring to childhood episodes: "I have no need to 'remember' them, I see them on a kind of internal screen, and

I need only describe what I see. To describe a scene, I need only relive it. And if somebody else has told me a story, it is not simply the content of the story that I have registered in my memory, but the entire scene: the position of the narrator, his or her clothes, the gestures, the mimicry, the sounds around us. . . ." On the question of the relationship between the particular and the general, between synthesis and analysis, and so forth, Bâ comments: "When we recount an event, the film plays from its beginning to its end, in its totality. For this reason, it is very difficult for an African of my generation to summarize. Either we recount the totality or we don't recount anything. We never get tired of listening to the same story over. Repetition, for us, is neither a shortcoming nor an imperfection."

Amadou Hampâté Bâ describes three specific elements that characterize African culture in general and its oral nature in particular: the understanding of temporality, the subdivision of the continent into geographic zones (to which he, too, makes reference), and the role of dreams and prophecies.

About chronology, or rather, the way in which time is experienced, he says:[10] "In African stories, in which the past is relived as a present experience, somehow *outside* time, there is a certain chaos that is problematic for Western rationality, but inside which we are perfectly at ease.[11] We wallow in the content of a story, like fish in a sea where the water molecules mix and form a living whole."

About the various African geographic zones, Hampâté Bâ explains that *an* Africa does not exist. Likewise there is no single man or African tradition that is valid for all the regions and the ethnicities contained on the continent. He highlights the fact that "important commonalities exist (the presence of the sacred in all things, a rapport between the visible and the invisible worlds, between the living and the dead, a sense of community, religious respect for the mother figure, etc.) but also great differences: the gods, sacred symbols, religious prohibitions, social customs that vary from one region to another, from one ethnic group to another, even from one village to another."

Finally, he comments on dreams and prophecy: "Another thing about African stories that sometimes confuses Westerners is the frequent presence of premonitory dreams, prophecies and other similar phenomena. But African life is woven with these kinds of happenings, which for us form part of life and we are not at all surprised by them. It was once common to see a man arrive by foot from a distant village exclusively to share with others the signs or the instructions that he had received in his dreams. Then he would return to his village as if it were nothing, like a courier charged with the delivery of a letter who was quite simply doing his job. . . . To a certain extent, these kinds of things . . . are still part of our lives."

While the grand fresco painted by Hampâté Bâ illuminates some of the issues concerning mental health, illness, and their treatment, a recent study entitled *Les représentations de la santé et de la maladie chez les Ivoiriens* (Memel-Fotê, 1998) attempts to analyse visions of the world and related representations of health, illness, and death in the Ivory Coast.[12] This study will guide us in the following considerations.

Despite differences of a secondary nature, the authors of this study individuate a substantial and profound unity of inspiration, structure, functioning, and logic in the visions of the world belonging to the interviewees. The unity in question concerns, first of all, the makeup and the formation of the world based on four elements. The primary element is fire—celestial energy that is manifested in heat and dryness and which corresponds to the dry seasons. Fire generates the second element, air. Air is tangible in heat and humidity and corresponds to the wet seasons. From air, in the form of rain, comes the third element, water. A synthesis of humidity, heat, and dryness, water is "the essential element of life, fetal life, precedent lives, the interior life that precedes external life" (Memel-Fotê, 1998, p. 21). From water comes the fourth element, the earth, synthesis of the three previous elements. From the earth are born, in chronological order, vegetation, minerals, animals, secondary beings [in the original text, *cadet*], and man, favoured among all animals.

The elaboration of this cosmology suggests that the world is divided into two spheres: one visible, the other invisible. In the invisible sphere, the celestial level beyond the heavens is the resting place of god and, according to some ethnic groups, also of primordial man, progenitor of all living beings. Another "zone" of the invisible sphere is the underground, divided into two areas: the village of the dead, where ancestors reside, and the village of the "jinns"[13] who reside in the mountains, the rivers, the trees, and the rocks. The invisible world is that from which, by definition, come causes, while the visible world is home to effects and all that concerns our existence. By definition, the visible world corresponds to the village of the human beings.

In the world, there are two times: day, when the sun's light renders everything clear, and night, when everything is hidden from sight—only diviners, healers, and wizards[14] can see; indeed, these people have inherited clairvoyance from god himself when he retired from the earth to take up residence in the heavens.

The principal characteristics of life are:

- *Universality*: the world consists of sky and earth, the primordial couple who put all beings into the world; these two womb and-blood siblings also include minerals.[15]
- *Positivity*: life is the opposite of death; it is necessary to produce and experience all positive events, in particular those connected to the body, to fecundation, matrimony, and procreation.
- *Eternity*: though men die, life is eternal, and so too the world may change but it cannot end. What, then, is the death of a single individual? A passage from one side to the other, a transformation, not an absolute loss. "One is declared dead when his or her respiration is no more, when blood no longer circulates, and when words and movements cease; following the funeral, if all rites pertaining the deceased's social status have been observed, the 'after' or the 'soul' reaches the village of the ancestors." Eternity is assured in two ways: the first is a rebirth in the invisible, underground world; the second, an earthly rebirth, implied by the transfer of the dead individual into a new being: an affiliated or married adult, or otherwise a child. "Children are men's response to death."

There is a myth originally from the Ivory Coast that offers us a version of this vision of the world and the dynamic of opposition between earth and sky:

> At that time the earth was covered in darkness. The Guela below did not have fire to see clearly. At that time, the light was held in the sky. At that time, the sky *was* the light. The Guela

on high had the sun to illuminate everything. The Guela on high saw that the Guela below had many beautiful playthings. He said:

"Give me some of your clay men, your women, your fish and your animals. I will give them life, and I will give you my sun's light."

The Guela below responded:

"I will only give you the clay fish and the animals and the plants. I will not give you the clay men and women."

The Guela on high insisted:

"I want the men and the women too."

The Guela below said:

"Very well, you will have them. But first make life enter into them."

So, the Guela on high made life enter the bodies of the men, the women, the fish, the animals and the plants. The men and the women stood up and began to walk, the fish swam, the animals got up and jumped around, the plants raised themselves up and started to grow.

"Now, Guela below, maintain your promise! I gave life to the men, the women, the fish, the animals and the plants that were once mere clay forms. I gave you the sun's light. Now maintain your promise."

But the Guela below didn't want to keep his promise. So the two Guelas argued and remained angry with one another until the end of time. Since then, the Guela on high has been trying to take back the life that he gave to the clay bodies of the men and the women, to the fish, and to the animals and the plants shaped by the Guela below. And every time the Guela on high succeeds in taking back a life from the men, the women, the fish, the animals, the plants to whom he had given it, a man, a woman, a fish, an animal or a plant dies. However, since the Guela below defends the life that the Guela on high gave to the men, the women, the fish, the animals, the plants, for as long as their dispute continues, men, women, fish, animals and plants will suffer sicknesses.

It is in this way when the harmattan blows.

It is in this way during war.

It is in this way during the storms.

The stars are precious stones that the Guela on high makes shine to attract the women towards him. The moon, the eye of the Guela on high. With this eye open or semi-open, the Guela

> on high watches the Guela below—his enemy—even at night, at which time he takes back the sun that he gave when he gave life to the men, the women, the fish, the animals, the plants. It was in this way before all things were on earth and in the sky. [reported in Gbaka Zady, 1989, pp. 12–13]

The representations of health, sickness, and death are directly correlated with this vision of the world. For our purposes, we shall deal only with those aspects most directly connected with ethnopsychiatric practices.

Representations of health use different vocabulary depending on ethnic group and can include the vocabulary of two or three different groups whose traditions transmit the idea of a complex and multidimensional reality. Health is always associated with a kind of superior quality of life, a fullness of being, relationships and activity. Such well-being is applied to the body when it is defended from suffering and is in good shape, this being expressed through external signs of freshness (as opposed to the overheated bodies of the ill), resistance to physical aggression and sickness, flexibility and mobility in all its forms (including rest, walking, running, dancing, and working), and, finally, the ability to reproduce.

But well-being is also that of the spirit: free from worry, in peace with itself, radiant in its relationships and activities. Health is not intended simply as an individual state of well-being, but is also social: it is peace, prosperity, and celebration within the community (family or village) and between communities. Health, like life itself, has a universal dimension (exception is made for jinns and spirits). It is compared with and related to many elements of the living world: the solidity and resistance of stones (even we say "strong as a rock"), the eclipses of astral bodies (factors in fertility), the earth's degree of vigour and vitality, the agility of animals, and so forth.

Even if the absolute origin of good health is attributed to god, every spirit of the invisible world, including ancestors and jinns, participates to varying degrees in its maintenance. Man, for his part, participates in the maintenance of good health by respecting religious, political, and social rules and balanced alimentary and sexual habits.

The representation of illness follows, at turns by opposition, the same logic. Illness is already present inside the body of each man and is provoked by his actions. From this idea, human beings appear predisposed to regression. This is an important point: as opposed to many other traditional visions that exonerate the subject from whatever individual responsibility there may be for his or her illness, assigning its causes to the supernatural world or to interpersonal relations, in this case the individual is directly involved. Regression to an unhealthy state can be manifested through pain and physical suffering, both associated with heat. The degradation of health in the form of heat evokes a final regression towards death.

Of particular interest to us is the fact that sickness can also strike the spirit, both directly and indirectly, through the suffering of the body. The term that indicates both forms of vital regression is *Tanto*, meaning the degradation of health at the hands of a mortal.

The concept of illness, then, is not unlike that of good health: illness is not a purely individual experience but a social fact involving relationships inside the community—misunderstandings, arguments, and the like—or external relationships between different communities—that is, between the community and the natural world (floods, epidemics, drought).

The *representation of death* in the cultures considered in this study posits a range of interpretations. Though death generally represents the end of physical life and can be caused by any kind of untreated illnesses (there is no net difference between serious and non-serious illnesses), this is not necessarily a negative thing. Indeed, through death, space is cleared for newborns, increasing their chances for life in situations characterized by a scarcity of resources. As in the case of sickness, death is a social fact and not an individual one.

God-heaven, whose will is decisive for all life, is at the origin of illness and death. However, various intermediate causes exist through which His will is expressed. First, there are causes originating in the invisible world: jinns (spirits), ancestors, and wizards. Second, there are human causes, both social, like the violation of sexual prohibitions (incest, fornication in open air, or in the *brousse* [bush] etc.) and individual (rancour, infidelity). On a third level, there are physical, environmental causes: sun, wind, and dust. These levels justify the interpretation of illness as a "wild" phenomenon.[16] The connotation is that illness is extraneous, hence the metaphor of illness "assailing" or "striking" the individual.

Death shares with health and sickness the characteristics of universality and eternity, unless the evil that brings it about is associated with astral bodies or jinns. Diverse ideas exist concerning death's relationship to universality and eternity. For which reason, some healers maintain that it is dangerous to examine these cases, and they believe that to speak of them might put their powers and even their lives at risk.[17] Others consider jinns mortal like men, and they therefore do not adhere to this taboo. The same type of contradiction concerns sicknesses and death caused by the astral bodies: some compare the existential conditions of the astral bodies to those of men, others distinguish between immortal astral bodies (the stars) and mortal ones (moon and sun). Health, illness, and death assume equivalent forms in the animal and vegetal worlds.[18]

Visions of the world, health, illness, and death and their consequences on healthcare systems

As in every healthcare system, traditional medicines in the Ivory Coast have their various components: the personal and its designation or formalization; fields of specific competence and specializations; methods of intervention, subdivided into diagnosis and cure; pharmacopoeia; professional deontology; collaboration with Western (or scientific) medicine; social and economic statutes; and so on These are all variables that originate in the different interpretations of health, illness, and death described above. It is not necessary to investigate all of these aspects. I consider it essential, however, to make note of the fact that so-called disorders of the spirit are subdivided into two principal diagnostic categories: the first (*Mpiakpé*) includes trauma provoked by the sight of blood "following an accident or a gunshot"; the second includes all other disorders.

In traditional visions, both conservative and innovative currents coexist and give life to three prevailing dynamics: "permanence" (conservation) of the traditional vision; "syncretism", or adaptation of the traditional and the modern; and "modernization".[19]

These dynamics are particularly interesting for our discussion, as they recall experiences with immigrant patients in our societies. Let us briefly examine them.

The *dynamic of conservation* influences all levels of the social and cultural reality: ideological and linguistic, practical and institutional. There is a fundamental continuity in the use of indigenous concepts concerning health, illness, and death and, by extension, the animal, vegetal, mineral worlds, jinns, and the spheres of the astral bodies. This continuity is ideological and is based on the existence of the village and the family—fundamental social structures. Even in urban conglomerations, a large part of the population—particularly in the slums—has its roots in the village, from which come alimentary customs, supplies, social habits, healers, and *devins-guérisseurs*.[20] When assailed by illness, even the urban population turns to the family, and not only the nuclear, modern family, but also the enlarged traditional family over which reigns either a patriarchal *(mandé/kru)* or matrilineal *(akan/gur)* head of the family. Today, as in the past, sickness provokes the family into action, and each member brings a material or moral contribution depending on his or her role.

This ideological continuity is behind the perpetuation of individual and collective practices, among which the ways in which healers' powers are transmitted, the ways of investigating sickness (diagnosis), therapies, and reticence to collaborate with modern medicine.

Syncretism is a dynamic that affirms a kind of coexistence and cultural reconciliation. There are various forms present in the terminology regarding health, illness, and death and in ideology, practice, and institutions. Turning our attention to terminology for a moment, we find several new and particularly interesting terms: *dotorosso* (Malinké), *dotorokaha* (Senufo), and *dotoroghé* (Beté), meaning literally "the village of the doctor", or hospital, health centre, dispensary. Often, traditional healers operating in urban contexts tend to distinguish themselves from their rural counterparts by adopting names that denote a level of nobility, like "doctor" or *tradipracticien*.[21] From such examples, the authors deduce that a process of construction of a new self-image by groups of traditional healers is underway. It might therefore be the case that fissures in the visions of the world and the representations of health, illness and death exist. In particular, the system could no longer remain integral in the Abe, Senufo and Malinké societies.

In these areas of syncretism, although health still maintains its relational and global content, it no longer covers a universal extension but, instead, is limited to certain social and cultural spaces. The main responsibility for health is, furthermore, attributed to humans.[22]

Cultural breaks of this kind are especially common among those healers who adhere to a monotheistic religion, although for the majority of them faith in one god or creator coexists without any apparent contradiction with the faith in jinns, ancestors, and witches. These healers generally adopt a "technological syncretism" in the tools and procedures of intervention. They use traditional as well as industrial materials in their investigation and symbolic treatment. Some associate the rites of the new religions to those of the previous ones, and the structure of their work swings between modern and traditional medicine, according to the back-and-forth flux of their own and their patients' anxieties and beliefs.[23]

The forms of *modernization* can be found in three principal social contexts, which in themselves are images of change: the city, the school, the hospital. Within these contexts, the subjects, which in different ways represent the major impulse for change, are the patients, the health workers, and the state; among the patients, youth, women, and those who practice a monotheist religion figure prominently.

Another Ivorian author, G. D. Tchetche, a Western-trained psychotherapist, suggests a partially different reading of these data, as he considers that the dynamic of change in terms of modernization is merely a superficial one (Tchetche, 1998). From his point of view, the Ivorian context is affected by a failure of traditional medicine, but this is in no way explained by the recognition of an interpretative or therapeutic superiority of Western psycho-psychiatric approaches. On the contrary, the latter represent a further articulation of the historical experience of Western colonialism, particularly European colonialism.

Thus, although "hospitalization in a Western psychiatric environment signals the total or partial failure of the traditional way of care, in reality this is to be explained in terms of the de-structuring of the family environment, the impact of Islam and other religions, the economic upturn linked to the contemporary changes and urbanization" (Tchetche, 1998, p. 121). In other words, for Tchetche the current change does not lead to any therapeutic improvement. He does not take issue with the efficiency of the traditional interventions of the past. However, he notes that these are no longer guaranteed, on the one hand, and that hospitalization has little to do with the therapeutic efficacy, on the other.[24]

The failure of traditional medicine has its roots in social dynamics: the distancing of the mad person from the family and the village; the conflictual change of the roles within the family and in some social categories such as that of the traditional healers; and the changes in the interpretation of madness and in the social status of those afflicted by it caused by the contact with the Western hospital. The removal from the customary place of life, caused by the hospitalization of the "mad person", induces a justification of fear and suspicion towards that person; as a result of his or her experience of asylum elsewhere, he or she becomes "other" and progressively, "as in Europe, an object of incomprehension and rejection".

How could this happen? As already mentioned above, in many cases the extended African family is no longer a structural reality. When a family member has a psycho-psychiatric problem, the weakening of the family structure and the village no longer enables the group to provide care. Moreover, hospitalization in a Western psychiatric environment is the result of such family destructuring. In a village, the ill person could be watched over collectively; in a city, this is no longer possible. Generally, there is a social pressure towards hospitalization, a pressure that frees the family from the hard and conflictual task of deciding whether to "abandon" (as the author puts it) the ill person in the hands of Western therapists. During the hospital stay, it could be easier to arrange a parallel treatment, traditional or Muslim, should the family desire. The influence of Islam seems to play a crucial role in this context as well. According to the author, it represents a refuge for the generation of fathers in particular, as it enables the maintenance of authority, which had been put in crisis by the breaking-up of the family.

Contrary to what has emerged from the research mentioned previously, according to Tchetche women are generally opposed to therapeutic changes. One of the reasons for their resistance is the social prestige guaranteed to them in the village through the cult of the "rabs". The attachment to this cult cannot be explained simply by a "convenience" of role; there is also the lasting belief that procreation depends on the agreement between ancestors and allied spirits. It follows that men, especially those in a paternal condition (which means up to the age of 50 years, since afterwards they often fall into the category of grandfather), are the most precarious social subjects, as they are immersed in a conflictual situation with respect to the elders, "who are still absorbed" by the old beliefs, and the women. Their recourse to syncretism seems truly exemplary. In fact, if on the one hand their adherence to Islam has led to the abandonment of the ancestral cults in their original form (group care of the patient, supported by drums, dances, exchange and circulation of goods, etc., as in the "rabs" ritual),[25] on the other, they have also created a new category of Muslim "rabs" rituals, which according to the author, "like all syncretic phenomena, reflects men's need to integrate the two registers of interpretation".[26]

The other social subject affected by the change taking place is the healer—and consequently the ill person. This process develops during discussions among the patient's relatives, who complain about the cost of the treatments by traditional or Muslim healers. Their discussions are justifiable in view of their actual situations. In the urban hub of Abidjan (an example that, in reality, represents a universal phenomenon), anyone can be a *marabout* or healer, since the social control of the elders is no longer possible in an urban context of continuous change. Thus, in a society in transition, the therapist no longer receives any institutional support for his or her work and tries to compensate for the loss of prestige with material benefits.

Nevertheless, the author highlights that the results of a study on "The African Mother in Relation to Schooling" (Tchetche, 1998, p. 126) indicate that 80% of the women interviewed confirmed that they went to a *marabout* before an exam or after their child received a grade that they considered too high. Therefore, according to the author, the *marabout* has not lost his image, neither in this example nor in relation to the cure of madness. He has simply become more expensive. In choosing how to take care of a family member, the main difference between the male and female points of view is that while men prefer the *marabout*, women consider the *n'döppkat* to be more suitable. Men's opposition to *n'döppkat* is due to their higher cost.[27]

The only "pathologies" on which there is total social and cultural consensus on the greater effectiveness of modern therapies are those related to the contact with the Western world: drug use, alcoholism, and stress. This peculiarity allows me to underline an important characteristic of "colonial" relations that continues to manifest itself in the contacts between Northern and Southern cultures. The reason why white Western medicine is considered in Africa to be more appropriate to some pathologies is very logical and concrete: these pathologies come from the West, from our contact with them. There is no principle of "extension" that goes on to acknowledge a greater total effectiveness of Western medicine in the treatment of psycho-psychiatric disturbances. This is a simple Western assumption: it is our unfounded presumption that people belonging to other cultures (and among these, many immigrants) have the single perspective of identifying themselves with our cultures, including the medical culture, in a kind of evolutionistic rush to catch up with a superior stage of the human being and thought.

I therefore insist on articulating a distinction between the logic of therapeutic effectiveness and that of the social practicability of the therapies, as they are two completely different orders of discourse, each with important practical implications on the health and psychiatric policy towards immigrants and others.

Sociocultural change and therapeutic effectiveness from an anthropological perspective

The failure of the traditional caregiving system for psychiatric "illnesses" has sociological causes. The characteristics of this process, which are extremely important to our discussion, have been elaborated by many authors. Forster (1976), for example, emphasizes that "the main issue in ethnomedicine is how to take into account the visions of the world and the prevailing views of health and illness, whose effects cannot be ignored, not only in terms of psychic balance but even on sensorial perceptions. . . . The people in question are often aware of the cultural dimension of their state of health and illness and for this reason do not accept the impersonal vision of Western medical science, as their views appear under many aspects and present themselves persuasively as a self-sufficient and well-founded system."

Mary Douglas expresses a different point of view on the way of reasoning of "primitive" people, one that is less "descriptive" and more "interpretative". She does not deal specifically with illness and health but more generally, with visions of the world and rituals as examples of the ways of thinking adopted in a particular society. From her perspective, the attitude of primitive people towards danger, which is identified as an indicator of a pre-modern or magic mentality, should not be understood in terms of an actual adherence to the magical thought, but, rather, as a necessity of group cohesion caused by the "political" fragility of the society: " When non-believers are accused of wreaking havoc on the weather, killing with lightning bolts and causing storms at sea, what should interest us is not a blind spot in the way of reasoning of primitive men but rather something related to the attribution of blame. . . . I have put forward the hypothesis that their political structure is more fragile than ours, so much so as to force them to resort to guilt and taboo, and I have mentioned the possibility that their political fragility takes into consideration what could instead appear to be a flaw in their rational faculties" (Douglas, 1998, pp. 7–8).

Thus, both Tchetche and Douglas conclude that the social component—unsustainability (Tchetche) and political fragility (Douglas)—play a crucial role with respect to the adherence (or not) to a "modernized" view of the world by so-called primitive people. However, the two interpretations have significantly different consequences in the therapeutic framework.

Following Douglas's hypothesis, we would arrive at a therapeutic approach characterized by collusion. In other words, according to this interpretation, the "primitive" does not really believe in what he or she says, but says it out of fear of making the vision of the world to which he or she belongs more fragile. Consequently, the primitive behaves *as if* he or she believed it. In this case, the therapist (ethnotherapist) should be aware that resorting to interpretations of the psychic disorder that locate its cause in forces belonging to the world of the invisible takes place *as if* he or she also believed it. In reality, both believe in something else.

If the hypotheses of reference are those of Tchetche, for whom the change in the vision of the world and of the health/illness system is more apparent than real, the resulting therapeutic approaches are closer to those theorized and practised by Nathan. In this case, it should be clear to the therapist (ethnotherapist) that even if the patient acts as if he or she no longer has a sense of belonging to the culture of origin, deep down there is a strong adherence. Consequently, the therapist must act through an intervention of strong "influence", promoting the patient's re-acknowledgement of his or her own deeper convictions.

My ethnopsychotherapeutic experience of several years and in different clinical contexts has allowed me to verify that with immigrant patients, the second hypothesis is the more valid and applicable one. At the same time, with many patients, perhaps a greater readiness on our part to play a role that is closer to the one described in the first hypothesis could lead to a reduction in the many drop-outs. We deal with this topic in greater detail in chapter three. As an extreme synthesis, we could say that the symptoms and visions of the world of immigrants are also in a migratory phase.

Whoever has had anthropological and psychotherapeutic training and work experience (as the author of this book has had) should be aware of the analogy between and complementarity of the two disciplines. Other authors have pointed out the similarity of the methods and tools used in both anthropological and psychoanalytic work;[28] I intend here to deal with the relationship between ethnographic methods and family psychotherapy methodologies. In order to be concise and clear, I shall continue to refer to the two Ivorian studies discussed above.

The fundamental questions regarding mental health put forth by the authors can be summarized as follows:

- To which general vision of the world does the Ivorian population refer?
- How do they define mental health, and what cultural significance do they give to it?
- To whom do they go in case of illness, and what are the results?
- What do they think is the best treatment?

In ethnographic work, it is necessary to use some devices in order to be fully trusted by the community that one intends to study, to minimize the risk of misunderstandings, suspicion, and the like, as these factors may invalidate the collection of information. In addition, only with time can one accumulate reliable information, especially when a study is being undertaken in areas that are rife with conflictual issues such as mental health. An illuminating example is an ethnographic study by J. Favret-Saada (1980) on witches in France, in the region of Bocage, where only after a long period of time did the people of the community begin to talk freely with the researcher about their personal experiences with witches. They wanted to be fully confident that the ethnographer was not a witch herself.

In many cases the members of the community being studied are reluctant to talk. They assume, often rightfully, that the researcher has such a superficial knowledge of their culture that it would be impossible to make him or her understand it in all of its nuances. It is not by chance that I have referred to studies conducted in the Ivory Coast by Ivorian researchers and therapists.

Finally, we come to the relationship between interpretative methods used in family therapy—those that allowed Tchetche to collect the information utilized above—and ethnographic methods. An understanding of what is behind the conscious formulations of those who furnish information is vital to both. I am not referring to the Freudian concept of the subconscious, but, rather, to fundamental ideas (presuppositions) taken for granted in the community, so much so that community members no longer even consider or discuss them. These kinds of ideas can emerge only after specific solicitations or after important, fundamental changes, or otherwise through ethnographic or psychotherapeutic work. Yet these fundamental assumptions in a culture largely determine all human behaviour. They are considerably more influential than the conscious thoughts that go to make up formal ideologies.[29] Whoever has worked in the field in Africa or in other continents with communities belonging to "other" cultures must be conscious of the hiatus that exists between what is declared, what is presumed (fruit of fundamental assumption), and what is really evident.[30]

The considerable space dedicated in this chapter to cultural change in Ivorian society serves as a point of reference with which I hope to clarify my point of view on the two further themes that concern psychotherapy with immigrants:

1. synchronism in the processes of social and cultural change, and, in particular, the relationship between individual and socially shared synchronism;
2. therapeutic efficacy, including interpretation of the cause(s) of disturbances (aetiology).

Let us briefly discuss the first point, giving particular attention to psychological-psychiatric disturbances. By "synchronism" I mean the phenomenon according to which, within a process of cultural change, when there is sufficient time, the people involved adapt to new values, points of view, beliefs, and so on. They maintain, however, a certain number of prior values, though these may be transformed. This occurs despite the fact that the two systems may be incompatible on a rational level. The existence of a universal process of synchronization testifies to man's profound necessity to integrate the old with the new, the past with the present, in order to give continuity, order, and sense to his being in the world.

Interpretations of the world and the rituals that represent them are continually being assembled, disassembled, and reassembled. As we saw in the first chapter of this book, this is evident in the evolution of fables, which, in their extreme wealth and diversity, have nonetheless maintained identical or similar structures. This fact confirms the pertinence of an autonomous "rule" of social phenomena: structural changes happen at a rate far different from that of cultural and social changes. A radical, structural change does not automatically correspond to a change in the culture of the individuals who experience this change. This is often the case because the individuals are *subjected* to change. The appeal to synchronism is one of the elements that allows identity, or similarity, between the past and the present to be maintained. In other words, within the process of change, synchronism is a kind of bridge between the past and the present and is essential for the integration between different points, times, and stages.

It is important to observe how synchronism manifests itself in different ways in different cultures. Fables are one rather recent example. In the ancient past, the recounting of fables included rituals (as happens today in cultures that are less affected by modernization)—generally, initiation rites and rites of passage.

We must now understand *how* a system changes and *why*. In this case, we are dealing with a system of interpretations, knowledge, and practices relating to sickness and, more specifically, to madness. If, as in the case of the Ivory Coast, the reason *why* is linked to unsustainability, it is nonetheless necessary for the traditional society to explain *how* these changes and mutations in the social environment happen. Change may come about through degeneration—that is, loss of efficiency. Regarding, however, the individual and social health, one may use the logic of compatibility with phenomena in other systems (economic, colonial, etc.).

My hypothesis is that synchronism, far from being a residual function, allows the old system to maintain prior objectives, or at least it allows it time to verify that the new system is more clearly suitable and does not bring about degradation. According to Propp, fables, for example, embody a new form, a new model, that society has slowly adopted as a substitute for ancient rites of passage.[31] In this lengthy process, the real objective of the ritual—to signal, pronounce, and legitimize through a kind of rehearsal the change in status of individuals within the society—is partly maintained and partially lost. Something has been maintained through the permanence of the "functions" that correspond to the structure of rites, but something has been progressively lost in the diminished context in which the new system/fable is used. From a familiar social context it has moved to being a secondary product for children, utilized in situations that are often marginal to social life and to dominant forms of communications and socialization. To conserve the effectiveness and the purpose of the rite/fable (passage from one status or role to another) we must attempt to maintain both the structure (the functions) and the context in which this structure was once effective. At the very least, we must recreate it symbolically.[32]

Shifting our attention to changes in medical systems (traditional versus Western) we are obliged to pose the question in two ways. In the first place, we must verify whether or not the characteristics that rendered the traditional system effective have been maintained in the Western system. (If so, as we say in jargon, the *baby has not been thrown out with the bathwater.*) Second, we must analyse the situations in which synchronism has more acute reasons to exist—for example, in traditional societies undergoing change and transformation, and in immigrants who have turned to Western therapies.

It is necessary to direct our attention to the second theme so as to understand *if, why,* and *how* forms, practices, rituals, and instruments used to animate prior systems could be effective. Anthropological interest in this matter dates from at least the beginning of the twentieth century, when Mauss, in 1926, called attention to the phenomenon of induced death by social suggestion, a phenomenon that he had personally seen (Mauss, 1965). In this case, while psychic conditioning is evident, no form of wilful self-destruction was evident in the victim. Beginning with this observation, and referring explicitly to Durkheim's thesis as explicated in *Elementary Forms of Religious Life,* Mauss deepened his investigations into the relationship between psychological and organic functions and social factors. "Sacred things are simply collective ideals, represented in the form of moral forces, and fixed on material objects, figures, movements, sounds, words. . . . These symbols are interiorized by individuals once the social fabric has started to unravel. . . . But once again, it is only through these things that individual consciousnesses, naturally closed to one another, can communicate reciprocally" (Durkheim, 1971).

More recently, the field of linguistics has uncovered an analogous procedure in the use of language.[33] Semiotics has attempted to construct "models of generative grammar of language", beginning with the assumption that the procedures of symbolization, which include the use of language, become operative only when the collective models start to become conscious.

The individuation of "generative grammar", common to both metaphoric symbolism and myth and to scientific logic, and the rules of transformation pertaining to both, allow us to make significant ground in the understanding of our difficulties. Valid assistance on this front comes from the work of Claude Lévi-Strauss and from structuralist anthropology. In 1949, in his studio, Lévi-Strauss hypothesized three determining elements to explain the symbolic effectiveness of shamanic interventions: (1) the shaman's belief in his own techniques; (2) the belief, confirmed by previous successes, of the subject in these cures; and (3) collective consensus "since the training of the shaman, and the intellectual satisfaction and affection he receives, is subject to collective adhesion that inaugurates, in turn, a new cycle" (Lévi-Strauss, 1962).[34]

Lévi-Strauss suggests that we also consider the effectiveness of shamanism from another point of view: that of the relationship between normal thought and pathological thought. The respective functions of these are: the ongoing schism in a given system and, in the second, the maintenance of unity. This would mean that to a certain degree the "mentally sound" person is an alienated individual who collaborates with the schism in society, whereas the "madman" would be that individual who does not accept life in a schizophrenic world founded on a schism between the world of symbols and the real world. "In every society, then, there would be a certain (variable) number of individuals who find themselves located . . . outside the system, or between two or more irreconcilable systems. The group asks of them, and imposes on them, the representation of predetermined varieties of compromise that are unrealizable on the collective level, and that they pretend to make imaginary transitions, to incarnate impossible syntheses. In all behaviors that are apparently aberrant, the 'protagonist' is simply translating the group's state and rendering tangible one or more of its many constants. Their peripheral position does not stop them from being an integral part of the total system. More precisely, if they were not the docile witnesses that they are in reality, the total system would risk disintegration of its local systems. It can be affirmed, then, that in every society the relationship between normal behaviors and particular behaviors is complementary" (Lévi-Strauss, 1965).

The madman, then, in order to return to the terminology used until now, is nothing other than the actor of an individual synchronism that allows him or her to connect the symbolic world with real systems through expedients, modalities of thought and behaviour, that are no longer part of the society, or, rather, are socially shared but in ambiguous ways. The effectiveness of the therapeutic intervention would therefore consist in creating, through appropriate rituals, a connection between modalities of thought belonging to these two worlds that partake of forms that are more thoroughly shared, creating in this way a passage—among various possibilities—from an individual synchronic form to a socially shared synchronic form.

It is not difficult to find similar elements in these interpretations of the causes of disturbances and mental disorders and the visions described in the first part of this chapter: those "subjugated" models of ethnopsychiatry or "ethnoiatry" (as we have called them) that we examined from a diachronic perspective. It is also useful to maintain elements of this vision of mental illness in approaches to family therapy. But we treat this theme further ahead.[35]

Continuing from the socio-anthropological interpretative perspective, we must now individuate *how*—that is, through which specific mechanisms—the three characteristics suggested by Lévi-Strauss would function. That is to say, with which relational and social interventions can one produce a corporeal change in a patient? It is a question that may seem superfluous to this discussion, given that we are dealing principally with psychic disorders, sicknesses that are not strictly the domain of biomedical expertise. However, I believe that these considerations are useful as an introduction to and an illumination of the following discussion relating more specifically to the ethnopsychiatric setting. It is sufficient to remember that, according to Lévi-Strauss, the effectiveness of shamanic therapy is based on a structural homology between operations of the mind and dynamics of the organism. For which reason, the manipulatory aspect of the cure consists in inducing an organic transformation through the actualization of a symbolic language, both received by the patient and, in turn, produced by the patient. In other words, the shaman intervenes in the relations that exist in the patient between symbol and the symbolized object, placing himself in relation with the mental functioning of the patient through a process in which causes, and the pathological situation in which he finds him/herself, are symbolized. For the sick person, the shaman is the person who is in most direct contact with monsters, spirits, and the forces inducing physiological disorder in him or her. The shaman knows the language of the invisible world, thanks to which he can induce a physiological restructuring in the patient "through a language that he provides to the sick person and with which he or she can express certain unformed and unformable states". "That the mythology of the shaman does not correspond to an objective reality is an unimportant fact: the afflicted person believes and is member of a society that believes." The cure would consist of making the mind accept pain that the body refuses to support; pain that, "thanks to myth, is substituted by the shaman by a unity in which everything has its reason for being . . . the afflicted person, having understood this, no longer limits him/herself to resignation: he or she heals."

Here, Lévi-Strauss provocatively introduces a comparison with Western therapeutic processes. Why, he asks, "when sick people in our society are offered a detailed explanation of the causes through the individuation of microbes, bacteria and viruses (through, that is, simple communication), why don't they heal? Paradoxically, because bacteria and viruses exist, while monsters do not exist. But "the relationship between microbe and illness is external in the mind of the Western patient, that is, a relationship of cause and effect. . . . While for the 'traditional' patient, the relationship between monster and illness is internal, whether he or she is aware of it or not. The relationship is one between symbol and symbolized object." Lévi-Strauss hypothesizes that the shamanic cure is a situation "midway between our organic medicine and certain psychological therapies like psychoanalysis. Its originality derives from the fact that it applies a method similar to the latter to organic dysfunction." "In both cases, conflict and resistance are dissolved not through consciousness, real or supposed, that the ill person progressively acquires, but this consciousness makes a specific experience possible, in the course of which conflicts manifest themselves in an order and on a level that permit free resolution and a final dissolution of symptoms" (Lévi-Strauss, 1998b, pp. 221–223).

Sociocultural change and therapeutic effectiveness in a psychological perspective

I would now like to highlight other interpretations of the effectiveness of shamanic therapy, interpretations that approach categories of Western thought and, in particular, of dynamic psychotherapy. I refer, as an example, to recent specialist studies, even if Lévi-Strauss was already moving in this direction to a certain degree when he hypothesized a duel similitude between the afflicted person and the shaman and between the shaman and the psychotherapist.[36]

The first interpretation that I intend to propose is from a description of the case of a Cambodian patient treated in a refugee camp at the Cambodian border in Thailand. The case is described analytically, together with numerous others, by J. P. Hiegel and C. Hiegel-Landrac (Hiegel & Hiegel-Landrac, 1996b). The authors were able to observe how at times, if disorders (including psychological disorders) are not encysted, it is possible to obtain astounding results through the use of traditional medicine. The case in question is that of an 8-year-old child named Vicheka, born with the umbilical cord wrapped around his neck. As he was cyanotic and unable to cry immediately after birth, he had to be resuscitated. He had always been a very difficult child, particularly with his mother. To escape from Cambodia, the family had had to separate, and the father, who had previously taken care of the child, was obliged to escape in a different way and at a different time than that of his family. Some time after their arrival in the refugee camp in Thailand, the mother decided to abandon Vicheka, because she was no longer able to face the child's behavioural problems, which had become increasingly serious and frequent. In particular, she was not able to tolerate the child's aggression towards her and his two young siblings, nor the incessant destruction of the family's few belongings.

The child was born during the period in which the Khmer Rouge had prohibited every form of religious practice. Vicheka's mother had not been able to give the offerings required by her culture when the child was born. On the premises of the Centre of Traditional Medicine in the camp, at the *krus*,[37] a *slator*[38] was prepared and was put inside the child's house. Two days later, Vicheka appeared smiling, calm, relaxed, happy, and affectionate. He visited the camp's psychiatrists regularly over the following year. His behaviour remained perfectly normal. According to the Khmer tradition, a child who is born with the umbilical cord wrapped around his or her neck develops mental disturbances, or at least suffers recurrent headaches, if the appropriate offering is not made at birth, and possibly repeated later in case of necessity.

Jean-Pierre Hiegel comments on this case, underlining that modern therapy faced with this type of syndrome would reason in organic terms, pronouncing a diagnosis of cerebral damage due to neonatal anoxia; or in psychoanalytic terms, would identify an oedipal relationship. These are diagnoses that for a Khmer child, living in a refugee camp, do not always appear to be particularly useful. The *krus*, in this case, gave the appropriate response, producing a family dynamic that can be understood also through our conceptual system. The mother–child dynamic can be summarized in this way: the mother knew that headaches, and possibly madness, would have marked the child's destiny, but, given the dictatorial conditions imposed by the Khmer Rouge, she could not practise the appropriate protective rituals. The place attributed to Vicheka since birth by the mother's unconscious was that of the lunatic, a role that the child had faithfully fulfilled until the suitable offering was made. The *slator*, relieving the mother of her sense of guilt, allowed her to hope that the child might become normal. From this "turn", the child himself felt authorized to demonstrate that which he had always been, without running the risk of losing his place in the family. He was cured in less than 48 hours.

Hiegel shows elsewhere that in the West, when children born in similar circumstances present similar problems, a favourable evolution can be noted thanks to psychotherapeutic sessions held exclusively with the parents. If a child is born cyanotic and does not cry immediately, all mothers, be they Western or Khmer, may believe that the child's brain has been damaged. The Khmer traditional belief system allows validation, under the cloak of magic, of an intervention whose character is clearly psychotherapeutic and which, provided that the mother–child relationship is not gravely neurotic, brings about immediate effects.

Here, then, we see a possible non-magical interpretation of the effectiveness of a specific traditional therapeutic intervention. There are many others, and reporting them would entail nothing more than reference to an encyclopaedia. The collections of studies edited, respectively, by Corin and Murphy (1979) and by Corin and Bibeau (1980) are essential for anyone who wants to pursue work in this field. An interesting point of view is presented in these studies by O. C. Ortigues and E. Ortigues, who offer a psychoanalytic interpretation of traditional Africa's diverse visions of the world, which are prevalently of a persecutory nature (Ortigues & Ortigues, 1973, quoted in Corin & Murphy, 1979, p. 164). Reflecting on the consequences of the particular oedipal situation of African children—as members of an extended family in which the natural father is not seen as a rival—these authors hypothesize that instead of the oedipal process being redirected to the entire group of elders (including dead ancestors), a situation too oppressing to be confronted, it is expressed through rivalry among brothers. But since this rivalry cannot be expressed directly due to a prohibition imposed by the community, it is converted into a general feeling of persecution.

The numerous interpretations, both anthropological and psychological, present in the literature are not free in any case from the fundamental conditions highlighted by Lévi-Strauss: adhesion between therapist and patient to the same culture and the contextualization in a reference group (community) that binds and reinforces the therapist–patient relationship.

The third area: ethnopsychiatry and alternative medicine

The growing interest in ethnopsychiatry can also be explained by the fact that anthropology and sociology have already introduced reflections of a general nature concerning the role and the meanings that illness has in culture and society. In addition, illness and recovery constitute fundamental elements of the social, cultural, and symbolic world of every community. Today we know that in many societies and cultures (among which, those we have already dealt with) a net schism between mind and body, between spirit and matter, such as that common in Western thought, does not exist. But we also know that structural similarities and differences exist between all societies and cultures, however different they are, in the way in which illness is caused, diagnosed, and treated.

According to Kleinman (1981), every health system is composed of three partially overlapping subsystems: the popular subsystem, the professional, and the "folk".[39] The popular subsystem represents the largest and least studied subsystem of all health systems, so much so that both in Western industrialized countries and in developing countries, between 70% and 90% percent of all pathological episodes fall within the defining boundaries of this system. The popular subsystem is always in communication with the other two systems, while the professional and the folk systems often do not communicate.

The clinical reality of the diverse subsystems and their components are extremely differentiated. However, the power to render illness and recovery social phenomena and to legitimize a certain construction of reality as "the one true clinical reality" are not equally distributed and depend largely on the level of institutionalization and legitimization of the subsystem.

In Western societies, the professional subsystem is constituted by so-called scientific medicine, but it is necessary to remember that in some countries—the best-known are China and India, but we have seen that this is also the case in the Ivory Coast and in most of Africa—real, verifiable autochthonous professional systems exist. In Western, industrialized countries, scientific allopathic medicine has been able to gain professional predominance, eliminating, controlling, and marginalizing other forms of medicine. For some of these other medicines, the process of marginalization has happened only in the twentieth century. Over the past twenty years, however, a certain reversal of this process has been noted.

In countries in which traditional cultures are not simply surviving, as in many of the so-called developing countries from which a majority of immigrants to Western countries come, "scientific" medicine is subject to a process of "indigenization", complementary to that of modernization and synchronization that we examined in the Ivory Coast study. This is a sort of cultural metabolization, similar to the process of popularization that medical concepts are subject to when they are introduced into a popular subsystem. Very often, the greatest problems of communication between patient and health system arise from an insufficient indigenization of scientific medicine, and doctors, psychologists, and researchers often think of the health system in its entirety as the only existing professional system.[40]

Naturally, this attitude persists in relationships between professionals of "scientific" medicine and members of "popular" or "folk" cultures, as is often the case with immigrants, in particular in the area of mental illness. Similarly, the readings that immigrants (bearers of values and knowledge, both "folk" and "popular") give to these kinds of relationships in their dealings with the host nation's health system offer us many illuminating interpretations. The ethnopsychiatric therapeutic practices used in many creolized Western societies can effectively be seen as an attempt to integrate the knowledge and practices of various folk and popular subsystems with the Western medical system. These ethnopsychiatric experiences can, in addition, be categorized in relation to a greater attention given to folk and popular subsystems belonging to immigrant patients.

For example, in the approach and in the clinical model of Nathan, the cultural origin and the characteristic folk therapeutic practices of the patient are taken into consideration almost exclusively. The approaches of Littlewood, of the Minkoweska Centre in Paris, and other European and American realities seem to accentuate further the relationship between popular subsystems. (For further information about the approaches and the experiences of ethnopsychiatry with immigrants, see chapter three.)

The presence in our societies of members of "other" cultures undoubtedly contributes to reinforcing recognition of official medicine's limits and the paradigms accompanying its practice (essentially linear-causal: the symptom is an indicator of the cause, the abolition of the symptom or the externalization of the cause produces a healing effect). The process is already underway among practitioners who tend to be more sensitive to professional medical subsystems. Awareness of the limits of the scientific vision is being accompanied by the presence of a more complex vision of both the causes and the process through which illness manifests itself. In less rigid and institutionalized forms of scientific thought, a different paradigm is emerging that revisits the traditional idea of illness as a corruption in harmony, as an interruption in the cosmic process that connects the individual to the environment and to the group. Sacks (1973) suggests possible areas of research in this direction when, recalling Alexandr Luria, he speaks of "romantic" and classic" as specific and distinct forms of thought. And Bruner (1986) identifies in the "narrative" and the "paradigmatic" two natural modalities of thought. In addition, elsewhere in the much diffused and legitimized field of psychotherapy, models and schools exist that are more or less open to the influence of new paradigms.

It is obvious that people who are rigidly determined to search out links to biological-genetic causality in mental illness will be rather disinclined to develop hybrid ideas—and even if they choose to, they will have few instruments with which to do so. Such people will be little inclined to mix their own interpretations with an interpretation of psychological malaise that involves supernatural causes, lack of respect for ancestors, or cultural norms belonging to the community and the family. Analogously, one who is open to recognizing the relational components in psychiatric pathology will have more instruments with which to recognize how, in other societies, relationships are founded on models and cultural practices that are different.

Immigrants are responsible for the existence of "other" concepts of health among us, but not only those. Their presence has revitalized concepts that were already present in our societies but were largely or slightly marginalized. Given that in all societies the tendency to identify a connection between biological order and social order exists, in what way and in which communities is illness explained in terms of social order? Is there some kind of correspondence between ethnic group and the importance given to social, cultural, and religious reasons for illness?

Whether one is a psychiatrist or a psychotherapist, one of the most common opening comments during a first meeting is: "I have never been sick, I've never slowed down for anything." This equivocation defines the illness more than any other physical state. In this case, the illness, as a socially connoted discourse, moves away from the medical model. The illness is not necessarily experienced as "destroyer" but, on the contrary, may represent an occasion to free oneself from a socially oppressive, suffocating role.

In socially connoted social representations of illness, there is a kind of equivalence between perception of social aggression and the illness itself. The individual must try to resist aggression. In fact, the perception of self, as happens in the case of immigrants, is that of being fundamentally healthy. It is the world that makes him or her ill. This representation of health and illness can be schematized in a double opposition: health versus sickness and the individual versus society. This is a representation that reminds us of themes that have existed for ages: corrupt air, for example, and above all the idea—classic in anthropology, in some ways present also in the studies of the Ivory Coast—of illness as exogenous and caused by a real or symbolic intrusion of a harmful object and/or the malevolent act of an unhealthy person (represented in this case by society). While for some marginal autochthonous groups in Western society (e.g., see Léger, 1983) that same society represents a singular "objectified" totality in which relationships and social interests neutralize themselves, in the ideas of "otherness" of illness, brought to the West by immigrants, the image of society does not exclude conflict.

The general processes of change that occur in society and in cultures help us, therefore, to recognize the existence of a certain proportion of the population—not only immigrants[41]—orientated towards practices and content that respond to needs not covered by official medicine. This phenomenon has characterized all advanced societies at least for the past twenty years. The diffusion of non-institutional medicine is, indeed, connected to the capacity to respond to these new types of needs. We are dealing with an indigenization of folk and popular practices. I do not believe that one can speak of a new phenomenon, inasmuch as all societies have always applied therapeutic practices in parallel to institutional ones that have often been complementary and have cohabited with official practices without friction.[42] This is due to the fact that no culture is ever able to give a complete institutional response to the question of healers.

It is, therefore, only a limit, a need to simplify our language and our thought, to speak of "our culture", of a Western culture, while in all sectors—even those concerning health and mental illness—there are multiple responses. It seems that, even in this sphere, there is one dominant culture and another subjugated.

Indeed, the request, the need, for health and/or healers does not completely coincide with the visible extent of this need: there is a latent dimension that is channelled in other directions and testifies to something profoundly felt and not entirely translatable into words or behaviours, hidden in the healer as it is hidden in the illness itself.

Such plurality exists to an even greater extent inside societies that we recognize as increasingly creolized. Traditional or alternative medicines are used to a notable degree in the West, even if it is a degree that is incomparable to the weight and the power of official medicine. This is not a new phenomenon. However, there is something different and specific, apart from its mass appeal, in the way it is manifested today. In this sense we must consider it a collective phenomenon, and one of the characteristics common to all collective phenomena during construction phases is the lack of language, symbols, points of semantic reference with which we can name what is being born. In this phase, collective phenomena typically use the available cultural patrimony to voice new needs to which responses are sought. Other times, they use socially marginalized experience to revitalize them.[43]

In our case, it may be useful to underline similarities and commonalities among many traditional medicines, and some ethnopsychiatric formulations, for the construction of a conceptually new language and conceptual models. Apart from the common vision of health as a continuity between people, community, and environment and illness as a break in this circuit/equilibrium,[44] it is also possible to compare and integrate language and concepts that come from "traditional" and "scientific" nosology. We have, in addition, often referred in the preceding sections to the work of Di Nola, Bibeau, and others, work that represents important benchmarks for the development of our work.

Furthermore, the holistic and circular model that is at the base of all the traditional practices tends to highlight the global interdependence of phenomena that comprise our experience, and responds to the need to abandon the linear causality that characterizes many sectors of our society. The paradigm of linear causality is in profound crisis. This is true not only in our field, but in our daily experience, ever increasingly characterized by uncertainty, plurality, turbulence, and differentiation. It is therefore natural that we move in the direction of research that focuses on connections rather than causes. Today we are in need of convincing theories of connection able to give sense to the experiences that we encounter in many spheres of our lives.

Many non-institutional healing practices are able to provide a response to the profound, constitutive needs of this culture of complexity, and they appear as an alternative to official medicine, taking advantage of the latter's failures and inadequacies. I think, however, that this function is temporary. It will be followed by a process in which the content of non-institutional healing practices will be exulted and from which a new paradigm will be born. Alternative practices, among these ethnopsychiatry (or ethnopsychiatries), contribute in a decisive way to the formation of a new paradigm. Their aims are to develop individual responsibility regarding illness and health that are not limited by social aspects and to adopt a non-biomedical model that focuses on the symbolic, relational, and cultural dimensions and is founded on non-linearity.

As for the relationship between official medicine and "other" practices, if we assign the role of collective phenomenon to the diffusion of these practices, they can be read as relationships between ordered institutions and movements. The institutions—in this case, official medicine—respond to the need for change usually in three ways, or a combination of all three. The first is refusal: an attempt to ignore that which the other brings that unveils the institution's lack and failures. The second is co-optation: the institutions respond by co-opting the new movement's elite and creating parallel institutions. In the variegated world of alternative practices, it is necessary to differentiate true, authentic "contra-institutions"—parallel institutions with their own market, their own elite, and their own institutional codes—and practices that are still in a nascent phase. The third response is reform: that is, institutional change that brings about the incorporation or creation of new institutions that embrace innovation with new energy.

In the process of forming a new paradigm—a process that removes the residual character of traditions and parallel practices and brings them into the debate—the construction of a new language that destroys both that of official medicine and that of traditional practice is vital. A new paradigm can be born only in the moment in which the old language is left behind. Until then, we continue to use unsuitable and inadequate words for something that cannot, as yet, be named.[45]

To delineate the border of this new paradigm in therapeutic terms, we might consider two afflictions that official medicine has been addressing with little success, and from which human beings suffer daily: chronic pain and psycho-psychiatric disorders. In other words, the kinds of illnesses to which social and even iatrogenic causes are relevant. Diverse medical practices—traditional and/or alternative—among these ethnopsychiatry have much to give in this direction. It is necessary to recognize plurality as the fundamental characteristic of the new paradigm under construction—plurality at the level of intervention, interpretative keys, language, and technique. The case described in the second part of the book illustrates the specific contribution of (ethno)psychotherapy at the theoretical, technical, and practical levels.

Conclusions

I would like to underline once more that the structure of a vision of the world does not change when the form through which it is expressed (ritual or fable) changes. Structural continuity—beyond the apparent and often superficial changes—is valid for the observable modifications in historical time, and for the same society in different periods, and for the changes derived from contact with "other" societies. They provoke some important observations for psychotherapy:

1. If (psycho)therapeutic rituals used in other traditional cultures are effective, the structure of these rituals (not necessarily the content) should be effective, at least for people coming from cultures similar to that of the therapeutic practice.
2. If syncretism, as a social category, is a phenomenon that one can find in all situations of cultural change, it must also be present within immigrant groups.
3. Consequently, the reflections and the numerous discoveries coming from psychotherapeutic work with immigrants—a category on which multiple factors of change have a great bearing—can be used, with necessary elaboration and specification coming case by case, even with people belonging to other social categories subject to change. In some ways, all of us are, at least a little bit, immigrants.

An implicit corollary to the third point is that a series of therapeutic rituals functions as a bridge, as a way of "integration," between a past and a present that is fractured. This hiatus is repaired in a way that sparks in the patient a feeling of being once again part of the world. But all this is understandable and communicable if the "mental illness" is explained as a response to a fracture, even a precocious fracture, that has occurred in the life of the patient.

Notes

1. Here, the meaning of *popular medicine* includes folkloric curative subsystems that other authors (e.g., Kleinman, 1981) distinguish from popular medicine, as discussed in the third section of this chapter.

2. "Ethnopsychiatry has always paid special attention to the study of 'superior' cultures, using the terminology and the epistemology of the superior cultures themselves, even when it has had as its reference point, primitive archaic and ethnicities, and has ignored the subjugation inside classes-based cultures" (Di Nola, 1981, p. 9).

3. Conflict between the generations—the generation of grandparents and their children-parents and grandchildren—can come close to the conflicted relationships noted between "erudite" and "submerged" or "profane" interpretations.

4. The next section describes how these categories correspond to those described by studies of "alternative" visions of the world, health, sickness, and death in cultures whose members are from "traditional" backgrounds. Note here, while postponing the argument for a deeper analysis to the following section, that the study of definitions of sickness and systems of cure in alternative cultures has brought to light interpretive schemes that are more sophisticated than the schemes (perhaps more simplistic) that were previously available in the Western biomedical paradigm. Many scholars and many schools are now moving towards research of new paradigms, having been made aware of the restrictive limits of the "erudite" biomedical model. Mariella Pandolfi, for example, referring specifically to psychological malaise in immigrants, underlines that "it is necessary to construct a methodology that incorporates rather than separates the complex aspects . . . of the migratory event. . . . This experience is one of life's most complex since it involves the individual and the group to which he belongs, his land or origin and that which welcomes him." It cannot be compressed by moving attention from diagnostic psychiatric categories to more exotic ones that often, in common language, have become known as "psychopathology of immigration." Pandolfi continues, proposing a project of medical and psychiatric anthropology that focuses on the study of two dimensions: that of the body, intended as "historical and problematic category and saturated with the imaginary" and that of "narration of the sickness that substitutes the sickness itself" (Pandolfi, 1993). Though it may be true that the tripartite, body–relations–myth foundation scheme distinguishes itself from the linear and irregular biomedical, psychiatric approach, it would be incorrect to affirm that the latter is representative of the Western model. However, it is true that psychoanalysis has fully ignored the third element of

the tripartite scheme. Kaës, for example, interpreting Freud, refers to a "genealogy of the psyche, of its instants and its interpsychic ramifications," that point to a double dimension: " the experience corporeal and the experience intersubjective" (Kaës, 1995, p. 17).

5. In the text, I use indiscriminately, on the one hand, the terms "traditional", "archaic", "subjugated", "other", or similar alternatives, and, on the other, "modern", "dominant", "Western", "scientific", and so forth, attributing to them, respectively, the same meaning.

6. The term was coined by Gilles Bibeau (1981) to describe this propensity of Western thought to compare everything. From another perspective and another discipline, Carlo Ginzburg (1979, 1998) has brilliantly discussed this propensity, underlining its necessities and risks. On this important theme, a more thorough discussion can be found in the second part of this present chapter, referring to the discourses of Bibeau.

7. In addition to the illuminating essay by Di Nola dealing with this theme in theoretical terms, apropos of clinical cases of Italian immigrants in German Switzerland, I refer the reader to Risso and Boker (1992). It is important to note that this double reading is useful for understanding many psychosomatic forms observed in immigrant patients—a difficult matter, in which nothing is simple and nothing can be taken for granted. While in subjugated visions there may be no schism between the psychic and the somatic, in so-called *sinistrosi*, for example, the symptom that we consider somatic because it so clearly assails the body of the patient may have psychic origins. At the same time, the immigrant patient, while presenting his or her symptoms in this way, often does not recognize and no longer accepts his or her own cultural origins. As far as the therapist is concerned, he or she does not know how to place the patient and is sometimes plagued by the suspicion that the patient is playing a game with an opulent society, seeking to "exploit" it as best he or she can, a game in which the therapist must participate endlessly. The case of the married couple K, mentioned in the previous chapter, belongs to such a typology.

8. The ambivalence of the "world of the powers" (saints and devils) described by Di Nola (1981, pp. 16–17), finds concrete applications in the case of San Donato, protector of epileptics and generally of all the nervous disorders or disturbances that can be ascribed to the psyche or the mind (San Donato was decapitated). In an essay by G. Lützenkirchen, "Il 'Male' di San Donato" (1981), the fact is confirmed that San Donato has both therapeutic and evil powers (see, in particular, p. 33). This information is of great interest given that the "ambiguity of the world of powers" is present in many African cultures. This, in turn, conditions and suggests the "format" of the therapeutic setting that we must adopt, a setting that should never be composed exclusively of patient and therapist, as this kind of meeting would expose the patient to certain risks—among them, the evil eye.

9. Amadou Hampâté Bâ, born ca. 1900 in Bandiagara (Mali) and died 15 March 1991 in Abidjan, was a member of the executive council of UNESCO. He was celebrated principally for his tireless efforts for oral cultures as well as for numerous works dedicated to culture and traditions. He is credited with the celebrated phrase: "In Africa, when an old man dies, an entire library burns." The annotations that follow are taken from the introduction to a personal

memoir, *Amkoullel l'enfant Peul* (1991: the stories were recorded, as the work was faithfully and completely oral.)

10. Clearly, Hampâté Bâ is referring here to modes of African narration, but, in my opinion, the same temporal dimensions apply to all of the other fundamental activities of quotidian life, and not only in African culture, but in most traditional cultures. (For a deeper analysis of the meanings of this modality of understanding the temporal dimension and its significance for the interpretation of sickness—and, by extension, its prevention and cure—see Augé & Herzlich, 1983, pp. 7–27.)

11. Tobie Nathan refers to the same concept in his work, identifying societies that adopt this modality of thought as *"a universi multipli"* in order to distinguish them from those Western, *"a universo unico"*. In this latter, there is no longer the awareness of the existence of other universes—in particular, a universe (or universes) that is invisible. I shall return to this point and to its therapeutic implications.

12. Memel-Fotê's study is part of a research project commissioned by the World Health Organization, with the aim of collecting sufficient information to clarify public health policies through a re-evaluation of the effectiveness of African medicine. The principal ethnicities and subgroups that make up the population of the Ivory Coast and were part of this study are mandé, dan, kweni, malinké, gur, seufo, lobi, akan, baoulé, abê, kru, dida.

13. *"Génies"* appears in French in the text. However, according to the ethnic group, these figures take a variety of names: *Mandebele-Kulo, Zrii, Xirii, Zlanbenu.* In other regions of Africa, not only sub-Saharan but also in the Barbary States, the terms used are similar: *Jinné, Ginay,* etc. All refer to the common root *genie, genitor, gene,* etc.

14. *Nyctosophes* in the French, from the Greek *nux, nuktòs* (night) and *sophòs* (who possesses wisdom); therefore, "wise one of the night."

15. This data is not unimportant for the choice of the material with which the healers construct their fetishes.

16. [*Translator's note*: The author uses the Italian word *selvaggio*, which has been translated as "wild" and refers to its etymological origins in the French word *brousse*, the bush, scrub. *Selvaggio*, therefore, would mean, "that which comes from the bush."]

17. It is not at all uncommon that the same fear is shared by the translators or cultural mediators with which we collaborate. At times, the mediators of the Geneva group do not explain the causes of their hesitancy to speak; probably they feel embarrassed and, as is the case with many patients, caught between two worlds: on the rational level, they believe that they ought not adhere any longer to traditional visions, but they prudently prefer not to violate rules or laws. As we will soon see, understanding this cognitive modality (and understanding the effects of cultural change) is fundamental for successful therapy.

18. The focus of this book does not allow me to completely analyse the material conditions of the lives of people who share these visions of the world, but I believe it is nonetheless useful to note an important point. Contact with nature, promiscuity in animals, pervasive conditioning imposed by the alternation of day/night and dark/light, and not least the changing seasons, bring with them admixture of alternative living worlds in the interpretation and

explanation of birth, sickness, and death. The rituals adopted in traditional cultures before great events in the life-and-death cycle are, in other words, strongly connected with what happens in other worlds. In this sense, it was illuminating for me (even from the theoretical point of view) to observe the birth of my son's pet cat. My son, Alvise, is used to living in contact with animals. The cat was in labour and Alvise, rather worried, kept it under tight surveillance. At the crucial moment, both of us witnessed the birth. I was under his direction, given that Alvise had thoroughly documented the coming event with the veterinarian. He was prepared and knew exactly the sequence of what would happen. One of the facts on which my son was informed and which was punctually verified immediately after the birth of three kittens was that the mother would eat the placenta that came with each kitten. I had never witnessed kittens being born before and, given my professional "interests", I began to connect this experience with rituals associated with the placenta among the Dogon of Mali, where I had worked for many years. In this, as in many other traditional cultures, the placenta must be eliminated after birth. Not observing these rituals can bring about negative consequences for the mother (sterility, for example) and/or for the child. In a much documented article based on an ample series of ethnographic studies on post-partum practices in African, Asiatic, European and Latin-American countries, and on interviews collected from almost two thousand Peruvians, Davidson (1985) posited a theory according to which the placenta and the rituals associated with it figure so permanently in traditional beliefs and practices due to its morphological characteristics and to its physiological properties. The study also underlines, however, psychosocial reasons: the ritual events delineate a portion of reality and thus create protection against anxiety by supplying an instrument of control over the health and well-being of the mother, the child, and the community. But this, while providing a convincing interpretation of the general functions of the rites, does not yet explain the roots of these convictions. Personally, I believe that an explanation may be found in the observation of animals, particularly those that have always been by man's side. Witnessing the birthing of Alvise's kittens brought with it a certain sequence of hypotheses regarding the elimination of the placenta; the same process may happen millions of times in the minds of people who live in direct contact with the animal world. From there, as is the case for many other important events in life, by imitation and successive differentiation, this act may have taken form as a specific and widespread cultural ritual.

19. With the term "modernization," the authors of the study refer to "innovations that aim for objective explanations and experimental efficaciousness of a scientific, universally applicable type" concerning themes such as health, sickness, and death (Memel-Fotê, 1998, p. 190).

20. As in all traditional societies, specializations exist among the healers of the Ivory Coast. Like bone adjusters, etc, healers cure sicknesses caused from within the visible world; *devins-guérisseurs* (called shamans in other societies) intervene in cases in which the sickness depends on the invisible world.

21. Literally, traditional doctor. In my field experience in Mali, I observed, on the other hand, that this denomination is common also among traditional healers active in the *brousse*.

22. The interpretation of this data is often very difficult and shows traces of the context and methodologies adopted. In this case, we are dealing with interviews and questionnaires given to people presumably in good health in the course of their "normal" lives. The material collected in clinical contexts from persons suffering health problems is quite different. In these cases, "modernized" visions of the world and of sickness often reveals themselves to be superficial (see Tchetche, 1998).

23. The same dynamic is well described and documented in Fiore (1998).

24. Furthermore, even we know this (or at least we suspect it). Nevertheless, we continue through many forms of cooperation and development to export hospitals and other structures that are economically unsustainable in Africa and elsewhere.

25. Similar rituals exist in geographically and culturally distant areas. It has been noted, for example, that there is an extreme similarity between the Zar cult, common in Ethiopia and Eritrea, and a ritual present in the rural Sardinian world. The same *tarantolismo* described and interpreted by de Martino (1961, 1973) has, in both its forms and its protagonists (women), many aspects in common with the rite to which the author here refers.

26. An analysis of the reasons for this commonly observed necessity is given in note 27.

27. The *marabouts* and the *n'döppkat* are, respectively, healers of the relatively more recent Muslim faith and healers/diviners able to put themselves in contact with the invisible world. The reasons for choosing one or the other are essentially economic and social. We return to this extremely important question below. I would like for a moment simply to underline the factors that usually characterize the therapeutic efficaciousness of the shamanic cure: (a) the competence of the healer and his conviction and capacity to communicate with the invisible world; (b) adhesion to the same visions on the part of the afflicted person, his family, and his *entourage* (village, extended family); (c) the active participation of the community in ritual cures. The current change does not consist in a lack of cultural adhesion, but depends upon the difficulty of practicing rites due to urbanization. As a consequence, a sort of collusion exists on the part of families who are undergoing change: we might say that healers "conveniently" feel exempt from a difficult role that does not simply involve economic strain and the employment of other individual resources (time, private premises, the time needed to stay with the patient, etc.) but also brings with it the risks involved in participating in a struggle against invisible forces (see note 17).

28. I refer in particular to Nathan, who, in turn, refers to Devereux (1978a).

29. An example of ethnographic work that is heading in this direction is represented by the work mentioned earlier of Mary Douglas (1998).

30. To distinguish between these subtle differences is not always easy. A clear example of this is the debate on methodological candour that characterized an Italian research group during field work in Mali among the Dogon. Bibeau and Charland (1994) critique as naïve and hurried the hypothesis sustained by the team apropos the determining effects of modernization on the Dogon psychopathology and the relative relapse in terms of the interpretation

of sickness and recourse to cures. In reality, despite the rebuttals published by some members of the same team in the successive number of the same journal (Coppo, Beneduce, and others) the most convincing position seems to be that expressed by Fiore (1998).

31. Also in this case, faith in the efficaciousness of previously utilized rituals had not been lost, but had become impossible to maintain following various changes (social, climatic, migratory, technological, etc.). Calvino seems to be of the same opinion when he comments on Propp's hypothesis: "The birth of many popular fables that have arrived to our time took place in the moment of society's passage from hunting and clan to the first communities based on agriculture; when, that is, the initiation rites fell into disuse and the secret tales that accompanied or proceeded them began to be narrated without a connection to the institutions and the practical functions to which they were originally linked. These fables lost every religious meaning and became stories of wonder, cruelty, fear" (Calvino, 1971, p. xxxv, note 2).

32. Though extremely interesting, for reasons of space I must conclude here this discussion of the cultural and social change and the function of syncretism. Readers interested in deepening their knowledge of this matter should refer to Lombardo, *Metafore della vita* (1984), in particular pp. 163–172 and 191–202. Instead of "syncretism," the author uses the terms "anti-structure" and "limitability" (for further information on limitability, see Turner, 1972); while my reference to syncretism suggests a process within a system, anti-structure and limitability are meant more as variables within a system. Perhaps it would be more appropriate to locate the term syncretism close to the process of "schismogenesis" (see Bateson, 1972).

33. I take up this argument from Lombardo (1984), p. 213.

34. The overlap of the three elements highlighted by Lévi-Strauss with those operating in the "dispositivo etno-terapeutico" proposed by Tobie Nathan, discussed in chapter three, is plainly evident.

35. A similar interpretation of schizophrenia, though utilizing other terms, can be found in the work of Devereux (in particular, 1978b).

36. After a brief mention in "La pensée sauvage" (Lévi-Strauss, 1962), solicited by Michel Leiris, who had judged the collocation too simple, Lévi-Strauss reaffirmed and clarified his hypothesis in the introduction to his work on Mauss (Lévi-Strauss, 1965).

37. The term *kru* means, in Khmer, all people in possession of wisdom. When the context is not sufficiently explicit, a second term is added that clarifies meaning. In this case, we are evidently dealing with people who possess traditional wisdom concerning rites linked to birth.

38. Offerings, generally composed of flowers and candles, with specific characteristics for different reasons.

39. "Folk" means, precisely, "that sector composed of professional traditional practices (traditional healers)". [In the original Italian version of this book, I preferred to use the English term.]

40. Taking into consideration that, in every country, the relationships between folk and popular subsystems are always broader and more significant than professional subsystems.

41. The relationship with "the other", made unavoidable by the presence

of immigrants, provokes self-referential processes that refer to numerous "others" around us. Simple but clear examples of this can be represented by adopted children coming from other cultures—from, that is, various emerging regionalisms and localisms, from our antique origins and cultural beliefs, etc. This process/movement concerns not only medicine but also other social practices—alimentation (biological), style of life, etc.—as is analysed in numerous studies (e.g., see Augé & Herzlich, 1983; Flick, 1992).

42. For further information on these themes, see Losi (1990, in particular chap. 2 and selected bibliography).

43. In the specific case of ethnopsychiatry, the lack of language depends on the homogeneity of classification criteria for symptoms, syndromes, and their cure and treatment. Official psychiatry can turn to extensive classifications like DSM-III and DSM-IV. However, far from representing a clear and unequivocal point of reference, these reference tools often represent a wall of arrogant psychiatric "certainty" that obstinately and obtusely refuses to admit biomedical models. In recent years, serious and systematic work has been done by some journals (in particular, *Culture, Medicine and Psychiatry*) that attempts to critically discuss the exclusive "voices" of DSM-IV from a transcultural perspective.

44. This kind of approach favours attention to environmental, ecological, and social dimensions of sickness and tradition. In this sense, many parallel medicines together with ethnopsychiatry paradoxically appear to be more modern than official medicine, which is hyper-specialized and therefore less sensitive to the systemic, relational, and interactive aspects of health and sickness.

45. The systematic project of the journal *Culture, Medicine and Psychiatry* (see note 43) is oriented in this direction.

CHAPTER THREE

Western psychotherapies adapted for migrants and ethnopsychotherapy

> For ten years, my Arab brain, which thinks in Arabic, has been grinding European concepts in such an absurd way that they are transforming them into bile and getting sick from it.
>
> Chraïbi, *Les boucs* (1955), p. 59

The epidemiological picture

Research on psychiatric problems of immigrants in European countries, widespread though such research may be, does not take the complexity of the problems sufficiently into account and does not reflect upon the complexity that should characterize the instruments of research that are used. The various research reports in question lead to descriptions and interpretations that are difficult to compare. The frequent discrepancies in the results usually reflect social, demographic, or cultural differences recorded among the groups studied, which lead to inevitable diagnostic uncertainties about syndromes with unusual symptomatic forms that are incomprehensible to the Western psycho-psychiatric worker. Added to these reasons is a true conceptual and methodological error: the ingenuous comparison of diverse problems forced into homogeneous definitions that fail to take into account different conceptions of the world and of health/illness/treatment that belong to the diverse cultures. Finally, there is the racism factor, whether manifest or latent, which often translates into diagnostic results that are unfavourable to certain immigrant/patient ethnic groups.

Despite such conspicuous limits, some studies provide epidemiological data that allow a cautious approximation. Many studies do not verify an increase of psychiatric problems for immigrants once they have arrived in the country of destination, while others show a much greater rate of diagnosis of schizophrenia and depression than that of the local population.

Many studies agree in pointing out the form through which immigrants present psychological-psychiatric affliction, which in many cases is somatized in psychiatric symptoms. Research on resident population samples living in the same community (community surveys) show "minor" symptoms of anxiety and depression among immigrants. However, it is necessary to note that these classifications are based on diagnostic repertoires that include the DSM-III or DSM-IV, which some researchers maintain are not effective in recognizing and representing the cultural diversity and significance that the symptoms can assume.

In addition, we know that, for "minor" and more serious symptoms, immigrant patients can turn to doctors who are not psychiatrists, to "alternative" healers, or to groups of volunteers, who can also manage to take care of them within their community. In making these choices, many factors come into play, including cultural barriers and the immigrant's legal status, legitimate or not.

Furthermore, in the country of arrival, as the family reunites on the one hand, and children are born in immigrant families or mixed with others on the other, the daily life of the immigrant families—their plans, concerns, dynamics—changes significantly. There is no doubt that two variables—the presence of an extended family and the length of the period of stay in the country of arrival—are directly correlated with a minor propensity for and probability of returning to the country of departure. It is also undoubtedly true that settling into a foreign country, which has been a widespread phenomenon in almost all European countries in the last twenty years, has an impact on the forms of the immigrant's psychic malaise. In the first phases of the migratory chain, if the problems essentially concern male immigrants who are young and single or who are living with other compatriots in the same conditions, the psychological-psychiatric affliction can be distributed among all of the family members in the phases that follow. Thus, while in the first phases the issues are related primarily to homesickness, solitude, uprootedness, anxiety, and possible episodes of acute dissociation, in the settling phases the malaise begins to concern family relationships—parent–child, the ways of understanding authority, male–female roles, and so forth. In other words, important changes in lifestyle and daily material culture bring corresponding changes in psychiatric problems, their forms, and the chosen interlocutors.

In France, for example, in the last two decades the process of immigration has resulted in a disproportionate increase in women immigrants with respect to the local female population. This, in turn, has brought about an increase in the birth rate: geographically disaggregated data have shown that the number of births among North African and Turkish women has increased, while it has decreased for European women. In mixed couples, this tendency has followed a positive trend (i.e. growth) when compared with European birth rates, and negative when compared with North African, Turkish, or Moroccan birth rates.

It is obvious that fertility rates reflect and at the same time influence different models of relationships and parental roles and consequently throughout the entire family, both nuclear and extended. These are merely a few example of concrete social and cultural changes that cross immigration societies (*creolized or multiethnic*) but, with different times and modalities, those of emigration societies as well.

In fact, the process of immigration into an unknown society and being cut off from one's origins—even if prepared, well-organized, and gradual—brings considerable stress upon the family, correlated with significant changes in status and family roles. The most common are caused by the loss of work on the part of the father and consequently of his status and role within the family; the shift of the woman's role from one exclusively within the family to one in which she performs activities outside the home; the integration of the children, especially during adolescence, into local peer groups and thus who share values, culture(s), and languages extraneous to those of the parents; and the "adultization" of the children, even before puberty, with respect to their better understanding of the local language compared with the difficulties their parents have communicating with the outside world.

I have already highlighted the fact that despite the many studies and research on the psychiatric morbidity of immigrants, the information derived from them is frequently unreliable or conflicting, for three types of reasons:

- methodological differences in the research (particular subgroups or insufficient number, samples that cannot be compared and/ or are not random, etc.);
- diagnostic difficulties due to language or cultural barriers, to xenophobia expressed more or less directly, and also to modes of expressing symptom(s) that are not encountered in Western diagnostic practice;
- lack of comparability between data concerning the local group and the group of immigrants, since the epidemiological differences between the groups can be merely the reflection of a different use of services, at least official ones.

A study conducted by the World Health Organization's (WHO) Regional Office for Europe (Gupta, 1991) shows different epidemiological situations for six European countries (France, Germany, Italy, Holland, Portugal, and the United Kingdom), as well as different levels of depth of the data. In France, for example, the frequency of psychiatric problems among immigrants does not seem to be different from that shown in the local population. However, it must be emphasized that, given the immigrants' work conditions and transition period from one culture to another, their symptoms can manifest themselves in unexpected shapes and forms. Three modalities are illustrated as an example of how depression can be expressed among immigrants. One is entirely similar to that of the rest of the population; a second takes an acute form ("delirium reaction"); the third manifests itself as physical pain, somatic. Going into further detail, we see that the second form, the "delirium reaction", is prominent above all in recently arrived young North African immigrants and manifests itself suddenly, without warning signs. Given the characteristics of immigration trends in France (recent arrivals are limited to those joining their families or seeking political asylum), the incidence of this form is in decline. Nevertheless, there are frequent diagnostic errors offering an excessively pessimistic diagnosis and viewing this form of depression as a medical problem, whereas the treatment should often be a more benevolent one because of the reactive nature of the symptom.

In the third case, relative to "somatic or somatized depression", the immigrants who suffer from this are primarily North African men and women of the first migratory generation, between age 30 and 50 years, who did not immigrate recently and have low working qualifications. This form of depression is preceded by or associated with psychosomatic problems (often peptic ulcers or dermatological disturbances) or follow a traumatic event, usually physical (workplace accident) or psychological (loss of a job, abortion, etc.). In this type of depression it is common to observe symptoms of a physical nature (aches and pains, headache, dizziness, gastrointestinal problems, impotence) as well as psychological (psychomotor slowness, lethargy, insomnia, sadness). This depressive form tends to last for a long time and is difficult to treat, especially in cases of "compensating neurosis" resulting from accidents at work, the major problem for many immigrants.

With respect to Germany, the data provided by WHO appear even more contradictory. In fact, while some data suggest a high prevalence of psychiatric disturbances in the first three months after arrival in the host country (among the Turks it can be as high as 33%), other studies show that the level of psychiatric hospitalization is lower among immigrants than among the host population, especially with regard to diagnoses of schizophrenia, alcoholism, and organic syndromes of the brain. Studies carried out in other regions of Germany show the exact opposite.

The only epidemiological data and clinical observations that appear constantly in all the countries studied concerns the psychiatric problems manifested through psychosomatic symptoms, which, it is commonly believed, could signify a different modality, culturally connotated, of expressing psychic malaise in conditions of life and work that are particularly difficult and precarious, or are experienced as such. Personally, I would include the difficulty of speaking the language of the host country, which makes it difficult to communicate emotions or feelings that can only be expressed in the mother tongue. It is also true, as we shall soon see, that in many traditional cultures there are formal taboos against direct communication of a personal, intimate problem in a dual situation, the very situation that characterizes almost all psychotherapies in the West, as well as the meetings with the doctor.

The inherent difficulties that arise from interpreting results of studies that have been conducted using instruments that are insufficiently sensitive to complex problems (i.e. transcultural, dynamic, diverse, eclectic) lead to the following questions:

1. Can the methodological difficulties in undertaking epidemiological research on immigrant patients be overcome given our current level of knowledge?
2. If the response to the first question is at least partly affirmative, what directions could be pursued to conduct a more satisfactory research (e.g., field studies of various communities and/or ethnic groups in their own context)?

A response to the second question has been in the process of experimentation for several years through a study of transcultural psychiatric epidemiology,[1] essentially qualitative, which, it is hoped, will provide a future orientation in the field of quantitative research as well. Taking these studies into account, we shall now consider the clinical experiences conducted in Europe that hold the greatest interest.

Several European clinical experiences

The therapeutic model for working with immigrants that has been written about, discussed, and debated most in recent years is undoubtedly the one being tested in Paris under the direction of Tobie Nathan. Therefore, it seems inevitable that a good part of the next pages should be dedicated to this model, as well as because both my experience in Geneva and that of the other collaborators in this book are similar to many aspects of this model. Other experiences in Europe do exist. We shall examine Italian ones in the case studies collected in the second part of this volume; here I shall point out the most significant ones among some other countries.

The C. W. Laeken Centre in Brussels (Centrum voor Welzijnszorg te Laeken) is a mental health centre with the declared objective of following the psychological well-being of its patients through a multidisciplinary approach. (For a lengthier description of the activity and the design of the centre, see Leman & Gailly, 1991.) The Centre's psychologists and anthropologists know the languages and cultures of their patients extremely well. Some of the Centre's members are of allochthonous (mixed) origin, so that the relationship between therapist and patient generally does not present communication problems in terms of linguistics or culture. The model of functioning is decisively Western, and the sessions are conducted as a meeting between a therapist (in some cases, two) and the patient in a "classical" setting.

The theories and concepts used by the therapists at the Centre are systemic, behaviouralist, or psychodynamic, even if it is not uncommon that in relationship to the points of view expressed by the patients, explanations for their malaise that rely on traditional concepts (*maraboutage,* witchcraft, etc.) can be accepted. In cases when the therapist sees value, the possibility that the patient will be sent to traditional healers in Belgium or in the country of origin is neither excluded nor infrequent.

According to the people in charge, the Laeken Centre model, which is very similar to that of the Minkowska Centre in Paris, "is the closest to the classical Western model and is part of the fabric of fragmentary therapies that are well known in the West. . . . The drop-out rate, which remains high, is still less serious than the drop-out rates attributed to linguistic barriers" (Leman & Gailly, 1991, p. 136).

Littlewood and his colleagues in London work in an analogous spirit, but the issue of linguistic barriers is not resolved by using allochthonous psychotherapists with the same origins as the patient, as in Brussels and at the Minkowska Centre in Paris. Against the backdrop of the experiences of Brussels and the Minkowska Centre, as Leman and Gailly record from the Laeken Centre (Leman & Gailly, 1991, pp. 136–137),[2] another important theoretical and organizational reference point is presented that cannot be overlooked insofar as it deals with transcultural psychiatry: that of Collomb in Dakar. Into his Western team, Collomb (1973) introduced at least one traditional healer. Although the therapists from the two different cultures tried to interact and coordinate their work, patients saw each of them separately. According to Leman and Gailly, this approach could not aspire to achieve better results than the Centres in Brussels or in Minkowska, because it was proposing an essentially bicultural approach rather than an interdisciplinary one.

The experience of Nathan and the wealth of written material that accompanies it should be considered indisputably "other".[3] In his therapeutic method, Nathan introduces several significant variations with respect to the other experiences. Above all, he adopts a pluri-cultural approach. His team is made up of at least fifteen therapists of different national or ethnic origins: French, Spanish, Wolof (Senegal), Bakongo (Zaire and Congo-Brazzaville), Berber (Morocco), Kabili (Algeria), Arab, Malinké (Mali), Antillan, and so on. The presence of many therapists, of whom one is the primary and the others co-therapists, brings the patients into the framework not of dual therapy but of a group. In this way, the patients recognize that they are in a therapeutic context that is similar to that of traditional healers and where they can bring their problems and be understood. On the basis of the work of Lévi-Strauss, we identified in chapter two the essential components of traditional therapies, and now we see how Nathan's purview reproduces that situation both symbolically and, in many aspects, concretely. Within his therapeutic structure, there is a single therapist surrounded by a group of colleagues functioning as co-therapists. This prevents the frequent blocks that can take place in the patient due to the sensation that a dual therapeutic framework, like all relationships involving two people, has a sexual connotation (defined from a Western point of view as transference) or can be exposed to the dangers of witchcraft. In terms of the definition of the roles of the primary therapist and the co-therapists, one fundamental rule should be respected: only the primary therapist can question the patient directly, even in cases when the patient turns to a co-therapist. On the one hand, this rule hand strengthens the power of the primary therapist; on the other, it allows the patient to choose the explanatory hypothesis that he or she feels is most suitable among the many possible explanations put forward by co-therapists in the course of a session, sometimes even in a theatrical way.[4]

In chapter one, we have shown a series of elements that are useful for recognizing the complexity of the experiences of those whom we call, perhaps summarily, immigrants. We have also seen that the variables that play into the formation of a complex and diversified experience like migration are not even remotely considered in terms of understanding the roots of the migrants, either at the level of the comparative epidemiological research or, even less so, at the therapeutic level.

The apparatus Tobie Nathan has invented, and which has been used by us in Geneva for a number of years, offers a very different setting from any Western therapeutic approach. I believe it provides a satisfactory response to the complexity of the immigrant's malaise. The therapists are seated in a circle, and the patient is either received alone or is accompanied by family members or friends, at his or her discretion. If the patient does not know French sufficiently well (but not only in this case), a translator is present, or, rather, a cultural mediator who knows and shares the patient's culture and can speak with the patient in his or her mother tongue. This is an extremely important element for creating a relationship and a bond between the patient and the mediator and between the patient and the group.

The introduction of a mediator, even in situations in which the immigrant knows French well, has a decisive theoretical value. Language, as is known, is created by a group of speakers and, in turn, creates the speakers as individuals. The term Nathan prefers (for its evocative excess, I suspect), is "fabrication"; Nathan also uses it in reference to other subjects (especially with respect to rites of passage, as we shall see later). With this arrangement, the setting reinforces the process of continual and reciprocal interaction between language, identity, and speakers. To have a translator or cultural mediator allows a group of therapists and co-therapists who come from different countries with different mother tongues to speak "about" language, about the meaning that a certain thing has within respective mother tongues. Thus, a situation is created in which the patient links up and can "crystallize" his or her own symptom within one of the meanings proposed within the group, the one that allows the patient to identify him/herself better and to understand more easily how, why, and what the reason might be for that " thing" that has brought the patient to that place which makes him or her feel so badly. In other words, the situation enables the patient to feel that he or she is understood and protected, to make sense of the personal problem, and to activate a positive therapeutic alliance in which the he or she can play an active role.

The eventuality (very frequent in our sessions in Geneva) that the patient will "crystallize" the explanation of his or her own symptom within an interpretation of the world or of illness that is "other" with respect to the dominant one in the West becomes a topic of constant discussion among non-"ethnic" therapists who observe our experiences. And it is precisely this sort of event that stimulates the most fecund elaborations. I shall try to elaborate briefly on the points that are fundamental for understanding Nathan's approach[5]—above all, the change of the framework, of the setting. In Nathan's vision, it is precisely this change that marks the shift from ethnopsychiatry *tout court* to modern ethnopsychiatry. The introduction of the linguistic issue and the translator has overturned certain common presuppositions of Western psychotherapy.[6] The patient's words can no longer be interpreted according to psychoanalytic criteria. The primary need is to understand the meaning of *those* words literally. For this reason, wherever possible, the patient is asked to talk about some significant passages of his or her discourse in his or her mother tongue, even if the patient is perfectly fluent in French. The translator becomes a representative of that language and of that culture. At this point, the translator's presence alone is no longer sufficient—a "translator of the translator" is needed. The function of the group, of its discussions, is placed within this dynamic. The translator, the group, and the patient no longer have the problem of communicating in one language, but of speaking "of and about" language. Language becomes a subject of discussion.

The presence of the translator introduces the possibility that all interlocutors agree, a possibility that did not exist before. This happens through an open discussion, which, with respect to the patient–therapist relationship in Western psychotherapies, expands the context to a world that is more actual and global, represented by the expressed opinions of the co-therapists, who strengthen and stimulate the patient's ability to "have his or her say". Language has the function of putting people into agreement. To speak of language means to speak of something that can let the participants agree on a certain subject. In other words, language is an object that is "fabricated" by a group, which in turn "fabricates" the individuals of the group, one by one. The group fabricates the language, and the language fabricates the individual.

From this first observation, Nathan extrapolates that the difference between human beings is in the objects (including language) that they fabricate. But there are other "objects" constructed by people. Nathan refers in particular to therapeutic objects, to fetishes, to the "things" constructed in the course of the sessions and given to the patient to complement the prescriptions. These are "things" that have a function of essential mediation to stimulate the communication of the patient with the people, affects, rules, and material culture of the country of origin, as well as with those worlds that are "other" than human and that concretely form part of the patient's culture.

What effects do the prescriptions have, and how can they be understood? In chapter two, but also partially in chapter one, we have seen that in many "other" cultures the interpretation of the world and of illness implies the existence of additional realities that touch and interact with the actual world of people. Many immigrants, but also everyone who belongs to marginalized cultures (therefore, even us to a certain extent), do not live in society as a "single universe" where only the rational level and the world of people exist, as our modernized society wants to suggest. We live in a society in which other universes also exist and interact: the world of the living; of the dead (ancestors); and, depending on the culture, of worlds inhabited by different types of forces and spirits, of good and of evil. The fact that ethnopsychiatry recognizes the possibility of such an existential reality gives a strong stimulus for the patients to become open. They almost always find themselves at ease within a brief period of time and tell their story. They talk about their problems and offer—when they have one—a "lay" interpretation of the causes of their affliction. At the same time, the communicative dynamic created by the setting brings the patient into an environment that is familiar, which rebuilds the "psychic shell" that had been shattered in the course of the migration experience.

Another aid to maintaining the link between patient and therapeutic group, and therefore of this new sense of belonging and identity, comes from the use of prescriptions. This is not to say that all therapists give the same meaning to prescriptions. In the application of Nathan's model in Geneva, different therapists in our group have different training: I come from a background of family therapy, others from psychoanalytic therapy (various schools and tendencies). My understanding of prescriptions is principally that of focusing on the relationships with important people who have been left behind, in the country of origin, in the village, those who have died, those who are living—the latter because there is always one of them, often in the extended family, who offers a form of protection or of aggression for the patient.

As for those who are dead, the prescription has an effect on the intrapsychic dynamics of the patient that is independent of his or her adherence to religious or cultural beliefs, because the world of the dead always exists. And often it has some bearing on psychic disorders. Prescriptions are always directed at accompanying the patient in moving towards parents, family, relations that are not set and were left in suspense in the course of the migration; the patient is therefore assisted to undergo movements of return towards a world of which he or she no longer feels a part, amplified by the distance. This is often a world from which the patient has fled, which has never been elaborated, and which presumably is represented through symptoms. A psychoanalyst would most likely add other meanings, which might be shared. During a seminar in which I had presented a case that our Geneva group had handled with this approach, a psychoanalyst proposed the notion of "symbolic realization" to interpret the meaning of the prescription.[7]

The "therapeutic power" of this type of ethnopsychiatric apparatus is also due to the communication procedure that opens the first session. The patient is introduced to the co-therapists by the primary therapist; one co-therapist comes from this country, another comes from that, and so on. In this way, a strong metacommunication is exchanged—coming from a group that has experienced emigration—that legitimizes all the countries of origin, all the languages, and therefore each and every culture.

Some patients do not accept this situation and do not join in the communication game. Often a patient arrives at our sessions brimming over with ideas, diagnoses, prescriptions, prognoses, which he or she has no power to verify, but which he or she accepts, or thinks he or she accepts. In other words, the patient is a "Westernized" patient. These are the most difficult cases to deal with and often give rise to "drop-outs". But sometimes the patients only appear to accept the "Western" model of interpretation of their illness. With such patients it can take two or three sessions before communication can begin and they start to explain what they really think. There are two basic reasons for this, both of which are tied to the understandable need for reassurance in such an unknown context. The first comes from the concern about "not being considered mad", which has already happened several times to many of them in their dealings with "official" medicine and psychiatry. The second is the need to verify if the place in which they find themselves not only offers the possibility of being understood, but also has sufficient therapeutic power to combat the power that caused their illness.

On many occasions we have become aware of the existence of this second issue through the behaviour of the translator/cultural mediator: at some point in the treatment, after certain issues had been touched on relating to the causes of the malaise and the patient's disorder, the latter has informed us that he or she would not be participating in the next session. In this way, we have learned that, when the therapeutic group is not perceived as sufficiently powerful, talking about certain things brings risks for everyone present, including the translator/mediator and the therapists. In fact, this type of dynamic sets active forces in motion. The language constructed in the group, the symbols recalled and experienced through the prescriptions, create—or "fabricate"—concrete things, modifications in the people and the relationships, even in relationship between different worlds of power. This kind of session is partially oriented towards listening, but it is especially focused on change (see, in particular, Nathan, 1994; Pichot & Nathan, 1998, pp. 37–73). When the prescription given to a patient by the therapeutic group or by the patient him/herself foresees the construction of a fetish, talisman, or other protective object, it appears obvious that the protective presence extends outside the group and even beyond the context of the session. (The case of Armand described in part II is an example of this.)

It is clear that this therapeutic structure results in a duration of treatment that is brief, even if it has not been rigidly pre-established: the duration will depend on the difficulty of the case. This type of problem is also found in family therapies: after the period of the so-called invariable prescriptions, which suggest a rather rigid therapeutic path, other more elastic prospectives are often considered. Unfortunately, as so often happens within a discipline that is in the process of being formed, even in the sphere of ethnopsychiatry elements of debate assume more a connotation of clash and rupture than reciprocal enrichment. So the questions of the construction of fetishes and the interpretation of points of view (traditional or not) of immigrant patients has already provoked more than one break-up within Nathan's working group. It seems useful to discuss these two elements of debate/clash in greater depth, because of their significance within ethnopsychoanalytic theory.

The question of fetishes

The translator or the cultural mediator can explain to us how problems that these patients are bringing into the session are faced within the culture from which they come. The translator not only explains it, but also discusses it with the patient and with us. From Nathan's perspective, this is the "fabrication" of a language common to the group, which constitutes it and constitutes the individual members. The translator is not a neutral instrument offering an aseptic linguistic understanding of precodified and preconstituted meanings, but the essential element in the construction of a common base. In other words, the importance of the translator's function is not due so much to the communication of the contents being translated as to the metacommunication implied by his or her presence and in the use the therapist and the group make of it. In fact, if we use the same logic with which we explain the functions of language and the translator to understand what happens in the course of this sort of session, we need to agree that the groups fabricate the therapeutic apparatus and that the therapeutic apparatus fabricates the patients. Two possible options for therapists follow: to fabricate fetishes or, vice-versa, not to fabricate fetishes.

In the first case, what should we do? Should we learn to adopt the techniques of traditional healers? Tobie Nathan seems to be oriented in this direction: within his group, objects and fetishes are habitually constructed, sometimes completely similar to those used in the traditional culture that is part of the patient's background. Others think that this is not realistic, and that a therapeutic context and a training would be required that are not possible in the West, because of the thousands of languages and cultures in the world.

The second theme of debate (and clash), closely linked to the first, concerns the interpretation from the patient's point of view of the causes of his or her disorder. The type of ethnopsychotherapy set up by Nathan is developing steadily in the direction of taking it for granted, or acting as if, the immigrant patient accepts his or her own culture of origin in a more or less conscious way. The entire therapeutic intervention, including the construction of fetishes, is therefore oriented to helping the patient reacquire awareness of his or her own belonging, not in theoretical but in concrete terms, just as the construction and use of a fetish are concrete. In the course of the session, therefore, extremely strong and "influential" actions are taken. However, many scholars, including Rose-Marie Moro, emphasize how immigrants, precisely because of the experiences and changes connected to migration, are no longer immersed in the culture they left, but live perennially between two worlds, sitting on two stools, and therefore it is impossible to have an intervention that simply reconstructs the tradition.

I am convinced that this polemic is fictitious on many counts, and I shall try briefly to explain why. In our experience in Geneva, in fact, elements emerge that could favour or oppose Nathan's position. Undoubtedly, when we intervened following his approach to the letter, we experienced a number of drop-outs. In other words, if we have pushed highly "Westernized" patients towards hypothetical interpretations of their original culture in a way that is too rigid, sometimes we lose them, whereas at other times the intervention is effective. Perhaps the different outcomes of the interventions depend in part on the diverse composition of the immigrants in the two contexts: in Geneva they are thoroughly mixed, while in Paris most come from former French colonies. But it could depend on the therapists' different experiences, capacities, and healing powers. It remains to be said that, based on our experience, I do not believe that either hypothesis can be adhered to completely.

Undoubtedly, this therapeutic apparatus is extremely active and plays a major role in the "construction" of people. Its peculiarity, independently of the use made of it, comes from the strong push to de-psychologize the patient, through the formal legitimization of the patient's interpretations. From my point of view, to orient oneself towards one or the other ethnotherapeutic strategy (towards traditional interpretations or not), it could be helpful to refer to two different points of view: those of Lévi-Strauss and Douglas, already discussed in this book. Lévi-Strauss (1962) identifies three conditions that make the therapeutic intervention of a shaman effective: the shaman-medicine man-therapist agrees with the explanation of the world and of illness offered by the culture he belongs to; the patient agrees with the same theory, with the same hypothetical explanation; and the community of reference agrees as well. Traditional treatments never take place in meetings of two people (therapist and patient), but always in a "choral" situation, in which even the community can take an active part. In the therapeutic setting described above, this kind of situation is reproduced, symbolically and in other ways as well.

According to Mary Douglas's hypothesis, the "traditional" explanation given by the patient, the group of reference, and by the shaman himself is a simulation (Douglas, 1998). No one believes in it, but they perform this ritual to oppose the social and political fragility of the community to which they belong.[8] This collusion between shaman, patient, and the community allows them to behave "as if" and is therefore effective in every case.

Within the ethnopsychiatric therapeutic framework, the patient, the primary therapist, and the co-therapists function as a symbolic representation of a community. My hypothesis is that treatment will work to the extent that this triad provides a meeting ground between the hypotheses of the therapists and those of the patient but is indifferent to any shift towards one or the other of the situations described by Lévi-Strauss or Douglas. Cases of drop-out can be attributed to an insufficient capacity of the therapists to grasp which of the two interpretations is actually being used in that moment, in that situation, with that patient.

Fabrication of fetishes and fabrication of men

Nathan's insistence on using the term "fabrication" is tied to another theoretical point that is fundamental for understanding his point of view. We have already pointed it out, but now it is necessary to deepen our understanding, through a structural analysis, of the functioning of the setting or therapeutic apparatus as well as the relevant mechanisms of rites of passage in traditional societies. This last issue is, in turn, connected to the interpretation of traditional societies as societies with multiple universes. We have already seen what a society with multiple universes means, but at this point the interest lies in the connection between this reality (or this way of looking at reality in traditional societies) and the meaning of the rites of passage or initiation, whose structure is inseparable from that of the multiple universe. As Nathalie Zajde (1998) emphasizes, referring to Bateson for structural analyses of rituals,[9] it is important to distinguish between two great systems in the modality of transmitting knowledge. "Western culture has opted for a transmission through the *education of children*, cultures of initiation have opted for a deliberate *fabrication* of new beings" (p. 227).

The techniques of initiation imply traumas that can achieve their goal only when they involve the presence of the whole society. The passage of the candidate to initiation from one social category to another is not at all "natural" or linear; the initiate experiences a drastic change, a metamorphosis brought about by the intervention of specific social actors, the initiators. Among the latter are people capable of entering into contact with other universes. In this process of transformation, four phases can be distinguished (see Houseman, 1986). In the first phase, the positive characteristics of the initiate are brought to light (beauty, strength, courage, etc.), positive pronouncements that will guarantee the success of the initiation—that is, the passage and transformation from the actual state of a child to the imminent one of an adult. In the second phase, of destructuring, deconstructing, the objective is to dissolve, deconstruct, to literally crumble the initial identity of the candidate. This is followed by a third phase of reconstruction and a fourth of welcome into the community, through public recognition of the status of the initiate. To fully understand the process of annulling the former personality and "fabricating" of the new being, it is necessary to analyse in depth what happens in the course of the second and third phases.[10]

> In the deconstruction phase . . . the initiators ask the initiates to face specific ordeals such as: hunting an animal, gathering cola nuts, blowing through a horn, . . . lying on a bed of nettles, etc. All these actions are actually traumatic injunctions to the extent that they are systematically contradictory and paradoxical. In fact, the animal is no other than an initiator who follows the initiate, frightening and prodding him or her, the gathering of cola nuts should be done on a tree swarming with particularly aggressive ants, the horn is the anus of one of the initiators. At the end, the initiates need to say they enjoy lying on a bed of nettles. [Zajde, 1998, p. 229]

Through these experiences, the

> novices find themselves in an insoluble conceptual contradiction, obliged to agree to things that are clearly not true. . . . They are put in situations that are upside down and in which it is necessary to find a way to confirm that things which are obviously different and contradictory are identical. Now, and this is the secret of the ordeals, these conditions are both arbitrary, and . . . non-existent; in no way can they be deduced from an analysis of the same elements [of observation of reality]. [Houseman, 1986, p. 37]

According to Zajde, what binds the initiates in some way and prevents them from escaping from this nonsensical situation is "the constant pressure inflicted through fear and physical pain", evidently practiced by the initiators with the consent and participation of the community. This phase of deconstruction is followed by one of reconstruction, which leads initiates to adopt their new status and new identity. This phase, carried out through modalities that are typical of every initiation society (taking special drinks or food, accomplishing the final ordeals, which are not humiliating like the earlier ones, etc.), redefines the initiates as initiated. (In my description in chapter six of the case of Armand, the suffrage of Evelyne's dead husband and the subsequent funeral rituals can be considered part of this phase.)

The perennial duration of the effects of initiation is guaranteed by the superhuman statute of the test, which bestows the determining aspect of belonging to a society with multiple universes. In fact, the secret meaning of the rituals the initiates go through is the patrimony of members of the community who, as I have noted above, have the privilege of dealing with other universes, inhabited by ancestors, spirits, divinities. Zajde emphasizes most opportunely that in societies with multiple universes (and initiation), these ritualistic elements recur systematically not only in initiation rites, but "in all types of (collective) action, for example in those aiming to modify the state of a disorder (therapeutic action), or to accompany a natural transformation (birth, funeral rite)" (Zajde, 1998, p. 230).[11]

It is now clear that the therapeutic apparatus invented by Nathan tries to offer a space for representation, partly symbolic, and an occasion for "re-initiation", to members of traditional societies immigrated into Western society. His model can be summarized as follows:

On the part of the patient

- Migrant patients always refer (in more or less conscious or ambivalent ways) to a system of traditional thought, of origins, which includes theories of illness and consequent remedies.
- In these aetiological theories, the disorder is always caused by an external cause (intervention of the spirit world, maraboutage, djinn, witchcraft, the evil eye, curses, etc.).
- The person's "disorder" is the reflection of a break in his or her family ties (with ancestors, family) or affiliation (the community).

On the part of the therapist

- The healer or therapist does not act directly on the patient but through "mediators" between the person who is ill, his or her social group, and the invisible world.

- The objectives can be seen as part of a traditional aetiology and individuation of prescriptions that remedy the disorder.
- This type of intervention enables the patients to represent their own illness through a way of thinking from their culture of origin (re-affiliation/belonging) and to "re-inscribe" themselves in the family network and social relationships of the cultural group of origin (renewing family ties).

It is obvious how this scheme represents an updating of the procedures used in family therapies through an increasing sensibility to cultural issues. As I have pointed out, the polemic and conflicts within the small group of therapists who are experimenting with ethnopsychotherapeutic approaches could be avoided. Not for the sake of peace and quiet, or as a tactical choice of unity in the face of much more radical critics—often obtuse and incompetent—coming out of "academic" psychiatry, so much as because the different ways of working are not necessarily different and incompatible theoretical approaches but reflect the diversity of training and understanding of therapists who constitute the working groups. But above all because, as I have often emphasized, more than theories and theoretical diversity or divergence, this is a matter of therapeutic sensitivity in the construction of a space and common language that is rich in meaning and shared by the patient and the therapist(s).

Therapeutic effectiveness has a common denominator in all psychotherapeutic apparatus:

1. the asymmetry in communication between therapist(s) and patient;
2. the sharing of a space (language) that is rich in meaning.

In Nathan's apparatus, these two elements assume very special characteristics in terms of the roles taken on by the therapist and patient and the introduction of the figure of the translator/cultural mediator. These variations determine just how powerful Nathan's apparatus will be with respect to the patient. This "influence", often claimed by Nathan as the essential characteristic of his ethnopsychiatry, can be used, in my opinion, through hybridization with the working hypotheses I described in the first chapter. I am referring to the use of fable, understood as structure and functions *à la* Propp, as a relapse into initiation rites of post-traditional societies. In other words, Nathan's apparatus is used to reconstruct a therapeutic space in which the migrant patients can be re-initiated into their culture, literally reconnected with their family and affiliations. In this sense, the apparatus itself represents a relapse, just as the fable does ("learned" and professionally reasoned and constructed) into initiation rites. As a result, the apparatus, like the fable, contains within itself the functions and passages we have seen in Propp's analyses in the first chapter. Therefore, the way of looking at the process of re-initiation, re-affiliation, through the analogy with the functions Propp sets forth allows us to position the patient, through consolidated criteria, in a precise point and phase in the course of acquiring an active role, like the hero in the fables. We shall see in the case of Armand how this variation has been helpful.

In conclusion, I would like add several details, motivated by the awareness of how easy it can be to create confusion and misunderstanding using the hypothesis of fables. Some difficulties already encountered have brought me almost to the point of abandoning them, but friends and colleagues persuaded me that it is important to talk about it, even as a fundamental subject within the context of this book about it. I feel it is definitely the wisest choice, even at the risk of discussing something controversial and oversimplified, especially for anyone seeking polemics. To avoid some of the easier misunderstandings and in the interests of clarity, I would like to list these points:

1. In the course of ethnopsychotherapy sessions, fables are not told. It is the meaning and the kernel within their structure that offers the therapist a guide that can be used as reference.
2. In the experience in Geneva, the use of fable (in the modality explained in point 1) did not constitute an interpretative scheme shared by all the components of the ethnopsychiatric group but, rather, my personal re-interpretation of what takes place in sessions and, at the same time, my personal orientation when formulating questions and interacting with patients (ethno-systemic-narrative).[12]
3. The emphasis attributed to fables, like all the conventions

expressed in the first part of the book, even if they have been stimulated by work with colleagues in Geneva, represent, for better or worse, my convictions alone and are therefore my responsibility.

Notes

1. An international comparative research model (INECOM), established by Gilles Bibeau and Ellen Corin of the University of Montreal, dealing with systems of signs and meanings and activity concerning mental health. In addition to Canadian scholars, researchers from African, Asian, European and Latin America participate in the project. (For a more detailed discussion of this approach, see Bibeau, 1996.)

2. I refer to this analysis not knowing it directly, but, through extrapolation in their articles, from the experience of Littlewood and collaborators (Littlewood, 1984–85, 1991; Littlewood & Lipsedge, 1982).

3. Among Nathan's vast bibliography, I must necessarily select a limited number of texts: *Le sperme du diable* (1988); *La folie des autre* (1986); *Principes d'ethnopsychanalyse* (1993); *L'influence qui guérit* (1994); *Médecins et sorciers* (Nathan & Stengers, 1995); and *Psychothérapies* (Nathan, Blanchet, Ionescu, & Zadje, 1998). From this last collection the essay of Nathalie Zajde (1998), "Le traumatisme", is particularly recommended. In this essay, the author, comparing the meaning of the experience of trauma in various cultures, clearly describes what culturally belonging to a multiple-universe society means and the implications of this for therapeutic work. It is also useful to recall that Nathan and his group regularly publish works of theoretical reflection on ethnopsychoanalysis in *Nouvelle Revue d'Ethnopsychiatrie.*

4. In this type of setting or "therapeutic arrangement," as Nathan calls it, it is rather easy for the patient to choose the aetiological and therapeutic hypothesis that seems most familiar to and understanding of him or her. For Nathan, "A symptom can be . . . considered a *significant fluctuant* (C. Lévi-Strauss) that the ritual, thanks to its gift for separation, would assimilate in function of its own categories." The psychiatrist ends up considering the neuroleptic either a filter for love or a poison. And further: "The symptom is a sort of significant fluctuant waiting for therapeutic ritual that crystallizes it in the same way in which Stendhal speaks of crystallization in love" (Nathan, 1986).

5. For those who desire a deeper analysis of this approach, I recommend the literature proposed in note 4 and the general bibliography of this present volume. It must be mentioned, however, that reading the books in this bibliography is not enough to begin ethnopsychotherapeutic practice, even and perhaps above all for those therapists already trained in Western schools; it is necessary—as is the case for the training of therapists in all disciplines—to pursue theoretical and practical training.

6. Excluding, in my opinion, some approaches that form part of family therapy, as will be seen in the reading of this chapter and from my version of the case of Armand in chapter six.

7. I refer to the contribution of Gian Paolo Lai, who during one of my seminars in Milan in December 1998 related that "in Marche [a region of Italy] in 1300, when someone had a stomach-ache or disturbance, Sant'Antonio of Tolentino told them to put his or her stomach-ache in a sack and place it near the bridge, and the first person to pass would go away with the stomach-ache. The people were very careful that a dog and not a person passed first!" On the same occasion, Lai informed us that in the 1940s, a Swiss psychoanalyst from Geneva operated what he called—and which in psychoanalysis we still call—"symbolic realization": that is, he used prescriptions very similar to those utilized today in ethnopsychiatry. From one point of psychoanalytic view, the prescription worked in the same way that ethnopsychiatric settings "fabricate" effective therapy. For which reason, "if the Swiss psychiatrist said something, the patient . . . took it as truth." (For a complete reading of these seminar reports, see *Prospettive Sociali e Sanitarie*, Vol. 4, February 1999.)

8. Such fragility is certainly common to many immigrant communities.

9. In her text, Zajde—Nathan's co-therapist—discusses rites of passage through the lens of the communicative analysis proposed by Gregory Bateson in *Naven* (1936).

10. It is in this analysis in particular that Zajde refers to the contribution of Bateson cited in note 9 and to the fieldwork by Michael Houseman (1986), in which the author had already applied the categories of Bateson.

11. In the subsequent pages of his wonderful essay, Zajde places the experience of limited states (common among children of immigrants in societies in which the rites of "voluntary induction of trauma" are eliminated) near to the impossibility of legitimization and maintenance of such practices.

12. As I explained in the preface, eight years have passed since the original writing of this book in Italian and its current version in English. In this period, several experiences in my clinical practice have brought me to define my approach as no longer being generically ethnopsychiatric but, rather, as being ethno-systemic-narrative. (The main references to the meaning of this identification are contained in Losi, 2004, and Losi & Papadopoulos, 2004.)

PART II

CHAPTER FOUR

Psychotherapeutic practice with migrant families: the case of a young child traumatized by war

Saskia von Overbeck Ottino

An 8-year-old boy, "Armand", and a 10-year-old girl, "Gloria", were sent to me in connection with my specialization in adult and child psychiatry and in ethnopsychiatry. A specialist opinion was requested on the psychological states of the children and the credibility of their testimony with respect to a request for asylum. At the same time, a paediatric-psychiatric and transcultural approach was required for this family from Zaire, who were in great psychological difficulty.

The two children (I shall speak especially about Armand, but since their experiences were similar, I shall also touch upon Gloria to clarify the exposition) are the oldest of five children. They had just been reunited with their mother in Switzerland, who had thought they were dead, executed in Zaire. In fact, two years earlier, when the family was living in Zaire, Armand and Gloria had been seized by soldiers, along with their father. In all likelihood, they had been imprisoned. Having received no news of them, their mother was convinced they had been killed. After a number of threats, the mother was forced to flee Zaire with her three youngest children. Completely unexpectedly, the two older children reappeared two years later. Only Gloria could remember anything that had happened: all three had been imprisoned, then their father was executed in front of them. After they had managed to be released from prison, the children were taken in by an "uncle", in the broader sense of the word, and then sent to their mother in Switzerland.

The mother found Armand "completely changed", "gone mad". At the time of the trauma (he was 6 years old) he was growing up well, was sociable and clean, slept peacefully, and was beginning to learn to read and write at school. Now he is silent, withdrawn into himself, incontinent, and often has nightmares at night and wakes up screaming. At school, where he has been put into a lower class, he stays in a corner, mute, as if absent. Yet Armand has not lost everything he has learned: rather, it seems that he has withdrawn into an interactive cloister. This is apparent in several phrases that are coherent in both their formulation and context: "You can buy me some roller skates. . . ." This phrase, for instance, is an expression of the investment which, in spite of everything, he makes in the external world and his desire to succeed in identifying with his companions. He also seems to have maintained some level of communication, of contact with reality, as well as a good orientation in time, space, and context. Getting off the bus in front of my office, he sometimes says, "We are going to the doctor."

Armand refuses to be separated from his mother for the examination. He looks his age. During the interview he is very serious, if not "closed". He is completely silent except for a warning ("leave me alone") he gives to his younger brother, who was trying to take his toys; in this case, he finds the appropriate words. If he is not offered any stimulus, he fiddles compulsively with the miniature cars or occupies himself with his drawings, which are of excellent quality. If stimulated, he accepts brief exchanges with the examiner and follows certain suggested games well. Analogously, he seems quite attentive to certain exchanges between his mother and the examiner. (When we established a relationship between his incontinence and his wish to remain a baby rather than assume a more grown-up role, of big brother, which would put him in danger, like his father, he asked to go to the bathroom.) In this sense and despite his apparent withdrawal, "as if in his own world", he is very much present and able to understand what is going on.

Summing up, he is an inhibited child, blocked in his capacities to think, feel, and communicate, despite his linguistic competence, and with an apparently well-preserved ability to understand what is going on around him. He presents a withdrawal, if not a detachment, from the world around him, an important regression with respect to cleanliness and acquisition of experiences, as well as sleep disturbances.

A certain number of the elements lead us to think that the disturbances presented by this child are acute and reactive, rather than being chronic disturbances preceding the traumatic events. His mother's anamnesis confirms this impression.

Gloria has also changed completely since her arrival in Switzerland. Once she was happy, open, growing well. Now she is sad, closed within herself, stingy with words. Yet she was the one to tell her mother first and then the Swiss authorities, in the course of a hearing, how she and her brother and their father had been captured and imprisoned and then how their father had been seized and executed. She would not say anything else about those events, other than that together with her brother she had been received by a paternal "uncle" who mistreated them. Then they were entrusted to a woman who sent them to their mother in Switzerland. Since their arrival, Gloria has usually been immersed in her own thoughts, has trouble sleeping, and has nightmares. At school she was silent at first and shut herself in the bathrooms (later she explained that she was afraid that her classmates would ask questions). Little by little she managed to stay in the class and make a few friends. Yet, she is still very reserved and often distracted, immersed in thoughts she does not reveal.

In the examination, Gloria shows herself to be a sweet and pleasant young girl. She is always silent in the presence of her mother, as if on the defensive. Only once with the examiner did she open up a little, although she remained very reserved. She began to whisper, afraid she might be heard in the adjacent consulting-room. She has mastered French well but she does not talk spontaneously and answers any questions put to her very concisely. When discussions touch on painful and distressing episodes from her past, she only shakes her head. She remains very serious throughout the talks and never smiles. When she is not stimulated, she stays in her chair as if paralysed. When stimulated, she presents a repetitive scenario, appearing separated from the external world, completely absorbed by her own story. The theme often repeated is that of a "daddy-doll" devoured by a crocodile. A "daughter-doll" is part of the scene but can do nothing to help him and becomes very sad. The "mother-doll" is far away and did not see anything. When the "daughter-doll" finds her and tells her what has happened, the "mother-doll" treats her like a liar. Then the "daughter-doll" goes to the doctor to make the "daddy-doll" well again, but "it is too late". Finally the "daughter-doll" touches the "daddy-doll" and revives him. Themes of imminent danger with the need for escape are frequent. Gloria seems very caught up in this kind of game, which animates her. This contrasts with the block that overtakes her as soon as she leaves these scenarios.

Summing up, Gloria, like her brother but to a lesser degree, is struck by a hibernation or paralysis of her psychic processes, which seem to function adequately in themselves, but as if cut off. She shows a good capacity to learn from reality and distinguish it from play. The themes played out do not allow an affirmation that they constitute her particular reflection of experienced reality, because almost all of the themes can surface in the games of countless "normal" children. However, their structure, some details that strongly recall many events referred to above, their psychic consequences (sense of impotence, guilt, fear of not being believed, etc.), and the importance of the severing and ruptures, make them compatible with the repetitive story games described in syndromes of post-traumatic stress.

Armand and Gloria's mother, "Evelyne", is a profoundly depressed woman. In the course of our talks, she presents herself prostrate, often absent, and tells her story in a plaintive, monotonous voice. She has not managed to pull herself together after losing her husband, she weeps every time she thinks of him, and she lists the misfortunes that have happened to her since then. The story of her life is a long sequence of losses and abandonments that are making her all but mute and incapable of taking care of her children.

Evelyne was born in a village in Lower Zaire. She lost both parents when she was 5 years old, in unclear circumstances. Witchcraft had been mentioned (common in that region), since there were strong clashes within the family, provoked by the fact that Evelyne's father had money but did not share it with the rest of the family. Probably in order to be distanced from the clan, Evelyne was brought up by an "uncle", who was actually a friend of her parents. She was not happy in his house in the city. She met her future husband "on the street"; several friends made the wedding arrangements since the husband's parents were opposed to his marrying a woman from a different ethnic group and, what is more, "without family". Despite the precariousness of the relationship (in terms of its cultural and family recognition) and despite the fears of vengeance through witchcraft on the part of her mother-in-law, the marriage started off well. It began to deteriorate when her husband took an interest in politics. The arguments were sometimes resolved by Evelyne going away temporarily with some of the children. At the time of one of these absences, during which the father was left alone with the older children, Gloria and Armand, he was arrested and all three were taken away. Believing that her husband and the older children were dead, and fearing retaliation on herself and the other three children, she left the country and arrived in Switzerland. As we have seen, only two years later was she reunited with Armand and Gloria and learned the story of her husband's death.

As one can notice, Evelyne's story includes a certain number of cultural hypotheses and representations. For instance, she naturally uses cultural hypotheses when she finds herself alone and desperate in Switzerland, and then when she finds her children changed. She maintains that her mother-in-law was persecuting her with an evil spirit, and it is for that reason that she feels "dead" and her son is "mad". On the other hand, she went to a sorcerer of fetishes (traditional therapy), without much success. With respect to Armand, she is unsure about the necessity of a traditional (African) form of healing or, rather, a brain scan.

The mixture of cultural representation and recourse to "scientific" medicine is common in immigrant families. The modalities of functioning are often exclusive and reductive: either one or the other. In this way, neither system of representation can play the protective or containing role. On the contrary, if the intention is to embrace the complexity of the situation and allow an optimal therapeutic alliance, the advantages to therapists of considering as equally important the various modes of representing the difficulties and of structuring them in complementary rather than exclusionary terms are now well known (Devereux, 1970; Moro & Nathan, 1989). This allows a maximum of "entry points" that give access to the complexity of this type of situation, characterized, in this case, by a block in the psychic processes. We shall see, in the course of treatment, how we took both cultural representations and psychotherapeutic aspects into account and how we used their "enfolding" potentials.

Concerning the first part of my task (providing a specialist opinion on the psychological health of Armand and Gloria and the credibility of their testimony), we concluded that both showed signs of a post-traumatic stress syndrome (PTSD: in children, the composite picture of regressions, sleep disturbances, separation difficulties, scholastic aversion, phobias, behaviour disturbances, withdrawal, reliving experiences through play, etc.: Grappe, 1995; Terr, 1991). The disturbances presented by the two children seemed to be reactive in nature, although, in this case, it was difficult to form a judgement on any pathology before the trauma. Although the subjects of Gloria's games evoked a repetitive post-traumatic story game, this could not be considered proof of the truthfulness of the facts evoked. On the contrary, the two children presented a considerable inhibition of psychological functioning (especially Armand) while they kept a good understanding of reality and good cognitive abilities (especially Gloria). This allowed us to think that the children tended to say too little rather than too much. Gloria in particular had the ability to distinguish true from false, as well as the intellectual equipment to report facts without excessive distortion. At the same time, their mother presented a serious depressive state with loss of vitality, absence, and such inhibition that it was hard to imagine that she had the physical resources to urge her children to make false testimonies. Taking these different elements into consideration, we concluded that there were no medical or legal reasons to doubt the facts Gloria reported. On the certificate, we indicated the need for a paedopsychiatric examination of the children, and we also expressed concern about the psychological consequences, for the children and for the mother, that could result from a premature return to their country.

Once the certificate was written, the prospect of therapy for Armand seemed much more complex and had implications, as we have seen, for the family therapy as well.

The therapy of Armand and his family

Armand's situation poses the problem of the complexity of a therapy that includes a child and his family, in exile and with a serious trauma. Moreover, this family had few psychosocial resources with which to support themselves because, already in their home country, and before the political events, there had been numerous difficulties, ruptures, and losses of points of reference.

In this type of situation, certain specific lines of work that need to be taken into consideration are added to the usual psychotherapeutic aspects (Overbeck Ottino, 1999).

Problems related to trauma

Here the trauma, which was real and extremely violent, struck not only Armand but also his entire family. First of all, it was essential to consider the psychic effraction or rupture to which the child's hibernation of psychic mechanisms bears witness: the disorganization of several aspects of his psychological growth and his loss of self-esteem and of support capacities for his highly deteriorated internal imago (Grappe, 1995; Grubrich-Simitis, 1981; Pynoos & Eth, 1986; Terr, 1991). It was also important to take into consideration the reciprocal interactive aspects, especially between parents and children. In fact, such parents—traumatized themselves and faced with their incapacity to protect their children—are strongly shaken in their parental and containing functions. Immersed in their pain, filled with guilt over not succeeding in protecting their children from collective violence, they are often unable to listen to them or to identify with their horror. On the contrary, they are often inclined to erase, to restore at all costs, what was unbearable and unavoidable (Grappe, 1995; Zivcic, 1993). "In this fragile balance, they try to make exile function as a rebirth" (Grubrich-Simitis, 1981; Sironi, 1995). They push their children to forget, to adapt themselves as swiftly as possible to the structures of the place that receives them, encouraging the development of mechanisms of negation and of adopting a kind of "false self" that so often we find from the clinical point of view. This tendency to negate the impact of trauma is also shared at times by the receiving structures: it seems easier to consider only the neurotic conflicts of a child and, eventually, the impact of exile. But the effects of a violence that everyone would like to forget tend to become concealed (Sironi, 1995). Children lack "authorized" spaces in which they can express their own conflicts. If they are too happy, they forget too quickly. If they are too sad, they remember too markedly the misfortunes they have experienced. Analogously, when they play, naturally they play war games. For them it is vital, but for their parents it is unbearable and deadly. Yet it is indispensable that they play: "Playing has two sides: one that is oriented towards the past, the other towards the future. Games allow children to symbolically find a way out of unresolved problems of the past and to confront the conflicts of the present either symbolically or directly. For the child, it also constitutes an essential tool that prepares him or her for future tasks" (Bettelheim, cited by M. Szatan, 1995). The stories of Armand and Gloria made their mother weep, strengthening in them the ineluctable sense of guilt at having been the cause of the dramas that annihilated their parents. The first opted, at that time, for autistic withdrawal, the second for silent reserve.

The same PTSD, visibly reflected by interior distress, which afflicts the great majority of traumatized children (50–80% of children in the effected areas: Grappe, 1995), presents therapeutic difficulties connected with the psychic block and with the incessant reactivation of the trauma by "little" events in daily life (excessive vigilance). The more the trauma was intense, long-lasting, and repeated and the longer the period before a therapeutic intervention, the greater the block (Grappe, 1995). Finally, the suffering expressed varies according to the age and development of cognitive capacities. The younger the child, the more the impact of the trauma is influenced by the reaction of the parents to the event and by their behaviour after the event (Bonnie et al., 1991; Gozlan &

Salignon, 1995; Grubrich-Simitis, 1981; Sironi, 1995; Szatan, 1995). This highlights the importance of including the parents in the treatment of traumatized children (Grappe, 1995; Zivcic, 1993).

A therapy should include a space for the child to express him/herself, a support for the parents, a work of orientation on the relationships between parents and children, and a psychotherapeutic technique that takes into account the specific features of the traumatic impact (Overbeck Ottino, 1998).

Problems related to exile

To leave one's own country, be separated from dear ones, break with one's cultural references, and find oneself in a different culture, faced with a different language and customs, with no clear future—this "passage" that immigrants experience is always at the source of individual, family, and social crises. Changes of this sort require more than simple adaptation and seem to produce a genuine change in the psychic organization, an interior upheaval (de Coulon & von Overbeck, 1992; Grinberg & Grinberg, 1989). Some authors even argue that the rupture caused by exile could produce a genuine split in the ego (e.g., Pierre, 1993). In any case, it seems that something on the order of a caesura is produced that defines a before and an after, a here and a there, often accentuated by the sense of creating a distance from a "traumatic there", which blocks the access to mechanisms and resources that had been present before. Then the patients tend to become operatives, deprived of history. Psychic solutions, once more harmonious, become concrete and rigid, since a possible solution is now identified only in the body and in acting (psychosomatization, accidents, violence).

Exile also separates an individual from his or her own cultural representations of the world—life, death, illness, and so forth. These representations, which until that time belonged to the outer world and were in line with the representations of the inner world on the basis of a culturally codified grid, now lack points of reference and lose their own coherence and efficiency because of the discrepancy between the inner and the outer worlds. The latter is perceived as alien, disturbing, threatening, often incomprehensible, even more when the culture of the receiving country is rigid or made up of representations that are very different from those of the culture of origin (Moro & Nathan, 1989). Nevertheless, as we shall see with Armand, these cultural representations make up an important therapeutic resource. In Evelyne's case, they allowed her to maintain a (cultural) coherence, a continuum in the chaos surrounding her: the trauma, the metamorphoses of her children, and their preceding history are held together by these representations. The cultural coherence enables her and her children to remain in a protective shell—precarious undoubtedly, but at least a shared one. It also allows us to perceive the degree of discomfort, exposure, and vulnerability of this family and its lack of a protective shell, which is found at intrapsychic, systemic, social, and cultural levels.

In the course of the therapy, it is therefore a priority to take into account the impact of migration, which may constitute a trauma itself, and to listen to the patients' cultural theories, linking them with the emerging fantasies and affective qualities of the conflicts they are experiencing (Overbeck Ottino, 1999).

Family aspects

As we have seen, exile (Moro, 1994) and trauma (Zivcic, 1993) strike not only the child, but also the entire family; generally it is recommended that treatments that take the family aspects into account be encouraged (Grappe, 1995; Szatan, 1995; Zivcic, 1993). Working with the parents, or in their presence, allows them to understand the child, better identify themselves with his or her needs, and maintain a more appropriate distance (somewhere between too much distance and fusion). Often, it is also necessary to offer the parents support with respect to a specific problem they are experiencing and with their difficulties in social adaptation. In this way, they can improve their function as a container and become much more able to help their child in overcoming a traumatic situation (Overbeck Ottino, 1998a).

Aspects related to social precariousness

The patients are often people who have requested asylum and who risk expulsion. They usually receive complete social assistance, live in minute quarters, and are in contact with other families who are in exile and traumatized but are from different cultures and share neither their language nor their living habits. Often they have to relocate in the course of therapy and the children need to change school and integrate into another new environment. These conditions, added to the conditions created by traumas and exile, make spontaneous access to psychiatric treatments very difficult, so much so that psychiatry and psychology are often assimilated with the "madness". Moreover, the psychosocial network is generally quite complex and experienced in a disjointed way, analogous with the subjective experience these families have gone through, between traumas, exile, and difficult integration. The coherence of the network encourages internal coherence as well, and in this sense the treatments should be part of a network constituted of complementary and interdependent rings. This is one of the particularities of working with exiled people, also a result of their precarious circumstances.

In order to maintain a therapeutic coherence that respects the complementary nature of the intrapsychic, systemic, situational, cultural, and social aspects, we opted for a psychotherapeutic practice integrated into a network, in which each component has a specific role. This psychotherapeutic work would be complicated by the fact that it would deal not only with Armand but also Gloria (although less frequently), and at times there would also be occasion to see the other children in the family. This complexity, arising from the need to take into consideration concrete elements as well as elements of a psychic reality as yet undiscovered, prompted us to re-examine customary models of treatment. Only with a certain agility of the apparatus and the psychotherapeutic work, at least at the beginning, could we hope to be able to get close to the psychic reality of this type of patient. This means being flexible with the framework, with the temporal dates, and with our orthodoxy.[1]

The network was established in relation to the people and places in which Evelyne's family had already had an investment.

They had met together four or five times a year until now (two years of therapy) and were composed of the following:

- The social worker from the public social service responsible for the family. This figure would manage all practical and financial aspects and the request for refugee status for Evelyne and her children.
- A female medical internist, with expertise in working with migrants, whom Evelyne had met during the clinical exams conducted as soon as she arrived in Switzerland; she was to be the privileged psychological support, "between body and soul".
- An ethnopsychiatrist, Franceline James, with visits every fifteen days, for Evelyne at first, and later for Armand; the visits would continue for a year and a half.
- A school nurse who was to be responsible for the solid integration and academic progress of the five children.
- A nurse from the service for the protection of youth. She was brought in at a particularly troublesome time. At first she assumed a monitoring role (she was the one who would guarantee the "real" security of the situation) and later on a role of providing family support, in particular offering the children afternoon outings that were used for learning as well as fun.
- I was also part of the network, responsible for providing the therapy of the entire family from a paediopsychiatric point of view: closer individual attention to Gloria and Armand, regular sessions with the mother and children in order to strengthen the mother–child relationship, periodic assessments of the other children (in two years, there were a total of 41 appointments, of which 27 were concerned with Armand and 18 of those with Armand exclusively, 6 with Armand and his mother, 2 with Armand and Gloria, 1 with the whole family; the remaining 14 concerned either Gloria or the other children).

Armand

First impressions and the beginning of treatment

The first meetings with Armand were extremely striking: already in the waiting-room, this 8-year-old child seemed completely excluded from the world, and I thought back to his mother's phrases: "he's mad". He followed her into my studio like a robot: neither I nor the others, nor the surroundings, seemed to exist. In the consulting-room, he fiddled awkwardly and indifferently with pencils, animals, toy cars, and so on.

At the beginning, in this disorder, there were the expressions of the mother, a story made of catastrophes, abandonments, and desperation, and the accounts of Gloria, highly evocative, as we have seen, to invade me and prevent me from sinking with Armand into a mortal void. The images provided distanced me from the "void" and immersed me even more in a universe that was "too full", unbearable. In place of nothing, there was too much. In place of an empty Armand, there was an Armand who struggled to render illegible, to annul the unthinkable: the "unconnectable". Behind the silence and the psychotic withdrawal, and at the price of isolation and disorder, a nucleus had survived. Armand was no longer a subject: he was an insensitive appendix of the mother. He did not want her attention and even seemed to ignore her, but when she left the consulting-room, he followed her, without saying anything, like a robot, without glancing at me or at the surroundings.

How could he have expressed himself better? The trauma was still so vivid, and his mother could not contain it: she broke down and wept at any evocation of past history. Deprived of a structure capable of containing his experiences and emotions, incapable of organizing the catastrophic interior disorder, Armand muddled the tracks of his history and showed attempts to adapt to his new life and to forget: "I'd like a Game Boy . . ." or, getting off the bus and recognizing the street of my consulting-room: "We're going to the doctor."

For months, Armand refused to stay alone with me in my consulting-room, so I saw him with his mother present and sometimes with his brothers and sisters as well.

Was he afraid of being alone, or of leaving his mother alone? Was it a need to see her, to have in her a more strongly containing disposition, to watch over her to be sure of not doing her any harm, of not losing her as he had lost his father? While Gloria's games evoked an absent mother who did not believe what was told to her, Armand, on the contrary, tended to mix himself up with his mother at the cost of his own identity. In the same way that he could no longer control his faeces, he controlled the internal objects, but only at the cost of archaic mechanisms of merging.

During the sessions, while Evelyne was talking, Armand meticulously explored my consulting-room, looked in the boxes, the drawers, and so on and took the telephone, showing pleasure for the first time. He also found it wonderful to take my armchair and make it spin. At first terrified by a box of toys that he had dropped, he later managed to laugh about it with me and accept my invitation to play with some pieces of wood. When I asked his mother if Armand knew how to write, Armand formed the letters of his name for me. Thus, without giving the impression, he was paying attention to the exchanges between his mother and me. As I have already said, when we brought up the subject of his incontinence and established a connection between his fear of assuming the role of big brother and eldest son and thus risking ending up like his father, and his choice to remain small and protected by his mother, he went to use the bathroom.

During this first period of therapy for Armand, a period that seemed quite grim, Gloria was again the one to offer a glimpse of life. She seemed to be happy to come to see me, and when they were all ill, she showed she was proud and happy to go to appointments alone. As we have seen, her games were those that showed more of the underlying conflicts: the losses, sense of guilt, impotence, fear of not being believed or fear of being criticized, sense of oedipal guilt, and so forth. These appeared regularly. Instead of abandoning herself to her imagination and her own associations, Gloria tried to make me tell stories. Were these attempts to establish a relationship with respect to her own mechanisms of rupture? A request made to the world of adults, to the good father, to tell a story that would provide structure, since Gloria had only dramatic stories to tell? Fear of not being believed? Fear that I wouldn't be able to understand, like her mother, what she had to say? Thus we oscillated between banal stories and stories that were more connected with the traumas they had experienced, as if it were a matter of taking the trauma and the conflicts experienced "in small doses". The split between play and not-play that had been operating before was slowly transformed into a kind of play "that could be taken in small doses". Certain emotions could be expressed: Gloria thought a great deal about her father and often felt sad. Although she remained rather closed with respect to her mother, Gloria was opening up. She appeared to be happier and was integrating well at school. This evolution, however, was taking place at the cost of a tendency towards excessive maturity[2]—both in the maternal role which she often assumed with great ability and also in her efforts at local integration—and of distancing herself from her emotions concerning the most traumatic aspects of her past. It did not seem, however, that these adjustments were based on a modality of the "false-ego" type, as one might fear in similar circumstances.

During the first months, reality was not kind to the family of Armand: on the one hand, a paternal uncle sent Evelyne a letter announcing: "I am making a present to you of the children, don't write to me again."[3] On the other, the Federal Office for Refugees expressed its suspicions about the truth of their statements and threatened expulsion. Banished by her own people, undesirable in Switzerland, what place could be found for this family in a treatment centre? Fortunately, working through a network enables places to be maintained for considering the surrounding reality and thus to conserve a space in which emotions, ghosts, and psychic reality can exist.

In sessions that followed, Armand began to open up and show better capacities of relating. The disorganized games were replaced by more symbolic stories or drawings that evoked themes of attack, revenge, and a sense of guilt. Drawing was his preferred way of communicating with me, and continued to be so. They were "story drawings", which he made without saying hardly a word; I had to make comments, just as I had to take up the stories of Gloria. At times he corrected me, or elaborated on what I was saying. The story of one of these first drawings (see Drawing 4.1) concerned the meeting between a sun and a cloud that had started to cry and then became a porcupine who was afraid. Then a bee was transformed into a doll, and then into a little boy who fell into the water and whose leg was devoured by a fish. Finally, I could get

DRAWING 4.1

a sense, together with Armand, of his emotions and his ghosts. I could give a name to the affects he evoked so clearly: sadness over the loss of the parental figures (sun and cloud), but also fear (the porcupine), rivalry followed by a sense of guilt (the bee-doll that stings and is transformed into a little boy), and finally the anguish of reprisals and castration (the leg devoured by the fish). Armand then announced the end of the story, but he had difficulty leaving my consulting-room and tried to find the objects that were part of our first interactional play: the telephone and the spinning chair. Perhaps that was an expression of his intention to verify whether I was always going to be ready to play with him, to reserve a place for him in my consulting-room, and if he could always trust the environment in which we were working.

Following that session, which took place six months after the beginning of treatment, Armand was able to stay alone, without his mother. Did I become less dangerous? Was Armand daring to take a step towards his own past, differentiating himself from his mother in a movement of individuation? In this period, images and, later, evocations of paternal figures appeared as well, and the incontinence disappeared. One might say that control over the sphincter went along with the evolution of a more pertinent distance between the ego and the objects in which it had invested itself.

With the process of individuation, other characters and investments in the external world appeared. Armand tried to create ties: he wanted to telephone his classmates from my consulting-room to tell them he had been at the doctor's, that he liked school, that he liked coming here, and that he would like to come Monday, Tuesday, Wednesday, and so on, a slightly maniacal flow, of course, but nevertheless connected with relationships and vital energy. One day on which he spoke a great deal, he even expressed his fear of going home, a fear that is displaced in conflicts about the television. He asked if he could talk about this at home, or he if needed to fear that he would make his mother angry or too sad.

He also spoke more outside. His mother and his teacher noticed that Armand was more engaged but also sadder and more reactive. He talked about his worries and his bitterness. He could communicate better with his classmates, but sometimes apparently insignificant events could make him sulk or could set off some crisis, causing him to run out of the classroom and threaten to kill himself.

Analogously, during the sessions, Armand oscillated between phases of hermetic silence and moments in which he expressed his own emotions: "At school, with my classmates, sometimes I am strong, and sometimes I'm less strong and I get angry. Sometimes I even start to fight and go to look for the teacher." This showed a better capacity to rule his affects and the possibility of seeking external assistance in times of difficulty.

Armand, therefore, was better, even if the excesses and the reactions of withdrawal were still frequent and were testimony to the fragility of his self-esteem, the lack of complications of his drives, and the precariousness of his internal objects. He still showed little readiness for confronting things that are normally confronted at his age: he was seriously behind scholastically, his play centred on conflicts, his relationships were unstable, and so forth.

Life emerged again with its wake of emotions and ghosts, but it seemed "too much". The events that followed made us think that this disorganized emergence we perceived in Armand concerned the whole family, to the point of jeopardizing their "equilibrium".

Reactivation of mourning and family crises

At the end of the first year of treatment, a domestic accident caused by one of Evelyne's younger children threw the family into a black period: three successive accidents, potentially dangerous (a fire and a flooding of the apartment, a car crash) and caused by another of the younger ones, sank the family into bewilderment and fear and forced them to leave their lodging while repair work was done. From our point of view, these events not only constituted a clear reflection of the family's bewilderment, but also revealed its poor functioning. This led us to question the appropriateness of our therapeutic framework. At the time, we became alarmed over the inability of the children and, more importantly, of the mother to maintain conditions of minimum safety. Could we go ahead in this way, underestimating a reality that was becoming dangerous? Faced with this lonely mother who was lacking any pragmatic sense, we felt disarmed. We had to consider strategies that would be more structured, if not more authoritarian. With our local means, we imagined a more intense therapy for her and a stay in an institute for mothers and children, in order to support her in her role as head of the family and to leave her time to be treated. She agreed to everything but carried within her a passive opposition, letting herself be talked out of it by her children, who took command in an act of omnipotence and generational inversion:[4] they will not go to an institute. They clearly expressed their fear of starting a vagabond life again, accompanied by uncertainty and fear of losing their mother. The logic of war and exile had taken the upper hand, and the entire family showed conspicuous signs of fright; the children presented behaviour disturbances, and the mother became even more abstract and absent than ever. Armand was upset to such a degree that the school decided to place him urgently in an "adaptation class". He reacted with sadness and rage, very disappointed at having to leave the friends he had finally managed to make. It is easy to imagine how all that had happened increased his sense of being the cause of these catastrophes.

In cases such as this, it is not a matter of judging the attitude of the school. The system is created in such a way that the newly arrived are generally integrated into a "normal" academic circuit, sometimes after an initial phase in a "welcoming class" to give the students just enough time to catch up with the language. The withdrawal from relations and the stagnation of linguistic and other acquisitions in general are attributed to the time the child needs in order to adapt. The distress and the seriousness of a situation are so barely perceptible that the child, inhibited and frozen (as Armand and his sister originally were), does not manifest evident symptoms and therefore creates no difficulties in class for the teacher. Unfortunately, the moment the child starts to open up, he or she often does so "in excess"—with crises of rage, depression, agitation, maniacal states, violent or dangerous behaviour—and this then presents a real problem for the teacher who is in charge of the whole class and is ill-equipped to deal with this type of excessive behaviour. The situation rapidly becomes unmanageable and often leads to a brusque change in disposition. Generally the child experiences the event as a sanction, while on the psychic level it signals progress, since affects and impulses are emerging, even if in a disordered manner.

Since this is part of the reality encountered in the course of treatment, it could also be said that the child, in this case Armand, is (finally) in a more suitable place and that the mourning and desperation produced by this confrontation can be elaborated in a continuum that is, by and large, more adequate.

On the level of therapy, this period of distress was indeed rich. After the event, we had the impression that the entire family, like Armand, was caught up in a process of reactivating their mourning for the father.

In any case, Armand expressed a sense of guilt concerning his own aggressive impulses, which had been staged symbolically through rather classical oedipal images. This was also the first time a father appeared in his drawings, where interactions between

DRAWING 4.2

father and son began to be represented: a little boy gets into bed and is shoved out by the father with a violent shove; then a tiny cat with a "naughty" air assails the father. This, after an interpretation that indicated the desire to take the father's place but fear that this would lead to retaliation, was followed by the father chasing the cat away and kissing the son. Another time he made a drawing (see Drawing 4.2), still very expressive, of a "devil behind a man", which showed quite well the precarious balance existing between the containing and protecting needs and imago and the destructive and persecutory ones. It was one of the rare times in which Armand made a drawing with a cultural connotation—the doll looked like a fetish (except for the necktie)—whereas after that drawing, all his characters were overburdened with "Western" attributes (see later drawings).

Thus, parental figures appeared ever more frequently in Armand's games and drawings. After the scenes described above, he would also represent a more complete family scene, but always carrying a threat: a father, a mother, a brother, and a newborn threatened by a giant octopus. Finally, one day, while his mother was talking about the family and the country, he drew a man (still an African-type figure) in a tomb (Drawing 4.3). I learned that there had not been a funeral for his father, a fact that Armand confirmed by etching a cross on the drawing!

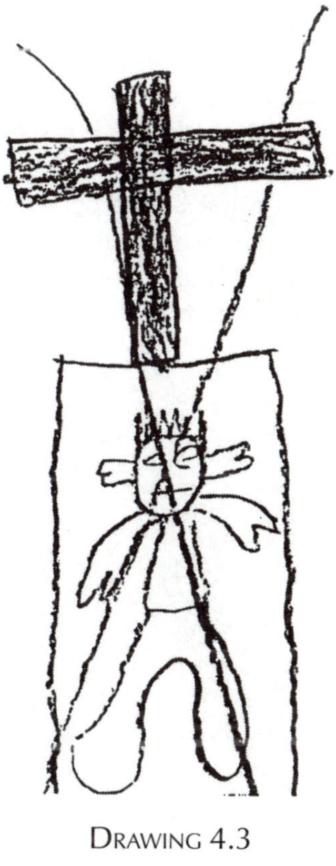

DRAWING 4.3

Elaboration of the mourning and the father's funeral

After that session, Armand spoke a great deal and at home wept about the death of his father. He was finally able to tell his mother how he had been killed in front of his eyes, how wicked the guards were, and what motives they had for doing it. During a discussion, I was present at one of the most moving moments of this treatment. Armand burst into tears and took refuge, sobbing, in the arms of his mother, who held him weeping. She had finally managed to assume a parental position and decided to organize a funeral. She asked me for an appointment with all the children to announce the event to them. I believed, then, that she was attributing to me the role of a third person, guarantor of the law, as well as offering maternal and paternal support, positioned somewhere between her cultural references and my own. Armand was very attentive to our organization, and for the first time I remembered that he was the oldest of the male children. A very meaningful drawing of this period (Drawing 4.4) shows a man in a coffin, a man-angel, and a small person with a veiled face. It would seem that a mortal-father, in his tomb (he bore some resemblance to the fetish man), lets himself be freed by a guardian angel-father, in a movement of organization of the persecuting and protecting parental imago. Was the small man the oldest son, keeping his face veiled in front of the difficulties of identifying himself with a destructive and menacing father?

DRAWING 4.4

In response to the mother's request, we organized a session for the whole family (we were always alarmed at the degree of family disorganization), in the course of which I had to deal with two things simultaneously: discuss a residential stay in an institute for the mother and children, and announce the mother's project of a funeral ceremony for their father. The first part of the discussion was very strenuous. The children were categorically opposed to the idea of the institute: they did not want to change the place where they lived and were afraid of losing their friends. I wondered if they were not also afraid of losing their mother (as they had lost their father), since she, in her total incapacity to contain her children, had fallen asleep during the discussion. The five children, in an act of maniacal omnipotence, became disruptive, attacked the plans presented to them, and brought my consulting-room into confusion. I had to assume an authoritarian parental role to reunite all of them and continue the session. After that, Evelyne became much more active in the discussion of the funeral arrangements: she had contacted a cousin (completely unknown to all of us until that moment) to ask for help with the ceremony. All the children agreed to the plans for the project and calmed down.

I was greatly relieved by the project of a ritual for mourning,[5] even if I continued to worry for the family's safety. Evelyne would do just enough so that we would not intervene more strongly: she would organize suitable holidays for the children, having uncovered unsuspected resources. Yet again, since I had often experienced this happening with traumatized families, I allowed myself to be guided as the situation evolved, confident that the proposal of a ritual for mourning would have a containing effect and present the best possible intercultural compromise in terms of the multiplication of modes for care.

Time proved us right: that period, filled with anguish and action on the part of various members of the family, seemed to lead to a reawakening for Armand (or was Armand the one who followed the evolution of his family?). In any case, it seemed that the present disorder had been connected to setting an elaboration of bereavement in motion, which required, for the survival of the family, "fixing" the father in some permanent place. The funeral, the ritualization of mourning, offered an opportunity to express depressive emotions and allowed the family to have an organizing shell again, on both the cultural and intrapsychic levels.[6] The ritualized distinction between the world of the dead and that of the living allowed the father's death to be made public (Evelyne had wanted to invite friends, acquaintances, and therapists). It also provided a setting that was culturally and psychologically suitable for the elaboration of mourning. The father's funeral was experienced positively by all of them and had a very soothing effect on the situation.

Elaboration of the trauma and the revival of fantasy life

The recognition of grieving for the father seemed to have initiated for Armand a true "elaboration of the trauma", analogous to the elaboration of the mourning. In his associations, fantasy themes typical of children of his age started to appear, although more connected to themes related to his trauma. The passage from one type to another was becoming more manageable now, even if his stories were often interrupted by outbursts of fear, confusion about categories (before–after, here–there, good–bad, persecutor–persecuted), and, at times, confusion about the reality of the trauma. However, these outbursts allowed the story to take shape with corresponding and appropriate affects. Thus, Armand made a drawing of a father who brought presents, but the presents cost dearly, and the father showed his teeth. Then ambulance drivers, at first kindly, became wicked and turned into soldiers who were coming to arrest a mother. The emerging of that reality led him to say, "Yes, I have seen people who kill." Silence was no longer absolute; the traumatic rupture found a role in a picture. It could take a shape and meaning and slowly become integrated into a more connected psychic functioning.

Armand still remained quite vulnerable to every important aggressive emotion, especially if it came from a man. He reacted violently, through withdrawal or an opposite emotion. One day he could evoke "a mean teacher" who "hit my fingers and kicked a little child . . . he is scary, he ought to be fired", demonstrating a persistent split between good and evil, but in which evil is better identified and projected towards the external world in an attempt to preserve the good parts. "But the lady teacher is very good."

The evocation of a good maternal figure suggested the anguish of losing his mother (a tiger killed a mommy-doll) and the emotions connected with the loss of his father: "I am sad for my father and sometimes I cry. . . ." These latter associations evoked feelings of impotence over not having been able to save his father and the absence of protective figures. After the burial of his father and the comfort of a protective cross, his anguish was directed again towards the loss of his mother ("Yes, I am afraid she will die . . ."). This was followed by games in which a maternal figure was threatened, but protected (killed but then saved by an ambulance), and appears frightening and at the same time protective (a mamma dinosaur protects her baby).

Thus, after the paternal figure, a maternal figure reappears, and I had to think about these long months in which the mother seemed truly dead, whereas today she seemed to be taking on a zest for life, in reality and also within Armand.

In Armand, the psychic effects of the trauma were perceptible on many levels. In particular, the imago was very fragile. There were also disturbances of identification because his parents and his country were wounded, and at times destroyed, in the unconscious. There were still difficulties related to impulse confusion, between good and bad, kind and aggressive, and so forth. The world, relational greed, phallic attributes, everything is immediately experienced as too aggressive and, possibly, as sources of reprisal. The necessary intrapsychic supports, made up of the good parts, were quite precarious, and, as has been shown, the reassuring objects rapidly transformed themselves into persecutory ones. The imagos of men in particular were especially fragile. The numerous phallic attributes given (necktie, earring, cigarette, pistol) are more threatening than reassuring (Drawing 4.5). One drawing (Drawing 4.6), which I called "Mr Half-and-Half", presents a sort of condensation of the split between good and evil, protector and persecutor of the imago (the little man is no longer swallowed up, as he was in the previous drawing, but can stay there, more tranquil, on the "good side") and a representation of a horror scene: a soldier (protective figure) kills; a father (good) abandons.

The search for stable imagos can be observed in all of Armand's drawings, up to the "Drawing of the Court" (Drawing 4.7), in which he is the one, the little man, who recognizes the criminal

DRAWING 4.5

under the policeman's uniform. It seemed then that the attempt to master the situation diminished to leave room for a more depressive sense of guilt (Drawing 4.8): an attempt to reunite the parental couple (Superman who reaches the cloud, this time both of them smiling) made the little man smile and then weep, and brought back a depressed paternal figure (Drawing 4.9). In the end, the processes of identification seemed to clash against a self-esteem that was seriously lacking ("No one loves me," he often said at school).

End of the first phase of treatment

Armand's therapy progressively became rich and harmonious. The drawings alternated with words and games full of pleasur-

DRAWING 4.6

able fantasies and emotions. Armand became more active, since he spontaneously brought much material and made associations. Analogously, since his mother could not accompany him every day, he started to come to the sessions alone, visibly content and proud of this step towards a greater mastery of his own external and internal life. (He was the only child of his age who, although coming from another part of the city, came to the session on his own.)

The external reflections were also favourable: the whole family was better, Evelyne was smiling, and for the first time I heard her say with satisfaction, "Things are fine at home with Armand." At school, even if he was still finding it hard to learn, Armand was making progress in his relationships with classmates and with teachers and presented only a smaller number of behaviour upsets.

DRAWING 4.7

The psychotherapeutic treatment was interrupted for several months because my maternity leave was starting. Armand responded, like other patients, with fantasies of loss, rivalry, and a great anxiety to know whether the child would be a boy or a girl, showing his capacities for transference.

At the last meeting of this first phase of treatment, he came with Gloria. From the very beginning of the treatment, I had suggested joint sessions to Gloria and Armand, believing it would have been easier for them to face their shared experience together. But they had not followed this suggestion, until this last meeting.

DRAWING 4.8

DRAWING 4.9

It was a surprising meeting, for many reasons: was it the reactivation of a common experience—that of "losing" me for several months—that brought Gloria and Armand so close? I had the impression that there was a genuine dialogue between them. I felt like a third party, witness and narrator at the same time: once again I was the one who had to compose phrases starting from their words, drawings, and indications. But they did not hide the rivalry existing between them: they asked if I thought it would be a boy or a girl. Naturally Gloria thought I would have a girl, and Armand was convinced it would be a boy, which allowed me to bring to light their fear of seeing a mother prefer one of her children, a baby boy, a baby girl, an older child, a younger one. Gloria and Armand then started to play a game for two, a game of hangman, a true and proper dialogue in which they created mysteries for each other and exchanged clues to help with the answers. I stayed on the side and commented on "the results". From time to time, Armand brought up the name of his little brother B____ (in association with my interpretation on rivalry with younger children). The following hidden words recall the sorts of thing small children love—*teddy bears, candies, baby bottles*—and evoke what young children ask of their mothers. Since I was acting as commentator, I allowed myself to remember some aspects of their shared experience: the sadness and fright they felt when they found themselves alone; their wish to run to a mother who would comfort them; the mystery they had to live with when encountering a chaotic world, ignorant of what others knew or understood, like a true hangman game in which the answers can never be found. Gloria and Armand were particularly attentive; at this point, Armand took up the game and gave a clue: "When a child is alone, who does he turn to?" Gloria had trouble finding the word *mother* but associated it with the hidden words *Planet Mars*—a strange condensation between the experience of an absent, distant mother and the experience of alienation of the children when they arrived in Switzerland, a disturbing world, which they had described to me as fearful. Then Gloria responded with the last hidden word: "It is someone who is with us in the consulting-room—Saskia" (my name), and she was worried about my food and my future.

In relation to these last propositions, clearly prompted by transference, we could evoke the sense of lack, the feeling of precariousness, and the fear of losing me, all references to their traumatic experience. Once again I distanced myself from psychotherapeutic orthodoxy by accepting Armand's request to write him a few lines when the child was born. Moreover, during my absence I could be reached on the telephone.

Armand and Gloria went away happy, relieved, with a cheerful, "Goodbye, see you soon."

One could say that the prospect of my absence reawakened in Armand and Gloria their mutual experience of loss and grief, which, this time, could be transformed into words in the course of the joint session. This time, the absence and separation could be foreseen and prepared for and the emotions and associated ghosts could be faced. On this occasion, brother and sister were able to break the ice with the game of hangman and re-evoked with me some of the elements of the painful phases, while facing the usual emotions connected with a separation in psychotherapy. In this way, traumatic aspects and fantasy life seemed to order themselves more harmoniously. However, I still felt the need to leave some concrete points of reference that could have not only a reassuring value but also a structuring one, for the evolution of the reliability of the objects of investment and of them, through the self-esteem of each child.

Conclusions

The problem posed by a patient like Armand is to understand whether it is possible to project and follow psychotherapeutic work that takes into account not only the functioning and the evolution of a child, but also the difficulties of an entire family and the factors connected with extreme traumas, exile, and social precariousness.

With Armand it seemed we had succeeded in progressively establishing a transference relationship, which allowed him to express his fantasies and affects and to begin the psychic elaboration. In the course of treatment, the evolution of the dynamic and economic aspects of his psychic functioning was made concrete with his symptomatic improvement. Starting from a withdrawal that was almost autistic, Armand allowed himself to start to become an individual, to live and express himself, even if at times in a disordered way. Among the phases of this evolution, we emphasized the progressive stabilization of a therapeutic alliance, the elaboration of the mourning for the father, the ritualizing of the mourning, the work on the trauma, and the reassumption of fantasy activity that was less dependent on trauma. Analogously, the drawings and games underwent an evolution in the therapeutic relationship: from meagre and repetitive sketches to complex fantasy scenes in which the traumatic scenes diminished in favour of the expression of an imaginative and "normal" fantasy life. In the end, the "said" began to substitute the "showing". This allowed for the verbalization of emotions and fantasies and a psychic elaboration, within which a work of connecting the fantasy life and the trauma could evolve.

Nevertheless, such evolution, as we have seen, was strongly determined by the decision to include: (1) family aspects (starting the therapy with Armand with his mother, supporting her, the family framework); (2) aspects linked to the trauma (difficulties with trust, excess wariness, psychic hibernation, exacerbation of certain psychic mechanisms, some ruptures, denial, isolation of affects, instability of the imago, upsets in the processes of identification, fragility of self-esteem, aspects of relationships and family); and (3) aspects connected to exile—in the case of Armand's mother, the value of her cultural representations was noted (especially in the treatments related to Franceline James's visit), while a softening of her relationship between her culture of origin and the culture of the receiving country did not (yet) take place. Similarly, with Armand, the ties to his country and life before the trauma did not go beyond several evocative drawings ("African" or "Western" attributes for the people). Such a configuration is often found in severely traumatized patients, as if it were difficult to establish links with cultural references before having established a certain psychic integrity shaken by the traumatic impact. The work that started with the organization of a grieving ritual had to be followed, so that Armand and his family could establish a more appropriate distance between their cultural resources and those of the receiving country.

Finally, the psychotherapeutic work could not have taken place without the consistency of a trusted, flexible, and stable network. The meetings, not very frequent but regular, were instrumental in monitoring the pertinence of the treatment and its impact on outside functioning. The network also functioned as a reassuring framework both for the family and the therapist, who in this way managed to always reserve a place for psychic reality, aware of the existence of a guarantor of the external reality.

In conclusion, for Armand, the reality of the trauma yielded step by step to the elaboration of the intrapsychic conflicts generated by the impact of the trauma or reawakened by the vicissitudes of existence. However, the impact of trauma, added to that of exile (a sort of cumulative trauma, intense, repeated, enduring, poorly contained by the family), produced breaches that were very difficult to close: we observed the fragility of the scattered impulses, the vulnerability of the imago, the difficulties with identification and the weakness of self-esteem. In fact, these are the weakest points of Armand's psychic functioning, and because of which his therapy has not ended. In addition, his entry into adolescence, with its numerous identity crises and shocks to the system, risks reviving a crisis situation for both Armand and his family: how will it be possible to integrate the power of adolescence with the ghosts of murder, loss, and abandonment? How will Evelyne deal with this period of return to discussion and confrontation? Clearly, therapy would be helpful during this period.

Many writers currently propose short interventions (debriefings) or group ones, but such strategies are mainly used in the immediacy of an emergency situation and somehow compensate for the poverty of therapeutic means available. Yet many clinics agree in recognizing the value of psychotherapeutic interventions in managing situations of collective violence and trauma, since they are about a high-risk population (academic failure, antisocial behaviour, addictive behaviour, psychiatric disturbances) for whom it is urgent to develop care and prevention strategies, not only on "home ground" but also in exile.

Notes

1. From a description by S. Amati, at a conference in Geneva, of a cycle of trauma.

2. Hyper-maturity is frequently noted in these situations, since the traumatic experience induces the child to evolve precociously, to "grow too fast" (see Sironi, 1995).

3. This uncle represented the last bastion of authority, but also of clan and cultural recognition; his "gift" was equal to distancing, an act that rendered Evelyne once again an orphan.

4. Exile, and even more so trauma, causes adolescents to learn the language and the norms of the country that hosts them very quickly. Quicker to adapt than their parents, they act as guides in a way that represents a real generational inversion.

5. Concerning the structuring and therapeutic functions of mourning rituals, see L. V. Thomas, *Anthropologie de la mort* (1975) and G. Rubin, "Fonctions structurantes et contenantes des rituels de deuil" (1996).

6. For the concept of psychic structures, see D. Houzel, "Le concept d'enveloppe psychique" (1987).

CHAPTER FIVE

The Child Sorcerer: the transmission of misfortune in a Kongo context. Description of an ethnopsychiatric treatment

Franceline James

Introduction: Kongo society

The term "Kongo" refers to an ethnic group that, in central Africa, occupies the entire lower stretch of the River Kongo. The river flows into the Atlantic Ocean, and the cities of Kinshasa and Brazzaville are located on its banks. At one time, the "Kongo" ethnic group constituted a great kingdom, the Kingdom of Kongo, which was famous in pre-colonial history and went on to become a complex society. Although it is impossible to fully describe the society here, for our purposes it is essential to mention two of its characteristics:

1. It is a matrilinear society: the child who is born belongs to the lineage of the mother. The maternal uncle has responsibility for and authority over the child (the father, in turn, is responsible for the children of his own sister). The lineage (all the descendants, living or dead, from a common female ancestor) determines the attitudes and behaviour of the individuals (Buakasa, 1973).
2. Representations of evil (mishaps, misfortunes, etc.), illness, and related procedures of reparation are highly complex and

sophisticated. An illness that does not get better or a misfortune that persists are considered the sign of a conflict within the community or the lineage, or even of an imbalance between the world of the ancestors and that of the living. These may also be caused by sorcery or witchcraft conducted by someone intending to harm another person. In fact, the Kongo people believe the universe is composed of two worlds: (a) the day-to-day visible world (inhabited by living people, animals, plants, minerals); and (b) the night-time and invisible world (inhabited by spirits and ancestors, both good and bad). Some exceptional people "see in both worlds": initiated into the night world, they can influence the visible world, both to protect the community by increasing the active force of the clan members (this is the case for all political leaders), as well as to cast a spell on a human being (this applies to the individual who uses his or her own influence on the invisible world for personal gain). People of this kind act out of jealousy or envy and turn exclusively to their own advantage the forces destined for the entire community; they represent the figure of the sorcerer, who has the powers of the night at his or her command and "eats" people (which means causes their death). The victim of such an aggression is defined as having been "eaten" in the world of the night. When his or her vital force is attacked, the person can even die (Kimpianga, 1997).

The ethnopsychiatric approach

Aware that this is the way of thinking in the Kongo, it seems impossible for us imagine how our classical medical treatments could address the difficulties and concerns of anyone coming from that world. Let us consider, with Tobie Nathan, that a human being is not constructed in a universally identical fashion, but is made, formed in his or her way of thinking, by the culture of origin. Let us then try to integrate the anthropological, cultural dimension into our understanding of individual psychological suffering of migrant patients. To allow this "complementary" approach (as George Devereux, the first theorist of ethnopsychiatry, defines it), we need the arrangement proposed by Tobie Nathan: a group of co-therapists, from different cultural backgrounds, welcomes the patients; the patients can express themselves in their own language thanks to the presence of an interpreter whose function is to work out a mediation between the patient's culture and ours (Nathan, 1996).

History of the treatment

Evelyne made her first ethnopsychiatric visit to the Psychiatric Institute of Geneva in April 1995, at the request of her assigned physician at the Centre of Community Health, which, in Geneva, handles those people who have requested asylum and who exhibit somatic problems. She was accompanied by her guardian (a member of the ELISA network [European Legal Network on Asylum], which was assisting her in the practical details of request for asylum). Our group received her with the assistance of a translator of Lingala, who also comes from Zaire.

Evelyne arrived in Switzerland in April 1993 with her three younger children (the youngest was just a few months old). She had wanted to go to Bale-Mulhouse to join a cousin who was living in France. But France refused her entry, and she was forced to remain in Switzerland and request asylum. The federal authorities rejected her request, and an appeal has been lodged.

Her tutor explained to us that, according to what Evelyne had said, her husband was active in politics. One day, several soldiers came to arrest him together with the two older children (a boy and a girl) while she was away with the younger ones. She was convinced that all of them had been killed.

Now, at the beginning of 1995 (in the period of the appeal), the two older children, who she had assumed were dead, appeared in Geneva. They were almost mute. It was only known that they had been prisoners in a military camp, and they had seen their father being killed.

The appeal Evelyne brought forward against expulsion was rejected by the Swiss authorities, who accused her of having lied about her identity (she had named only three children in her passport) and of having support in her own country because her two older children were able to get to Switzerland.

The tutor was completely impotent: every possible channel for lodging an appeal had been exhausted. And he was amazed at not managing to get in touch with Evelyne's family (a cousin in Mulhouse and a brother in Paris).

The contact with Evelyne was very difficult. Prostrate, weeping, she spoke in a barely audible voice that the interpreter seated next to her could scarcely understand. She was desperation personified. We started to understand that Evelyne felt like an orphan. Without her husband, there was no one she could count on. From the questions we asked, it emerged that the situation in Zaire had already been highly irregular: the lineage of the husband did not want to know about her. The oldest of her male children (who had recently arrived from Kinshasa) was often ill, and another child suffered from seizures of an epileptic type.

Faced with Evelyne's destroyed world, we immediately felt the need to resort to some links and connections, to reconstitute a shell. We asked the interpreter a few questions: in a situation like this, couldn't some form of sorcery be at work? The translator immediately accepted that hypothesis.

We continued: But the aggression against Evelyne through her children had begun long before, hadn't it? Evelyne immediately confirmed this: she lost her parents when she was very young (they were killed in a car crash when she was 5 years old). Then she was separated from her brother and sister. She never benefited from any material support and could not go to school. She was brought up by a family that was friendly with her father, but without kinship ties. She was not made welcome there, especially by the mother. She had always lived in misery.

We emphasized that her lineage had been the object of hostility for a long time. We noted that Evelyne spoke very submissively, as if she were wary of danger. She wept: she had never been happy, not with her husband, not in Europe. In her dreams, she has been seeing that life was short and that she would soon die.

We sketched out her genogram to understand how far back the curse may have stretched. We learned that her father had already been separated from his family. Then we could propose an interpretation: in this *mukongo* family of Lower Zaire (in which sorcerers are terribly feared), a serious menace had already been hovering over her parents. That was the reason the couple's children had been scattered. The wife of her father's friend who raised her knew, and for this reason she did not want to become affectionate with her. Evelyne had survived these ancient aggressions. It was in order to protect her that they had sent her away.

From that moment, the atmosphere of the session changed quite clearly. All of us could breathe. We felt united, "on the same wave length". Evelyne had raised her head. For the first time, she looked at us a bit. The interpreter confirmed the affirmations of Evelyne: curses follow individuals even after they leave a place, until things are put in order again.

Evelyne explained to us the meaning of her second African name: "It is mine, it belongs to me." Her father's name meant: "Something that is not mine, which belongs to others." These names speak of a long story of dispossession of the self. Evelyne was alone in the world; she seemed severely melancholic, and we were very worried about her.

The grave traumas this family has undergone have had a disorganizing effect that was hard to evaluate. At that moment, it was impossible to approach such material, which could be perceived only in its consequences of having ruptured psychic containers that were no longer protective: Evelyne was so profoundly crushed that it was difficult for us to imagine how she could cope with five children. Guided by the clinical reality, we tried to go by Evelyne's culture, which clearly offered her matrices of meaning that she might be able to use to understand reality and get her bearings again. In the attempt to establish a link between her and the elements of belonging, we decided to provide a fundamental containing function, from which it would be possible to elaborate the traumas and the losses she had suffered.

So we embarked on a treatment that lasted almost two years, with one session every fifteen days, and sometimes long interruptions during holidays (after the holidays, the patient usually missed a session or two). In the course of this long work, we had to take deaths, ancestors, and sorcerers into consideration and modify many ways of thinking established for our Western patients! I shall attempt to give an account of our work and of the framework of thought—or, rather, frameworks of thought—that we used.

Traditional aetiologies

Starting with the second session, Evelyne evoked two themes on which the most important part of our work with her focused: *the dead ones* who populated her dreams, ancient dead people, in decomposition, whom she could not identify. And her preoccupations about her first son, Armand (the second of her children, recently arrived in Geneva with his older sister). He was 8 years old but behaved like a much younger child. From the time of his arrest, he was always pretending to eat, not only between meals but also when he was sleeping. His mother suspected he had been bewitched during their separation. ("Eaten at night" is a message in code that everyone in Zaire recognizes, and it means an aggression on the part of a dreaded man-eating sorcerer. We shall find this significant on different occasions.)

We worked along the line of the traditional aetiology of attack on the part of a man-eating sorcerer, which causes suffering to the entire family. At the same time, the presence of the interpreter allowed the patient—so alone and for such a long time and who "belongs to someone else"—to find some sense or roots from which she had been cut off. On the other hand, the two themes proceeded together. We were struck by Evelyne's lack of links of belonging, unusual for an African. On the other hand, she gave the impression of having difficulty recognizing that she was originally a *mukongo*. Born in Kinshasa, she only spoke the vernacular language (Lingala). We understood that her parents had moved from Lower Zaire to the capital, and they had also experienced this strange cutting of family and kinship ties. When they were killed in an accident, their three children were scattered among neighbours. Evelyne had always lived abnormally alone. In such conditions, not even her husband's clan accepted her.

The social and family situation in the country of origin

The lack of protection from a clan, a family group, brought the same risk of rupture on all levels of the system: the oldest daughter, recently arrived from Zaire, had to undergo a federal hearing, in which she had to tell the story of her arrest by soldiers and describe the assassination of her father under her eyes and those of her brother. The following night she had a nightmare, in which her uncle, the brother of her father who had sent the two young children to Switzerland, gave her meat, but she refused to eat ("to eat the night" again represents the same idea of aggression on the part of a man-eating sorcerer and the threat of death). She was terrified and called for her mother. The two of them spent the rest of the night huddled together, reading the Bible. Then it was Evelyne's turn to have a frightening dream of aggressive sorcery, in which someone stuck a hand into her belly to rip out her guts. The following day she went to the hospital in Geneva with strong abdominal pain, but the doctors found nothing.

The use of this traditional representation undoubtedly allowed the daughter to do some sort of work of psychic linking of the trauma experienced, However, Evelyne could only hold a specular position with respect to her daughter. The mother was unable to offer a container for her daughter's anguish, pervaded as she was by the same fantasy of aggression that had overwhelmed her daughter and caused her to go to the hospital. It is necessary to emphasize here the cultural shortcomings of the doctors, who naturally were very embarrassed by this message, which a medicine man in her own country would have immediately understood.

Language as a cultural matrix that allows the anchoring of points of cultural reference

It is important to underline the role of the interpreter. He helped us for about half of this treatment. He was also *mukongo* and made a double link possible: between Evelyne and us, during the adaptation period; and between Evelyne and her origins, from which, as we have seen, she had been separated even within her family.

So the interpreter extended the range of traditional interpretations. Speaking Lingala, he allowed Evelyne to think about herself in the *mukongo* cultural world, and to think about herself with others, which he represented. Very sensitive, he sometimes assumed an almost pedagogical role, in part to the benefit of the group of co-therapists, but above all, in reality, to Evelyne, to whom he "presented" the *mukongo* world in all its complexity. At the same time, we noticed that Evelyne's trust in the group became deeper, while her older son channelled the idea of aggression on the part of a sorcerer for the whole family. Evelyne, very disturbed, described him while he talked in his sleep, making gestures of eating even in his sleep. He defecated in his underpants, and he presented behaviour problems at school.

Independently of Armand's individual psychopathology, it seemed to us that he and Evelyne had a closed-circle relationship, in which her incapacity to fill the maternal role of a protective container was echoed by Armand's disturbances. Both offered negative reinforcement of the other's difficulties. Was this situation connected to the fact that Armand, the second-born child, was the oldest of Evelyne's sons? Undoubtedly. In any case, we had the impression that the dead ones were struggling with us for Evelyne and that our group would have to embark on very difficult work with Armand, parallel with his individual therapy, to be able to treat the mother. We were also struck by the almost symbiotic closeness of the relationship Evelyne had with the interpreter seated beside her: she barely whispered, and only he could hear her, as if they were in a bubble.

When the summer was over, we learned that Evelyne's brother-in-law had broken off all contact with her. Now that the children had been sent to her, he wanted to have nothing more to do with her; she could never expect any help from him. Now she was entirely alone, completely abandoned. After the marked improvement, she fell again into a worrisome depressive state. Things were also going badly for the oldest son, according to Saskia von Overbeck. We agreed that Evelyne should bring him.

Starting with the ninth session, Armand accompanied his mother to our appointments (sometimes with one or the other of the younger children). He showed very worrying behaviour: he did not relate to anyone, but took refuge in a corner of our large room, next to a stereo. He played with the knobs and seemed to want to melt into the machine.

We learned that when he was 3 months old, he had an abnormally large head. A healer had said that the evil came from the father's side of the family.

As if to emphasize the significance of the broken psychic shell which allowed the aggression apparent in her son to emerge, Evelyne told us that several times in the past few days she had heard someone ring her doorbell at night. She was afraid. Armand put his hands over his ears. We remembered we were straddling two worlds: down there one can hear things from within and also things from outside. Evelyne started to cry; Armand began to sob. Our interpretation was that Armand felt that there was no one backing his mother up.

We continued trying to reconstruct the protective structures around this mother who had been abandoned with no mediation with respect to the haunting ghosts of death: at night, when she goes to check that her children are sound asleep, Armand seems dead to her. We evoked an angry ancestor who does not manage to be recognized. When the interpreter spoke of the interrogation to which a child in such a situation traditionally undergoes to identify the ancestor, Armand fell asleep as if pacified.

Evelyne lamented the fact that Armand behaved like a little baby; and, when he was asleep, he talked, he seemed to see people, to eat. At school he seemed to understand nothing, and he threw his food under his bed like a baby.

We were able to articulate our hypothesis: Evelyne and Armand were in the same psychic shell. Their shells were not separate. She saw no one backing him up.

Evelyne spoke of giving birth: it took place at the hospital in the presence of her husband, even though he did not follow the traditional procedure of burying the placenta (which normally should be done by the mother of the woman giving birth). We agreed that what had been left open from the birth experience had not been closed again. That was how Armand was attacked.

The evocation of this problem was soon followed by a series of catastrophes: the 4-year-old daughter was playing with matches and set her room on fire while Evelyne was in the shower; in the hotel where they found a temporary place to stay, there was flooding; the family had to move again. Social services intervened, the Protection of Children department planned to put the children into a shelter.

We also felt thrown. To remain in a single world, one must leave the other and close the door. But our group was completely divided in two, just like Evelyne. Some felt an immense, repressed anger; others, on the contrary, felt completely excluded, divided in two.

Armand was clearly not well again: he wept, he showed the same autistic behaviour we had witnessed some time before, and he tried to enter into the stereo as if he wanted to become a machine himself. According to his mother, he was convinced that, if his name were pronounced, he would be killed by the person who came to disturb him at night.

That gave us a chance to offer a frontal attack on the trauma, at the point where we saw the mother and son getting bogged down, reflecting each other. According to our terminology, we could say that we were taking an active position, in order to locate the aggressor clearly in external reality. This was the only instrument that would allow the subject to proceed to an organizing break (see Amati, 1979; Sironi, 1989). But we formulated it in terms of tradition, deciding to face the sorcerer, questioning him "above" Armand's head and thus forcing the child to "spit out the sorcery" into a recording machine (following a well-known procedure in Zaire). Armand, who up to that moment had never said a word, told us that a man came at night, offered him food, wanted to lead him into the forest, and dispatched him to do things. He had seen him eat people. Armand pronounced the name of his persecutor. For the entire session, Evelyne wept and was completely absorbed.

In the following session, Armand put himself outside the circle to draw. He commented on the drawing with a co-therapist who was near him: it was an enormous and threatening man who took up the entire space: in a corner was a tiny tomb; a weapon; in the ceiling, a hole that let something through (Drawing 5.1). We confined ourselves to listening to Armand's description of his drawings to the co-therapist, a man he felt close to. We did not make any comments or interpretations.

Evelyne had seen her husband in a dream, and he had entrusted the children to her. She was weeping. We declared that the time had come to bury him. Evelyne wanted to have a Mass said for him, which we would attend.

Armand showed us a second drawing: two men's heads. Armand was in his bed. The man offered him some sweets. The hole then was well defined, almost at the point of closing (Drawing 5.2).

DRAWING 5.1

DRAWING 5.2

We added: words are needed to close the hole in the ground when someone is buried, and also something we can perceive. After the Mass, we shall eat and drink together.

Armand quickly made a third drawing: he had been afraid, he had shouted, but he had injured the man because he kept a knife in his bed (Drawing 5.3).

In the following session, Armand drew a large black night bird, crossed by an arrow, perched on a red branch (Drawing 5.4). The co-therapist with whom he usually talked about his drawings gave him a bucket of modelling clay, which could be used to make shapes and plug holes. But he should not lose it or give the clay to anyone else; it belonged to the group, but Armand would be in charge of it.

Armand immediately began to model a figure. Surprise: it was undoubtedly a *mukongo* fetish with nails.

This was at the beginning of summer. Evelyne had planned a Mass in memory of her husband, which we would attend. To allow the dead man to rest in peace, the living must let him go.

DRAWING 5.3

DRAWING 5.4

Armand made a very vivid drawing: two dragons eating dead people, in front of a fortress, with a door well protected by iron grating (Drawing 5.5).

After the summer (the mourning ceremony had taken place), Armand was put into a special class, where he was well received. But he tore up the papers he needed to show his mother. As for Evelyne, she had a dream: she was drowning and a white woman came to find her. She was worried about her request for asylum, which continued to be pending. Armand was still screaming at night. He saw a man who wanted to carry him off to the cemetery. While he was sleeping, there was a bad smell; the man said it was the smell of the forest where he killed people and where he was going to take him.

During the times his mother was talking, Armand made drawings that looked more and more structured. In a series of seven that he had numbered, a battle between a monster—with horns and huge teeth, armed with a trident—and him. The monster wanted

DRAWING 5.5

the boy to get into a coffin, but the boy turned the trident against the monster and ended up burying him! "The monster wants to eat them all so he can be alone." In the end the monster became a skeleton in the coffin; his weapon was buried with him (Drawings 5.6 to 5.12).

In the twentieth session, Evelyne expressed her concern to us: Armand's teacher had called her because he continued to leave the class. But that did not happen just at school. This time we evoked her brother-in-law, who according to custom should have married her so she would not be by herself as well as to keep the children in their father's lineage. Instead, he had rejected her and left. While we went on with this accusation and referred it back to the judgement of the ancestors, Armand fell asleep. We established then that when grown-ups talk in this way, children can sleep. We accompanied him in his sleeping, and we proposed the induction that Armand could go back to his class at school because we were taking care of the things that concern grown-ups.

DRAWING 5.6

After this session, we learned that Armand was sleeping well, and so was Evelyne. Their dreams were pleasant, with no particular memories.

At the twenty-second session, Armand came into the circle and sat in a large armchair. We emphasized that each person was in his place, where the ancestors could watch over the big people, who in turn watched over the little ones.

Six months had passed since the Mass had been celebrated for her deceased husband; Evelyne now could put an end to her mourning. From this moment, in Africa, the woman was free and, for example, could remarry. Armand reacted. We suggested that Evelyne offer a meal to celebrate the conclusion of mourning. We were all aware that we could end the treatment.

At the final session, Armand made lively, colourful drawings. There was a multicoloured character, with one open eye and the other closed, smiling (Drawing 5.13). There were African animals (Drawings 5.14 and 5.15). We mentioned the responsibility of a

Drawing 5.7

Drawing 5.8

Drawing 5.9

Drawing 5.10

Drawing 5.11

Drawing 5.12

Drawing 5.13

Drawing 5.14

DRAWING 5.15

big brother towards the younger ones. Armand listened to us, intently.

This long treatment functioned on many different axes. We shall discuss three of them: traditional aetiologies that we made function in a sequence; the reconstruction of the psychic shells, which had deteriorated; and the passage from one world to another.

First axis

Above all is the use of the word "aetiology" in the plural: *aetiologies!* Actually, in a similar approach aetiology is not considered absolute scientific truth, but a framework of possible thought for the suffering of this patient (Nathan, 1988, p. 137).

Evelyne and her son were struggling with a suffering that was not merely connected to the losses or the shocks they had experienced. What made their situation difficult—and for those who tried to help them—was the fact that their suffering was, above all, impossible to put into words, because no one knew (not even them) in which context it had to be placed. It is this chaos that cannot possibly be shared that was the principal source of their suffering. But individual suffering is never of no significance: it is always, here as elsewhere, an invocation to a possible meaning, or invocation to a framework of meaning (James, 1994). What framework must we find in order to understand this woman from Zaire, cut off from her roots, dreadfully alone, who has lost everything? Or, rather: could we attempt to co-construct with her a pertinent framework?

As Tobie Nathan affirms very well, the symptom is a text without context (Nathan, 1994, p. 114). I have emphasized elsewhere (James, 1994) the risks of misunderstandings, which in general cannot be redressed, created by referring to our cultural context the text of a symptom manifested by someone whose personality was formed in another cultural context.

So we tried to explore the traditional meanings of what was not going well for Evelyne. It was obvious that the presence of an interpreter and/or a cultural reference point was indispensable for this part of our work.

But to think of aetiology as a framework, a form of containing (or, rather, a container that confers meaning on the contents: Anzieu, 1985), offered a highly flexible tool. In fact, even this framework evolved, and numerous different aetiologies were used successively to confer meaning to a situation and mobilize it.

From the outset, Evelyne's distress about her son's disturbances steered us towards an aetiology of aggression on the part of a sorcerer, whom she had also thought about (which had especially reinforced her sense of panic, because such an idea cannot be dealt with by a woman on her own). Her condition of extreme solitude from the very beginning of her story, highly unusual in Africa, allowed us to hypothesize that the attack arose from a distant time and to help explain the isolation of which she had been a victim since the time of her parents' death. A similar aetiology allowed us to understand, at the same time, Evelyne's extreme passivity, the remarkably disturbed behaviour of her son, and the aggressions and losses undergone by the entire family. So we were induced to receive them together, confirming our intuition that Armand's disturbances did not originate at the time of the tragic events of his father's arrest and assassination, but that he had always been considered a peculiar child.

The first aetiology was completed by the idea that, at the time of Armand's birth, certain fundamental rituals had been neglected, and thus he and his mother shared the same psychic shell: they only had one psychic shell for the two of them. This enabled us to face their merged relationship, which always bound them together, and help them to elaborate different feelings: Evelyne's idea of death projected on Armand, Armand's refusal to think about a third person between his mother and himself, and so forth.

Only at that point was it possible to set the process of mourning in motion, since our preceding attempts had come to nothing. Then we had accompanied (very concretely!) the family to confer a role on the father, locating him among the dead.

Second axis

Parallel with this use of successive aetiologies as a framework to contain suffering and confer a meaning that would allow things to move, our work consisted in reconstructing the psychic shells that had been lacerated by migration and the traumas they had suffered. Evelyne transmitted almost physically to us the sensation of being an egg without a shell, a sparrow without feathers or nest. Especially at the beginning, Evelyne whispered in Lingala beside the interpreter, and this dyad was also "framed" by the primary therapist, while the two, surrounded by the large group of co-therapists, constituted a true illustration of the multiple supports of the psyche described by Kaës (1979).

This functioning for multiple supports was merely topographical. In the course of the sessions, we continued to weave around Evelyne all the threads of possible understanding of her suffering, using all the codes at our disposal. In this way all our interventions quickly became half-breeds or *mongrels*. Using, on the one hand, traditional thinking on someone like Evelyne (re-transmitted by our African co-therapists) and, on the other, our corporeal countertransference, we based ourselves on all the elements (thoughts, fantasies, body sensations, etc.) provided by Evelyne to construct a fabric of thoughts.

So the idea of the co-construction of the psyche literally took shape for us (Moro, 1994, p. 35). In this co-construction, the role of

Armand was very important. This little boy with the strange head, so disconcerting at the beginning in his alienation, progressively established privileged links with one of the male co-therapists in our group, to whom he directed most of the comments on the drawings he had started to produce from the moment when we had succeeded in helping him make a break between himself and his badness (or sorcery).

Third axis

The third axis of our therapy, the *passage from one world to another*, was organized around Armand. The little boy was Evelyne's oldest son, and without doubt he bore the mother's unresolved problems with the paternal lineage even before the migration, and he had witnessed with his older sister the assassination of his father. After the family was reunited, his disturbances had become more obvious. But how could the passage between the two worlds take place if the disorders and violence that had enclosed Evelyne and Armand in a shared psychic shell served as their only protection? It was necessary to summon great patience to avoid disrupting their symbiosis before each of them could withstand a reciprocal distancing. The two themes of sorcery and mourning were elaborated at the same time. The boundary between inner and outer (spectacularly displayed in the session in which Armand "spit out the sorcery") and the boundary that separates the living from the dead managed to support them reciprocally.

At the same time, and as a consequence of this structuring separation, the "external layers" were reconstructed: we succeeded in evoking together with Evelyne the protective ancestors who watch over adults, who in turn are responsible for watching over children. As a visible sign of the reconstructed psychic layers, and from the contact re-established between the different levels, Armand fell asleep in the centre of the circle, completely tranquil.

The passage from one world to another, naturally, is not possible until the world of the migrant patients is completely reconstructed: their psychological world, as we have seen, but their cultural world as well, the world into which they were born, the world that forged them. From this point of view, no therapy in the country that receives them is thinkable if it does not reserve an authentic role, a role of legitimization, to the world the migrants left behind. And so we succeeded in accompanying Armand, the sorcerer child, up to the point where he could carry on the role of responsible big brother. But that would not have been possible if we had given to our theories the dominant role they claim to possess!

It is important to state that the two therapies described here were parallel. Armand and his mother had been referred to me and to Saskia von Overbeck from different channels. We made the decision to keep in touch by telephone from time to time, as needed, and to let Evelyne know about our exchanges. As I have said, Armand came to the session only because we had the sensation of not being able to help his mother without taking their dyadic relationship concretely into consideration. But that was possible only because the network described by Saskia von Overbeck was working, on the one hand, and, on the other, because Overbeck had a sufficiently agile concept of the work. This enabled our efforts to amount, beyond the strictly orthodox practice, to what seemed best for this family in difficulty.

As the description above shows, in the course of the entire therapy we continually used a multiplicity of codes—but not in a disorganized or impulsive way! Trained as Western therapists, we root ourselves in our psychodynamic understanding of the situation we are dealing with. But all our work, all the specific art of an ethnopsychiatric session, as we have learned from Tobie Nathan (1988), consists in letting our codes become relative and in building bridges: with the cultural code of the patient's ethnic origin; with his or her psychic suffering; and also between us, since the structure of the group is clearly essential for this work. (For the creation of psychic "bridges", see Kaës, 1979, p. 7.)

To enable migrant patients to elaborate the mourning of the world they have left, we need to abandon our certainties, our absolutes; we need to confront our modalities of thought with theirs, our practices with their practices. Only in this way can truly appropriate therapies be developed.

CHAPTER SIX

Armand and the "hole": therapy with a family from Zaire

Natale Losi

Armand's mother Evelyne is an ethnic *mukongo* from Zaire; at the time of our therapeutic support, she had been in Geneva as a refugee for about three years.[1] She had come to Switzerland with her three youngest children; she had believed that her two older children, Armand and Gloria, and their father had died in Zaire, in Kinshasa. In fact, after witnessing the arrest and subsequent killing of their father, they were eventually sent to join their mother in Geneva. Armand was highly traumatized, and in Switzerland his behaviour was always antisocial and extremely closed. In the course of his series of visits throughout the range of psycho-medical services in Switzerland, someone had even diagnosed him as autistic. It is with this experience behind him that Armand was sent to our ethnopsychiatric practice.[2]

I met Armand in the second half of 1995, during his seventh session. I was still not very familiar with the ethnopsychiatric group in Geneva, coordinated by Franceline James. I was almost unaware of the resources and networks of psychosocial support available through Geneva's social services; I was informed of the support that Evelyne's family, and in particular Armand, were receiving from Saskia von Overbeck—I knew her personally and admired her work—but I did not have up-to-date details as to how the therapy was proceeding under the direction of Franceline James.[3]

My exposition of the case of Armand does not present an interpretation after the fact (partially verifiable in the paragraphs indicated as "comment"), but it is a record of what I was thinking and perceiving at the time. I hope in this way to offer the reader a practical example of what I mean when I say that all our visions and our approaches are partial. The questions in some way implied are: How did Armand and his family manage to pull through? Was it due to the intervention of SvO or ours? Did my specific contribution, oriented by the internal structure inspired by fables, carry any weight? The questions are probably pointless, and each of us will remain with our own convictions, if any. Besides, only the patients can experience and value the usefulness of the support we offer.

I have chosen this case because it lends itself best to a description of my training path, through an engrossing experience, given that at the time I was starting out using a new therapeutic approach. The other main reason for this choice is the characteristic of this case as one that was played out "in a network" and with different approaches, a specific feature that well exemplifies and represents the principal message of the book: the necessity of therapeutic complexity and plurality. What is more, it is through this case that I started to develop the idea of using Propp's functions as a guide in therapeutic interactions, preparing a grid of interpretation for the migratory experience of our patients.

The first session

Only the mother and the translator come. Armand's mother is late and had skipped two previous sessions.[4] She explains why she had failed to come, why she is late today, and why Armand is not there. Immediately after the meeting with a social assistant who helped her with the practical necessities of integrating in Geneva, she went to a big department store to make some purchase, but when she was at the paying desk she realized that all her money had disappeared. She did not know whether it had been stolen or lost. In addition, on her way to our meeting she had stumbled and sprained her ankle. Armand was unable to come because his teacher would not let him leave school without a written notice from the service.

FJ: In this way, his teacher was trying to protect him.

The mother continues, saying that Armand still has the same problems, while the other children are fine. She is a fairly imposing woman, not beautiful, awkward in her movements, also because of her coat, which she keeps on even though the room is warm. She gives me the sensation of great suffering, almost desperation, of no longer knowing where, how, or to whom she can turn. She almost talks to herself. I have trouble understanding her murmuring. On the other hand, perhaps there is not much else to understand beyond the suffering that shows in the gaze of her large, sad, and afflicted eyes. I feel that the group expects something from me as well. I have recently arrived. I am the only non-African to have lived in Africa. I try to say that when we leave Africa, it always follows us. (I do not know the family history yet, and in this way am trying to link up with themes of homesickness for one's country.) But Evelyne does not seem to be listening. She is taken up in her own world, deep in the chair, holding on to its arms, wrapped in her heavy coat, a black beret on her head.

Someone in the group suggests that there is a code, a sign in the disappearance of money, as well as in the stumble that sprained her ankle. Evelyne responds to this suggestion, saying that she had already lost money in Kinshasa. She had thought at the time that it was a sign. She had spoken to her friends about it and they had agreed: it was a bad sign.

An African co-therapist specifies: "It is not indeed a bad sign! It is a sign! We say that we have bought someone's life."

Tr: Yes, it is a premonition, the disappearance of money. It is important to perform a ritual to make things right again.

FJ: Things are not in order when the ancestors have not been given their share.

African Co-T: When money disappears, it is a sign to go forward, but one can stumble violently.

FJ: In West Africa they say: "You can put a sea between yourself and your ancestors, but they will grow up again in your garden."

Group: It can be frightening to receive these signs; we felt alone, and we then realize we are in company.

We can feel guilty.

They are there, we can't ignore it. They also protect us.

It is an exchange, they protect us, but we have responsibilities towards them.

What thing . . . what message, what communication are we exchanging?

At this point I feel very confused. I did not understand the sense of many of the interventions, their theatrical feel. A deep silence falls among the group. Then someone mentions having a sensation of cold. I remember vividly how drowsy I was, almost unable to stay awake, feeling heavy, a sensation Evelyne probably shared, huddled in her chair. She looks asleep.

FJ points out that there is something double—an external: a task, a payment to make; and an inner: something to receive. There is a precise time for the outside and for the inside.

The group summarizes to Evelyne, repeatedly scanning the words, that "when we discover we are not alone we have responsibilities, we are protected, and the signs are remarkable."

Finally Evelyne is dismissed. We hoped to see her again in a month, and she will bring us her dreams.

Second session

Evelyne arrives with Armand and the two younger children, a boy and a girl. The children look very well cared for, the little girl has her hair in braids, and both Armand and his little brother (whom we will call "George") have short kinky hair. They have European names, not from their *mukongo* ethnic group, reflecting the "Christianization"(at least in its more formal aspects) of both Evelyne and her husband's family.

Armand is a handsome child, very tall for his age (8 years) and with an especially large head. Evelyne seems a bit more active than in the previous session. She is anxious about Armand's health. The school doctor had diagnosed a heart murmur, and tomorrow the child will be examined more thoroughly by a paediatrician.

Armand continues to have the usual scholastic difficulties; he has difficulty reading and doesn't want to do any homework. The translator thinks the child has a spirit that possesses him, which impels him: Armand is not like the others.

FJ, referring to Armand, says that he has something of a "double".

Someone in the group says that, watching Armand, one has the impression that he is a person with much experience; he has the face of an old man, and he has with heart problems.

FJ asks the translator if there is a name in Zaire for such a child.

Tr responds that there is, that this type of person is called a double, possessed. For children, it is as if their growth has been arrested.

I do not say anything. I feel that the group and especially the translator are performing an aggressive move with respect to Evelyne and, above all, Armand. The mother begins to weep silently. Armand starts to sob; he huddles in his chair, holding his head between his hands and knees. I get up to offer him some paper handkerchiefs. He throws them angrily to the ground. I gather them up and sit down again, upset. A thousand thoughts run through my head. Many doubts. I don't understand what the group is doing.

After a brief silence, FJ starts again.

FJ [*to Evelyne*]: Last time we spoke of signs [she was referring to the episodes of the disappearance of money and the stumble that had led to a sprained ankle]. The child, when he is born, is already designated. [*To the group*] Hasn't Evelyne already thought about this?

Evelyne: When Armand was 3 months old, his head looked abnormal, too big. A healer had told me that the evil came from his paternal side. His head has always stayed big.

Someone in the group: Can't the curse be shifted if the name is changed? The name can also be a mistake. Someone can be misnamed.

FJ: Yes. The signs multiply. Today it is the heart [*referring to the presumed heart murmur*].

Tr: If the heart starts to break down, the motor can't run any longer. The heart can be the principal target of attacks.

After a long silence, FJ asks Evelyne if she has had any dreams. The answer is yes, but Evelyne doesn't remember any of her dreams. She was awakened three times by the doorbell, but no one was at the door. Someone in the group comments that the doorbell sounds threatening when one is alone. The door of dreams closes.

Someone else says that in her country, in Iran, it is treated as a good omen, an announcement.

FJ: There have been signs for years, but it is impossible to grasp them when one is alone. They are too threatening. One doesn't feel protected. The things thrown back take life again, but a protective shell is needed so they can be felt.

Armand covers his ears with his hands.

The group continues to talk; someone says that when one is between two worlds, one feels things "within" and "outside." The scene of weeping is repeated. This time I do not move. Armand sobs.

Gr: Armand asks where his protector is.

Evelyne: No, B [*the name of a co-therapist*] is the one who asks that question.

Gr: Armand is the first son. He thinks there is no one to protect his mother.

Evelyne: He is troubled, he feels too alone, he would like the group to help him.

The group offers a suggestion. We ask his mother to do something with Armand to purify him. He will take a bath with herbs (parsley, wild onion, and mint) three times a week. Then FJ passes a piece of paper around. Each of us signs our names, and it is rolled up. Evelyne will tie it shut with string at home. Armand will carry it in his pocket all day and tuck it under his pillow at night. The next meeting will be in two weeks.

Comment. I start to understand that the group's strategy, although it was used harshly this time, is always aiming to induce in the patients a movement towards returning to and building up their own affective and cultural protective shell. This takes place through the continued appeal to their cultural interpretation and to unresolved questions, preceding the trauma of the father's killing.

The interventions of FJ take this form, supported by the specifications of the translator.[5]

From this point of view, the prescription chosen has a double significance. On the one hand, the little paper with our signatures summons the presence, even outside the session, of a powerful therapist who can combat "the worlds of power" that are negative and adversarial; on the other, the bath with herbs represents a task of presence and maternal competence (care of the child) and a re-appropriation of their respective roles (mother and son)—without taking into account that a warm and fragrant bath before bedtime is always relaxing.

I also work on my (counter-) transference with Armand, which moves me for what I imagine to be his sense of solitude and tragedy over the experience he has undergone, that of watching his father being brutally killed. I become aware of the way this experience draws me, as a father, into the fear of being absent (as if dead?) for my children who are not living with me.

It seems to me that I am starting to understand better what is going on in the sessions, but I am not entirely convinced that it is necessary to be so harsh, even theatrical, as the members of the group seemed to be, in recalling "traditional" interpretations of all the events that have been upsetting in the past or that are troubling the life of this family even now. I am not convinced, either, of the necessity of recalling traditional interpretations and using the language and cultural references of the *mukongo*, without then translating them into more Western categories.

Third session

Evelyne, Armand, and the translator/mediator are present.[6]

FJ [*to the group*]: Last time, Evelyne telephoned me to say she was sorry she could not come, because George had to go to the hospital after choking on a fish bone. [*Turning to Evelyne*] How is everything now?

Evelyne: He is home and all is well, but he wants to drink only milk.

FJ: Last time we were waiting for signs, from Evelyne and from

Armand. Have you had any dream? Or seen or heard anything?

Evelyne: Since December [*this is the beginning of February*] only Armand gives problems. He talks in his sleep, but he is not aware of it and doesn't remember. [*His mother has the impression that Armand sees people while he is sleeping, but can't talk.*] At school, he doesn't understand anything.

Tr: These are unequivocal signs. When a child understands nothing at school, everything is obscure; it is as if he is absent and can't manage to study. This sort of situation also happened to his sister [*Gloria, Armand's older sister*]. This was a curse on her parents, but the signs are now directed at the children.

FJ [*to Evelyne*]: I think that there is someone behind you. When a part of the person is not truly there, what happens? [*Still to Evelyne*] Would you ask Armand to sit on B's lap?

His mother asks Armand to sit on B's lap. B is a male co-therapist.

Armand goes there, but remains distant, tense. He cries. B is also tense and embarrassed. I hand him paper handkerchiefs. This time Armand accepts them.

Gr: Armand is angry; he has heard people saying that his grandparents were not happy about his birth. His mother has the impression that Armand behaves like a child who is much younger than he is.

Tr: Things are out of place.

FJ: There is a confusion of protective shells. Evelyne sees no one backing Armand.

Gr: There are two people in the same sack. Armand is cross because he doesn't have enough room. Everything is mixed up and confused because there is only one sack for two.

FJ: When one is crossed, it is important to be able to back up and, therefore, to have someone backing you.

Evelyne: Armand is different from other children. He acts like a baby. Sometimes he throws food under his bed.

FJ: It is sad to have to leave a communal sack, but it the first step for growing up.

Gr: Evelyne was left alone while she was giving birth. What was done with the placenta?

FJ [*to Evelyne*]: But does Armand know that someone or something was not right about his placenta? With his father's family?

Evelyne: I had no contact with my parents-in-law. But after six months I noticed a change in Armand. He had a huge head.

Tr: Usually the mother's mother takes the placenta and buries it. If it is the mother-in-law who does this, there is a risk that she will keep it for herself and, in so doing, will take away his [*turning to Armand*] intelligence, and the child will be retarded.

Evelyne says that her husband was at the hospital in Kinshasa when she gave birth, but he did not perform the ritual with the placenta.

FJ: And all of this has befallen Armand, the oldest boy. Something has not been done. Something has been opened but not closed again.

At the end of the session, FJ prescribes to Evelyne, in a pronounced and repeated way, to remember her dreams. She also asks her to watch Armand while he sleeps, but without waking him up, without touching him, without asking him questions. Then to return to bed and bring us her dreams the next time. She should do all this every evening. And she will tell us her dreams next time, in a month. Then we will see about the placenta, which has not been dealt with yet. It will be important to prepare something to enclose Armand, because he is now open. (In metaphoric language, because of the transitive nature of the placenta, this means that he has not become individualized yet. In figurative language, we shall see in the next sessions how the failure to bury the placenta according to ritual can be linked with the hole through which witches who wish to kill Armand can pass in his nightmares).

Comment. I begin to see more clearly and to agree to a greater extent with the group's strategy. For Armand, as for me, the group constitutes a new psychic protective covering, in which it is possible to recognize protection and to become an individual. For Armand, still caught in his mother's psychic shell, it will be possible to find someone backing him up who can help release him; for me, in the initial phase of migration, it will be possible to find remedy for the mourning of the departure from the old protective shell, my country, friends, house, language.

I remember a tale my mother often told us. It is the story about the wolf and the three little pigs. The wolf tries to eat the little pigs, who are brothers and are hidden inside their houses, built of straw, wood, and bricks. The first two save themselves by fleeing into the house of the third, which was built of bricks. I was the third child in the family. I start to reflect on the cues offered by fairy tales, on the hero and the association between migrant and hero (see chapters two and three). I was the hero in the story of the three little pigs and, what's more, I was a migrant. If I put Armand in this position as a hero (but how?), he will be able to find a way to get out of such a difficult situation.

Fifth session (about two months later)

Evelyne comes with her two youngest children. She is dressed entirely in black, the same colour as the beret she always wears. The children look very serious; they hold their heads high, almost haughtily, and look at us directly. Evelyne explains that the other times she left them with a friend, but today she was not able to.

FJ: How did you spend Easter?

Evelyne: Armand stayed with a friend who also has children. He hit my friend's children.

FJ: How did you spend your Easter?

Evelyne: Well.

FJ: Nothing more happened at night? [*she was alluding to the doorbell ringing and to Armand's nightmares*]

Evelyne: No.

FJ: And with the other children?

Evelyne: I am going with them to spend the day at a friend's house.

There is a long silence. I feel that Evelyne is particularly closed in herself, in her own world, in her own difficulties. FJ says she feels that Evelyne seems divided, on the one hand proud of her handsome children, on the other heavy-hearted because of her solitude.

Gr: Children tend to get into all sorts of trouble, until at a certain point one cannot even be asked to talk about it any longer. These children are happy, they get along. What does Evelyne think of her children?

There is no answer. Evelyne seems even more withdrawn. R, an African co-therapist, feels taken by contrasting and negative feelings, as happens in her interventions (as she will later confirm): feelings of excess, revenge, dissatisfaction, which she will discharge refusing all help from others. And she, African like the patient, has in this case a particular advantage over the other co-therapists, who feel even more powerless to deal with Evelyne's withdrawal.

FJ: Evelyne is asking if we, as parents, are proud of her. [*Turning to Evelyne*] Would you like to ask the children if they'd like to draw?

In an almost imperceptible voice, Evelyne asks her children to draw, and they timidly approached the table in the middle of the room, where coloured pens and paper are set out.

FJ: Do you sing with your children? Do you sing in your house?

Evelyne: Yes.

FJ: And do you yourself sing?

Evelyne: Yes.

Gr: A mother who sings is a gift. Evelyne has had to be very strong. She has given a great deal. Now she no longer wishes to receive or to give.

FJ: One needs time for weeping. But how can that time be found when there are so many children to care for?

Gr: Weeping doesn't help. The wish to hibernate, to sleep, the need for security, to be sure that "they" no longer want to return at night.

Evelyne remains immobile, looking downward, without showing any change in her expression. She does not reply to FJ's questions about how she herself feels about what the group is saying. FJ offers her a more comfortable chair, which we bring to her, and Evelyne sits on it without managing to relax more.

The group emphasizes that Evelyne has not left her purse for an instant. She is in exile and has to be ready to leave again at any moment. What is more, that purse must be full of concerns. Someone in the group says he feels pains in his body, another that he needs to pinch himself to be sure he is alive, another asks to sing a song. One co-therapist sings a lullaby. Another co-therapist stretches out on the floor, on the carpet. This produces a special atmosphere. The group say that what the song means doesn't matter.[7] What counts is to let yourself be consoled without feeling obliged to understand. FJ asks her to repeat the song, and the co-therapist sings a different one, explaining that she wants to sing it for the children. At a certain point in the song, R, the African co-therapist, takes on the melody of her Vietnam colleague, adding other sounds, increasing the magical effect of the atmosphere. But evidently my sensation is not shared by the group, who interrupt with laughter, which seems to me false, defensive. The colleague lying on the carpet stands up, saying that with the voices circulating in the air she had had the impression of finding herself within a container, like a bathtub. She thought the song sounded like the wind; there was no need to understand.

FJ draws out the conclusions of the session. The children stop drawing and listen. What we meant to say is that here in Switzerland, as in any other place, we have the right to feel like children, even when we are grown-up women with small children. It is important to feel understood when one needs to feel like a child.

The prescription is a continuation of that given in the previous session, which consisted of giving Armand a relaxing bath every evening and of Evelyne telling us about her dreams.

In the course of the discussion, a part of the group is oriented towards an effort to containing the depressive side of Evelyne; another part, including the African co-therapist, is in favour of activating it, showing rage and frustration. Many, including FJ, the primary therapist, are quite perplexed with the way the treatment is developing.

Comment. I am more and more convinced that the idea of the fable is pertinent. The one in the family who most catches my attention and engrosses me is Armand. However, the group at this time is especially working with his mother to help the child to play a more appropriate part in their family life. I feel that, by leading Evelyne towards a more active role, the group is inadvertently putting her in a position like that of a hero. Another observation, which is a recent one and did not come up at the time of the treatment, concerns the possible assimilation of this session to the original phase, that of rites of passage, described in chapter three.[8] It is also clear that the four phases in which Houseman subdivides the rituals are, in turn, aggregations of Propp's functions. For obvious reasons, in our experience we have occasions for meeting patients only at a certain point of their "fable" (often tragic), or, to drop the metaphor, of their migratory experience—that is, in a phase subsequent to, in the listing of functions by Propp, *the departure of the hero*. In the case of Armand's family in this session, we are working in the area of the following functions: *hero put to the test by the gift-giver* (whether through prescriptions or through a diagnostic confirmation of the actual trauma suffered by the children); *provision of a magic tool* (part of the prescriptions); *transfer of the hero* (instability continues in the family situation and particularly for Armand). It is obvious that some of the functions preceding these, according to Propp's description (such as distancing, prohibition, the trap), represent other episodes experienced by Armand and his family. Some of these connections will become clearer in the description of the next session.

Sixth session

At this session, six weeks later, Evelyne arrives with Armand and her two youngest children. The family's situation has been discussed with Tobie Nathan during his visit to Geneva for a seminar. His point of view, expressed, as is customary for him, in the language of reference of the patient's traditional culture, can be synthesized in this way:

> "Evelyne, in the *mukongo* tradition, after her husband's death, should have become the wife of her husband's brother. How-

ever, he sent her to Switzerland and doesn't want to have anything to do with her.[9] It could be that Evelyne hides the existence [past?] of a man in her life. What she shows to you in the group is probably destined for a man. Armand is an extremely active person, probably the bearer of witchcraft, and perhaps he himself is a witch. It is important to do something so the child can say things. It is important to make him 'spit out' his witchcraft, make him confess as if he were in a court or law before a judge, and record it. 'Spit it out' means put the witchcraft outside, permit him to exorcise it, eliminate it. Recording it will prove that it is outside him, that he has managed to get rid of it."

FJ [*to the group*]: Evelyne has been able to go back home to her apartment [*this is after one of her children had started a fire*]. Things are a bit better for the family. They have been offered the chance to go as guests to a "foyer"[10] for mothers and children, where she will be relieved of all domestic duties and get more help.

Gr: We have been worried about Evelyne, and there are still many things that are not clear: above all, who wishes her harm.

Armand sits and cries.

Evelyne: Armand has been crying since we left home to come here. But he doesn't want to say why.

FJ: It is probable that there is a man who wishes to harm him, and Evelyne must have had signs regarding this man. Here we want to explore this more.

Evelyne says that she has slept badly and very little recently. She doesn't get sleepy at night. Sometimes someone comes with a knife and wants to slit her throat. She wakes up and prays, reads the Bible. During this conversation, Armand appears more and more disturbed. He gets up from his chair and crawls under a little table at the edge of the group. He cries and kicks against the wall. He obsessively touches all the buttons of a stereo on the table. He is extremely agitated. He presses himself against the wall.

FJ: Armand is disturbed because we want to find out who is threatening him. He knows things, but he doesn't want to "spit them out". And his mother knows that Armand knows things and doesn't want to say them.

Evelyne: Sometimes, at night, he spoke with someone. This someone told Armand that he was about to be killed. If Armand told the name of this person, he too would be killed.

FJ: Armand knows he should say the name, but he is not sure that we can protect him. We know that Armand receives terrifying visits at night. That they give him things to eat and drink. Right here, inside our circle, is the place where he needs "to spit it out", not on the wall, and he knew that before coming here.

Armand starts to become calmer and to listen attentively to what we are saying.

Gr: And it is into this recording machine that he should "spit it out". It is solid, well protected, and will be closed up in a box. We are ready and decided and we are with him, with Armand.

FJ: Armand is afraid to say who is persecuting him, who is holding him slave.

The male co-therapist B invites Armand to come with him inside our circle. Armand lets himself be led by the hand peacefully. B crouches behind the child and suggests he speak into the recording machine.

Armand: Someone has been coming at night for a long time to give me food and forces me to follow him. [*Despite our repeated and insistent questions, Armand says he doesn't know the person.*] He takes me far away, into the forest, and asks me to do certain things.[11]

FJ: And he has told Armand he will also be able to do powerful things, just like him.

Armand: Yes, I have seen things, someone eating people.

FJ: They have threatened Armand, they have frightened him. He had to promise not to say anything, and since then he has been like a slave. Armand needs to say to the tape-recorder who this man is.

Armand: I don't know who he is. The man comes when I am

asleep and wants to take me away, and show me how to kill people.

FJ: He wants to send him to kill someone in particular, and Armand is afraid of going and being killed himself.

Gr: Armand could use a long tube of paper [*in the meantime, someone has prepared a tube of rolled-up paper, like a trumpet*] to announce the name of that person into the recording machine.

Armand: I am afraid to say it, because he is a witch.

Gr: Armand can blow several times in a row into the tube, very hard, to spit out the name.

Armand blows hard and repeatedly into the tube, with the opening towards the tape-recorder. The group encourages Armand's action, rhythmically repeating how brave and strong he is, and that the group is determined to protect him. Armand is visibly more tranquil.

FJ prescribes Armand to take a bath every evening, alone with his mother who will help him, before he goes to sleep, when the other children are already in bed. He should add mint leaves into the warm bathwater. The next meeting will take place in two weeks.

Group discussion

FJ feels uneasy; she has had the impression of playing an apprentice witch. The group assured her, saying that the ritual had been in the process of preparation since the beginning of the session. Evelyne's weeping was strong and subdued, and we felt she was extremely involved. Armand spoke little, while at first he was weeping, since he had learned he needed to come here. What they did was coherent with their world. The group pressure offered reassurance. Exorcising this force we have taken a burden from Armand.

Comment. It is clear from the way this session went how the serious trauma undergone by Armand—that of witnessing the assassination of his father—is "disguised" by the specific culture to which he belongs. Psychological literature on trauma abundantly documents the process of the internalization of guilt, and of the persecutor, on the part of those who witness torture and trauma. In this case, the therapeutic strategy was one of maintaining and reinforcing the symbolization of the persecutor, who could show himself to Armand through nightmares. What is more, both with Armand, and especially with Evelyne, the identification of the missing ritual of the placenta as one of the possible causes of the evil spell started to allow them to shift the sense of "evil" outside themselves and consequently to find redress through more appropriate means. In our case, such redress was constituted by the Mass and by a malleable piece of clay that I brought for Armand in the ninth session. At the same time, supporting this explanation (traditional aetiology) proposed by the therapist and supported by the group allowed Evelyne and Armand to find in us and experience with us a strong sense of adherence and protection—in other words, of reconstituting, through this support and this feeling, their shattered psychic protective shells. Finally, in the course of this session, to return to the model of the fables, we provided Armand and Evelyne with another "magic tool". Using Houseman's (1986) scheme, a series of positive qualities of Armand and his mother had been recalled at the beginning of the session. They had already been emphasized in the preceding session (first phase, of *positive connotation*), then the "ritual" of the tape-recorder was introduced for Armand's confession, which can be seen as an adapted form (specifically freed from the specificity of physical pain) of the second phase—of *deconstruction*—of that scheme.[12] As we shall see in the sessions that followed, the therapeutic work will be assimilated into the third and fourth phases of the scheme: *reconstruction* and *reception*.

Eighth session

Evelyne comes with Armand and the two youngest children. Two weeks have passed.

> *Evelyne:* The family is a bit better. But Armand screams and cries at night.

Armand sits at a little table outside the group circle and draws. Evelyne has dreamed of her husband, who has urged her to take care of the children (while she is telling us this, she stops and burst into tears).

FJ: Evelyne's husband has returned in a dream and has confirmed that she is the one who ought to take care of things. He is counting on her to do it.

Armand shows his first drawing to each of us, taking it around the circle. It is a large head of a threatening man, which takes up most of the page. A tiny tomb is in a corner (the dead father), a weapon, and a hole in the wall (which Armand tells us is his room) through which anyone or anything can pass.

FJ [*to the group*]: There are more people struck by witches. Even a child is between a dead father and one in the sky. In a dream, Evelyne's husband has let her know that the moment has arrived to bury him.

Armand goes forward and backward, between the inside of the group and the little table where he is drawing.

FJ [*continuing the discussion about burial, evidently symbolic*]: Evelyne has certainly thought about something to do.

Evelyne says she would like to have a Mass said for her husband, in a certain church in Geneva, and weeps with loud sobs.

FJ: The group would be pleased to join Evelyne at this Mass.

There is a discussion about timing: during the summer, the family will be guests in the "Foyer", and Evelyne will feel more supported. Armand will be changing classes in the autumn and will surely feel more at ease.

Armand goes around, showing us his second drawing. There are the faces of two men. We are still in his little room. Armand is sleeping in his bunk bed, and one of the men is offering him sweets. The hole in the wall is now almost completely closed.

FJ: What can be done to keep this hole closed?

Gr: When someone is being buried, first you dig a hole and then you close it. You put a cross on top and say something. When someone dies in a distant place, you say a Mass and make a ceremony for those who remain. You can also say some prayers that speak about the dead person, as they do in the synagogue every Friday evening. You can have an evening of remembrance, and have a meal and talk about the person who has died.

FJ: Those are not only words, but also something that is received, that is seen, and that is felt: all the things that close holes.

The organization of the Mass is discussed, as well as the need to call the brother-in-law in Paris. Evelyne says that she will also invite the cousins and brothers of her husband who are in France. Once the Mass is organized, we will then sort out what we should bring to eat and drink together. We will also bring something for Armand, so that he can close up the hole definitively. It is also important that the priest call Evelyne's husband by name, to give him a final farewell.

We reassure Armand that the tape-recorder is in the safe custody of the group, and we confirm the evening baths that he will take before going to bed. Before he leaves, Armand shows us his third drawing and explains, referring to the child that represents him in the drawing, "At first he was afraid, he kept shouting, but he killed the witch with a knife, which he now keeps in his bed." On the back of the page, for the first time, Armand has signed his name.

Ninth session

The family is almost complete: only Gloria, the firstborn, is missing. Two weeks have passed since the last meeting.

Evelyne has written to her cousin in France to find out whether he will come to the Mass. She has not yet received a reply and for this reason has not set a date.

The three oldest children are not at all pleased to be going to the "Foyer" because there is only one bathroom on each floor and they will not be able to see their friends. Evelyne has made an appointment to discuss this with the social worker. She complains about stomach aches and sleeping poorly.

While Evelyne is speaking, her children are around the small central table drawing, talking, and laughing. Armand seems to take on the role of the big brother who is listened to and respected. In order to be able to intervene with greater tranquillity and discretion, FJ asks a co-therapist to take the three youngest children out of the room. They follow him happily. Armand stays alone and continues drawing, with great concentration. After a short time he shows us his drawing. It shows a large nocturnal bird, perhaps a bat, with big wings. There is also an arrow at the top right of the page. It comes from the sky and goes through the bird. He has also drawn a small tree and the moon. Armand says that this bird comes at night, when he is washing (when his mother was giving him a bath?).

FJ informs Armand that someone in the group has brought him something to close the threatening holes in the wall, through which anything could pass. It is Armand who has this special work to do. He has to seal up the holes. I stand up and offer him a bucket of clay that I think he could use for the job. I tell him that it is clay, earth that can be modelled, and that he can make shapes and close up holes with it (*supplying the magic tool).*

> *FJ*: Armand should not lose this clay, nor divide it, nor scatter it. Armand will be responsible for it. This clay does not belong to him, but to the group. If he would like, he can make special shapes and dry them, but without losing them. It is for him to decide if his brothers can play with the clay with him and make sure that it is put back in its container. If they want to dry some clay figures, they should bring them here.

Armand takes up his new endeavour immediately. He starts to model a figure, with great concentration. While we continue with the mother's session, in a few minutes he has finished his work and shows it to us. It is a figure just like an African fetish against the effects of witchcraft. The fetish will stay with the group, who will take good care of it. Armand closes the container with the remaining clay. FJ reminds him to take it home and that it is useful for closing up holes. The next meeting will be in two weeks.

Tenth session

Evelyne has been able to organize the Mass for her husband. It will be in three days. Her cousin from Paris cannot come, but a friend of Evelyne's will be coming. She has spoken with her children, who will all be there. There will also be many co-therapists, all those in the group who can make it. The family will not be going to the "Foyer" because the children do not want to go. They have made other plans for the summer. Evelyne will stay alone with her youngest child.

Armand goes to fetch the fetish he modelled in the previous session, and he colours it with markers. Then he begins to draw. The group discusses the significance of the Mass and of funerals in different countries. Evelyne seems decisively more serene. After a short time Armand shows us his drawing. He has drawn a castle with two dragons that are eating dead people. Armand has drawn himself at the bottom of the page. The door to the fortress is well protected by bars. The next session will be held after the summer.

After the summer, we see the family, in different formations, three more times, with long intervals in between. The final session takes place in December, before the Christmas holidays. Armand appears to be fitting into school better, and his nightmares have ended. I am sorry to mark our definitive separation and to say goodbye. It seems to me, just as has happened several times in the past few months, that Armand could have another relapse, some form of regression. His mother, on the other hand, seems to have taken on a more appropriate and competent role, probably in part as a result of the celebration of the Mass and funeral ceremony for her husband, and the ritual of food and drink celebrating his memory, in which many members of the group had joined.

Before the final session I prepare a new little "magic tool" to protect Armand. It is a recording of a song by Francesco De Gregori, together with its translation into French on a piece of parchment paper. Armand will be able to listen to it any time he wishes, with a little Walkman that I give him along with the cassette. The song is *Buonanotte fiorellino* [Good Night Little Flower], and I read him the French translation as a final goodbye. I try to emphasize this part to him: "The little birds in the wind never get hurt;/their wings are bigger than me."

Conclusion

We have seen that this intervention, although complementary to the one described by Saskia von Overbeck, took place on three levels, or axes, as Franceline James called them in her summing up. If the therapy of von Overbeck was oriented towards Armand's greater individuation with respect to his mother, in the context of interpreting malaise to a child caused by the trauma of his father's killing, our intervention oriented Evelyne and, above all, Armand towards accepting a traditional interpretation of events that had preceded that trauma.

From this perspective, the therapeutic effectiveness of our intervention can be traced back to several key moments of the therapy.

I believe that a first major step in the therapeutic intervention can be identified in the third session[13] and in the identification of the missing ritual of Armand's placenta as one of the causes of his disorder, preceding the trauma connected with the killing of his father. It is probable that the reader will ask if I truly believe in this type of causal relationship and, consequently, in the effectiveness of a ritual of reparation.

To paraphrase the famous and frequently cited explanation given by Lévi-Strauss on the therapeutic effectiveness of the witch, the intervention functions precisely because the spirits do not exist (cf. chapter two). The originality of the ethnopsychiatric intervention consists in the fact that, transposing Lévi-Strauss's reasoning, "conflicts and resistance dissolve not through the knowledge, real or supposed, that the sick person acquires progressively" of the causes of his problems "but because this knowledge makes it possible to have a specific experience, in the course of which conflicts become real and with an order and plan through which they can develop and finally dissolve" (Lévi-Strauss, 1998b). This is, in my interpretation, what began to happen in the sessions starting from Evelyne's acceptance of the explanation of the cause of many of Armand's problems and family troubles through traditional aetiology (the missing ritual with the placenta). On the basis of this first step, it became possible in the fifth session to reinforce Evelyne's sense of the support the group was offering her, as if she were a little girl needing protection. In this way she felt she belonged to something again, to someone, acquiring a psychic and cultural shell that gave her a sense of protection.

A second turning-point in the therapy can be traced back to the fifth session. Evelyne let herself go completely. We saw that in this session the group of co-therapists was divided. One part showed intolerance and reactivity to Evelyne's increasingly depressive side; the other, on the contrary, welcomed it. In the end, Franceline James proposed to Evelyne this interpretation of the session: "What we have wanted to say is that here in Switzerland, as in any other place, we have the right to feel we are children, even when we are adult women with small children. It is important to feel understood when one needs to feel like a child again"—a way of offering support and acceptance or welcome.

It is through the experience gained in this session that, in my opinion, Evelyne finally felt wrapped in a new protective container. Not so much for the content of the communications, but for the suggestion offered by the means (songs, movement, and body positions) through which this communication was transmitted, a suggestion that is hard to express in written descriptions and that therefore I am not sure to have rendered with respect to its communicative power. The turning-point in this session concerned Evelyne above all.

Armand's turning-point came in the next session. As we have seen, in that session Evelyne was already more active and participative. But Armand was in tears and opposed in every way to joining the group from the moment he left home with his mother to come to the session. For him, the turning-point in the session came at two different points: the acceptance of a traditional interpretation (witchcraft) and the recognition of the protection offered by the group (new protective psychic shell). This was the fundamental moment for starting to let go of his symptom(s), "spitting out" whatever he knew into the recording machine. The modality of working with Armand in that session followed the general mechanism of symbolic realization (see chapter three, note 7). In Armand's case, the effectiveness of the mechanism came about through the intrinsic power of the group's injunction/induction to Armand (which as we have seen, through the specific therapeutic apparatus, "makes" a therapist extremely powerful), and also because the injunction fitted with the culture to which the child belonged. The structural similarity of the mechanism of exorcism/ elimination of witchcraft used with Armand (within/outside, in a protected place) with what Gian Paolo Lai has related to us, recalling a fourteenth-century saint, Sant'Antonio of Tolentino, is remarkable. This similarity brings us to consider the continuity, in time and space, of the "subjugated" therapeutic techniques, which cannot be superficially cast aside as superstitions.

Then, in the eighth session, the therapeutic work was again important, above all for Evelyne. The dream in which her husband appeared was interpreted as a request on the part of the deceased for a proper burial to allow him to finally enter into the world of the deceased. The communication that took place through this interpretation of the dream had a double value. If, in fact, on the one hand his symbolic funeral allowed him to rest in peace, on the other for Evelyne it implied the recognition of her own capacity to take adequate care of her children. This was made possible by the celebration of the Mass and the rituals connected with it that we have mentioned, in which many members of our group also participated.

Finally, the ninth and final sessions confirmed for Armand his definitive change in status: from a world of connection with spirits, of confusion about his protective shell and his mother's (placenta), to the world of human beings, in his role of eldest son, protected by a more able mother and by the group.

Finally, as a family therapist, it is impossible for me not to translate the therapy with Armand and his family into an interpretation compatible with the categories of that specific therapy. From this interpretation, the case can be viewed as a "disguise", using the specific culture of the patients, of a family therapy approach that wisely mixes typical prescriptions of the "paradoxical" period with tri-generational approaches. As for the first aspect, we have already seen in the preceding pages how paradoxical prescriptions (see note 12) can be traced back to a form that is up to date and culturally acceptable in Western societies for the second of the rites-of-passage phases (see the frequently cited analysis of Houseman, 1986). As for the second aspect, to be able to assimilate the ethnopsychiatric treatment with tri-generational approaches,[14] it is necessary to say that, in both cases, the causes of the disorders are sought not in the subject who is occasionally the bearer of them, but in the relationships within the family, including members from different generations. In the specific approach of ethnopsychiatry, the relationships in question do not only concern the living family members, but extend to the ancestors and to beings belonging to other worlds, who often appear in the living and in their symptoms.

In conclusion, I would like to point out that, unfortunately, the research on the effectiveness of psychotherapies and their methodological limitations is still poorly developed. And even less developed is the research that is sensitive to the specific qualities of transcultural psychotherapies. Therefore, I do not believe we can know whether Armand and his family will continue well in facing a life that up to now has certainly not been easy for them. Despite the lack of "scientific" controls, I would like to hope that, without our help, Armand and his family would have lived a life even more difficult than the one that awaits them.

Notes

1. In this chapter I use the same pseudonyms used by my colleagues Saskia von Overbeck (SvO) Ottino and Franceline James (FJ). The abbreviation Tr is used to indicate the translator or cultural mediator and Gr to indicate the group in its entirety. In other cases, my co-therapists will be indicated with their initials. With the exception of specific cases, my interventions can be assimilated with those of the group. The case of Armand was dealt with in more than twenty sessions, lasting almost two years, an unusually long period testifying to the difficulties encountered. From comparison of my chapter with those of my colleagues, the reader, I hope, will have a concrete example of both the possible complementary nature of ethnopsychiatric and physiotherapeutic (the latter more consonant with Western thinking) treatments and the possible interpretative differences within ethnotherapy.

2. The therapeutic setting/arrangement used in our sessions included a principal therapist and a certain number of co-therapists. On the workings of this particular arrangement, see chapter three.

3. My interpretation of the case is not necessarily shared by all the group but is, rather, the fruit of my own work. Independently from their conclusions and possible differences of opinion, I am infinitely grateful to all my colleagues in the group for having helped me to understand many things that I previously knew only in theory. Their notes on the sittings were extremely helpful for the completion of mine, which were written systematically while returning home after every meeting, at times disturbed, at times doubtful, at times lacking faith and perplexed, and at other times relieved. Finally, I was more convinced and satisfied than ever with their/our work.

4. By "first session", I refer to the first session at which I started to follow the case, which, as already mentioned, was the seventh session for the group. (Ethnopsychiatry patients often find benefits from even fewer sittings.)

5. The three axis on which therapeutic interventions revolve—the recuperation of traditional aetiology; the reconstruction of the psychic wrappings that have been torn away; the passage between two worlds (original land and host country)—receive a more detailed treatment in the case study written by Franceline James (see chapter five).

6. Unexpectedly, more than two months had passed before this session took place. In the meantime, several domestic "incidents" happened, about which SvO and FJ speak in their chapters, and one of the children was hospitalized.

7. In truth, it was a Vietnamese song that nobody understood with the exception of the co-therapist who sang it.

8. See in particular Houseman (1986) and the relevant discussion in chapter three in this book. In summary, the phases into which Houseman subdivided initiation rituals are: (1) initial, comprising positive exhortations of the initiate's character; (2) deconstruction, in which the initiate is subjected to "paradoxical" tests; (3) reconstruction or the fabrication of the individual; (4) finally, welcoming and legitimization of his or her new status.

9. Entrapment, damage (Propp's functions).

10. Literally "hearth" or "fireside": a protected place of welcome in a house or a community.

11. Armand is reporting on the content of his nightmares—a man passing through a hole in the wall of the room where Armand sleeps. This is the hole that must be closed, the one that had not been closed, or blocked up, through an appropriate ritual concerning the placenta at Armand's birth.

12. From the point of view of family therapy, this phase is connected to the paradoxical prescriptions that were used, above all, in the 1970s and 1980s (e.g., see Selvini Palazzoli et al., 1975; Selvini Palazzoli, Cirillo, Selvini, & Sorrentino, 1988).

13. According to my numeration, which, as I have already mentioned (note 4) does not correspond to the actual number of the treatment sessions.

14. In addition to my version of this case, I refer, in particular, to the previous interpretation reported by Franceline James (chapter five), in which the incident that caused the death of Evelyne's parents when the former was very young is discussed. The elements working against this woman therefore preceded the events initially mentioned during the sittings.

REFERENCES

AA.VV. (1998). *Psychothérapies*. Paris: Odile Jacob.

Amati, S. (1979). Récupérer la honte. In: R. Kaës et al., *Crise, rupture, dépassement*. Paris: Dunod.

Anger, I. (1995). *Theory and Practice: Psychological Projects under War Conditions in Bosnia-Herzegovinia and Croatia*. Brussels: Echo/Ectf.

Anzieu, D. (Ed.) (1985). *Les envelopes psychiques*. Paris: Dunod.

Arendt, H. (1982). *L'impérialisme*. Paris: Fayard.

Arendt, H. (1987). Nous autres réfugiés. In: *La tradition cachée*. Paris: Christian Bourgois.

Augé, M., & Herzlich, C. (Eds.) (1983). *In senso del male, antropologia, storia e sociologia della malattia*. Milan: il Saggiatore.

Bateson, G. (1936). *Naven* (2nd. edition). Stanford, CA: Stanford University Press, 1958.

Bateson, G. (1972). *Steps to an Ecology of Mind*. New York: Ballantine Books.

Bibeau, G. (1981). Préalables à une épidémiologie anthropologique de la dépression. *Psycholopathologie Africaine, 17* (1–3): 96–116.

Bibeau, G. (1996). Antropologi nel campo della salute mentale. Un programma finalizzato alla ricerca qualitative. *AM—Rivista della Società italiana di antropologia medica, 1–2* (October): 23–55.

Bibeau, G., & Charland, C. (1994). Sur la piste des errances du renard pâle. Les recherches d'une équipe italo-malienne sur le haut-plateau dogon. *Psychologie Africaine, 26* (3): 341–386.

Bonnie, L., et al. (1991). Children and disaster: Age, gender and parental effects on PTSD symptoms. *Journal of the American Academy of Child and Adolescent Psychiatry, 30* (6): 945–951.

Booth, H. (1992). *The Migration Process in Britain and West Germany: Two Demographic Studies of Migrant Populations*. Research in Ethnic Relations Series. Avebury: Ashgate Publishing.

Braun de Dunayevich, J., & Pelento, M. L. (1989). Les vicissitudes de la pulsion de savoir dans certains deuils spéciaux. In: J. Puget & R. Kaës (Eds.), *Violence d'État et psychoanalyse* (pp. 86–105). Paris: Dunod.

Bruner, J. (1986). Two modes of thought. In: *Actual Minds, Possible Worlds* (pp. 11–43). Cambridge, MA: Harvard University Press.

Buakasa, T. K. M. (1973). *L'impensé du discours*. Kinshasa & Brussels: UNAZA-CEDAF, Université Nationale du Zaïre.

Calvino, I. (1971). Introduzione. In: *Fiabe Italiane*. Turin: Einaudi.

Calvo, F. (1977). *Qué es ser emigrante*. Barcelona: Editorial La Gaya Ciencia.

Chauvenet, A. (1996). La situation des réfugiés. In: A. Chauvenet, V. Despret, & J. M. Lemaire, *Clinique de la reconstruction. Une expérience avec des réfugiés en ex-Yougoslavie*. Paris: L'Harmattan.

Chauvenet, A., Despret, V., & Lemaire, J. M. (1996). *Clinique de la reconstruction. Une expérience avec des réfugiés en ex-Yougoslavie*. Paris: L'Harmattan.

Chraïbi, D. (1955). *Les boucs*. Paris: Denoël.

Collomb, H. (1973). Rencontre de deux systèmes de soins. À propos de thérapeutique des maladies mentales en Afrique. *Social Science and Medicine*.

Corin, E., & Bibeau, G. (1980). Psychiatric perspectives in Africa, Part II: The traditional viewpoint. *Transcultural Psychiatric Research Review, 17*: 205–233.

Corin, E., & Murphy, H. B. M. (1979). Psychiatric perspectives in Africa, Part I: The Western viewpoint. *Transcultural Psychiatric Research Review, 16*: 147–178.

Davidson, J. R. (1985). The shadow of the life: Psychological explanations for placenta rituals. *Culture, Medicine and Psychiatry, 9*: 75–92.

Decornoy, J. (1996a). Profughi, rifugiati, migranti. Un'umanità di "stranieri" senza fissa dimora. *Le Monde Diplomatique—Il Manifesto*, February.

Decornoy, J. (1996b). Sirene senza frontiere. *Le Monde Diplomatique—Il Manifesto*, February.

de Coulon, N., & von Overbeck, S. (1992). Migration et crise. Les mécanismes d'inversion. *L'Évolution psychiatrique, 57* (3): 439–454.

de Martino, E. (1961). *La terra del rimorso*. Milan: il Saggiatore.

de Martino, E. (1973). *Il mondo magico*. Turin: Bollati Boringhieri.

Devereux, G. (1970). *Saggi di etnopsichiatria generale*. Paris: Gallimard.

Devereux, G. (1978a). La psicoanalisi, strumento di analisi etnologica. Dati di fatto e implicazioni teoriche. In: *Saggi di etnopsichiatria generale* (pp. 316–331). Rome: Armando.

Devereux, G. (1978b). Una teoria sociologica della schizofrenia. In: *Saggi di etnopsichiatria generale* (pp. 198–225). Rome: Armando.

Di Nola, A. (1981). Introduzione. In: G. Lützenkirchen et al., *Mal di Luna*. Rome: Newton Compton.

Douglas, M. (1998). *Purezza e pericolo. Un'analisi dei concetti di contaminazione e tabù*. Bologna: il Mulino.

Durkheim, E. (1971). *Le forme elementari della vita religiosa*. Milan: Comunità.

Eitinger, L. (1981). Feeling at home: Immigrants' psychological problems. In: L. Eitinger & D. Schwarz, *Strangers in the World* (pp. 84–106). Bern: Hans Huber.

Erikson, H. E. (1968). Identity and uprootedness. In: *Uprooting and Resettlement* (pp. 44–75). London/New York: World Federation for Mental Health.

Favret-Saada, J. (1980). *Deadly Words: Witchcraft in the Bocage*. Cambridge: Cambridge University Press.

Ferenczi, S. (1968). *Oeuvres complètes, IV*. Paris: Payot.

Fiore B. (1998). Medicina Dogon tra Islam e tradizione. In: V. Lanternari & M. L. Ciminelli (Eds.), *Medicina, Magia, Religione, Valori* (pp. 367–390). Naples: Liguori.

Flick, U. (1992). *La perception quotidienne de la santé et de la maladie*. Paris: L'Harmattan.

Forster, G. M. (1976). Disease etiologies in non-Western medical systems. *American Anthropologist, 78*: 773–782.

Frigessi, D. (1993). Il modello patologico dell'immigrazione. In: V. Di Micco & P. Martelli (Eds.), *Passaggi di confine. Etnopsichiatriae migrazioni*. Naples: Liguori.

Garza-Guerrero, A. C. (1974). Culture shock: Its mourning and the vicissitudes of identity. *Journal of the American Psycho-Analytical Association, 22* (2).

Gbaka Zady, R. (1989). *La nostra Africa, l'avventura di crescere nel continente nero,* ed. CIDIS. Roma/Perugia: Palombi Editore.

Ginzburg, C. (1979). Spie, radici di un paradigma indiziario. In: A. Gargani (Ed.), *Crisi della ragione* (pp. 59–106). Turin: Einaudi.

Ginzburg, C. (1998). *Occhiacci di legno.* Milan: Feltrinelli.

Goffman, E. (1968). *Asylums. Le istituzioni totali: I meccanismi dell'esclusione e della violenza.* Turin: Einaudi.

Gozlan, Y., & Salignon, P. (1995). Soutien psychologique auprès des ex détenus bosniaques musulmans et de leurs familles. La mission Médecins sans Frontières. In: M. R. Moro & S. Lebovici (Eds.), *Psychiatrie humanitaire en ex-Yougoslavie et en Arménie face au traumatisme.* Paris: PUF.

Grappe, M. (1993). L'action humanitaire et les camps de réfugiés. In: V. Nahoum & M. Grappe (Eds.), *Vukovar, Sarajevo . . . La guerre en ex-Yougoslavie* (pp. 243–260). Paris: Esprit.

Grappe, M. (1995). La guerre en ex Yuogoslavie. Un regard sur les enfant réfugiés. In: M. R. Moro & S. Lebovicic (Eds.), *Psychiatrie humanitaire en ex-Yougoslavie et en Arménie. Face au traumatisme.* Paris: PUF.

Grinberg, L., & Grinberg, R. (1990). *Psicoanalisi dell'emigrazione e dell'esilio.* Milan: Angeli.

Grubrich-Simitis, I. (1981). Extreme traumatization as cumulative trauma: Psychoanalytic investigation of the effects of concentration camp experiences on survivors and their children. *Psychoanalytic Study of the Child, 36.*

Gupta, S. (1991). *The Mental Health Problems of Migrants: Report from Six European Countries.* Copenhagen: WHO.

Hampâté Bâ, A. (1991). *Amkoullel l'enfant Peul,* Paris: Actes Sud.

Held, T. (1988). La psychanalyse allemande et la question du traumatisme réel. *Revue Française de Psychanalyse, 6*: 1422.

Hertz, D. G. (1981). The stress of migration. In: L. Eitinger & P. Schwarz (Eds.), *Strangers in the World* (pp. 70–83). Bern: Hans Huber.

Hertz, R. (1928). *Étude sur la représentation de la mort. Sociologie religieuse et folklore.* Paris: PUF.

Hiegel, J. P., & Hiegel-Landrac, C. (1996a). Quand les victimes ont commis des atrocités. In: *Vivre et revivre au camp de Khao I Dang. Une psychiatrie humanitaire* (pp. 351–399). Paris: Fayard.

Hiegel, J. P., & Hiegel-Landrac, C. (1996a). *Vivre et revivre au camp de Khao I Dang. Une psychiatrie humanitaire.* Paris: Fayard.

Houseman, M. (1986). Notes sur quelques propriétés générals de la transformation initiatique. *Nouvelle Revue d'Ethnopsychiatrie, 6*: 31–40.

Houzel, D. (1987). Le concept d'enveloppe psychique. In: D. Anzieu (Ed.), *Les envelopes psychiques.* Paris: Dunod.

James, F. (1994). La signification culturelle du symptôme. *Psychothérapies, 2*: 77–83.

Janigro, N. (1994). *Dizionario di un paese che scompare.* Rome: Manifestolibri.

Janovic, C. S. (1975). Introduzione. In: V. Ja. Propp, *Edipo alla luce del folklore* (pp. vii–xviii). Turin: Einaudi.

Kaës, R. (1979). *Crise, rupture et dépassement.* Paris: Dunod.

Kaës, R. (1989). Introduzione. In: J. Puget & R. Kaës (Eds.), *Violence d'État et psychoanalyse* (pp. xi–xvi). Paris: Dunod.

Kaës, R. (1995). Introduzione. In: AA.VV., *Trasmissione della vita psichica tra generazioni.* Rome: Borla.

Kimpianga, M. M. (1997). La psychothérapie dans le système médicale traditionnel et le prophétisme chez les Kongo du Zaïre. *Psychopatologie Africaine, 13* (2).

Kleinman, A. (1981). *Patients and Healers in the Context of Culture: An Exploration of the Borderland between Anthropology, Medicine, and Psychiatry.* Berkeley, CA: University of California Press.

Léger, D. (1983). Le comunità apocalittiche neorurali in Francia. In: M. Augé & C. Herzlick (Eds.), *In senso del male, antropologia, storia e sociologia della malattia* (pp. 239–259). Milan: il Saggiatore.

Leman, J., & Gailly, A. (Eds.), (1991). *L'interaction soignant-soigné dans un contexte multiculturel et interdisciplinaire.* Brussels: De Boeck.

Lévi-Strauss, C. (1965). Introduzione all'opera di Marcel Mauss. In: M. Mauss, *Teoria generale della magia e altri saggi* (pp. xxv–xxvi). Turin: Einaudi.

Lévi-Strauss, C. (1962). La pensée sauvage. Paris: Plons.

Lévi-Strauss, C. (1998a). *Antropologia strutturale.* Milan: il Saggiatore.

Lévi-Strauss, C. (1998b). L'efficacia simbolica. In: *Antropologia strutturale.* Milan: il Saggiatore.

Littlewood, R. (1984–85). La migration des syndromes liés à la culture. *Psychopathologie Africaine, 20* (1): 5-16.

Littlewood, R., & Lipsedge, M. (1982). *Aliens and Alienists: Ethnic Minorities in Psychiatry*. Harmondsworth: Penguin.

Lombardo, M. G. (1984). Metafore della vita. Analisi per un progetto d'intersezione tra medicina e scienze umane del simbolismo. In: AA.VV., *Saggi di medicina e scienze umane.* Milan: Scientific Institute of S. Raffaele Hospital.

Losi, N. (1990). *Gli amici dell'acqua. Medici, pazienti e medicine alternative.* Milan: Angeli.

Losi, N. (1995). *I progetti per il futuro dei profughi della ex Jugoslavia ospiti nei centri di accoglienza in Italia.* Rome: International Organization for Migration.

Losi, N. (1996). Doppio, riscatto, imbroglio: categorie per la comprensione della follia degli altri. *Rivista Italiana di Gruppoanalisi, 11* (2): 129–151.

Losi, N. (2004). The white egg of the white hen. Or: Therapy of mixed couples in the ethno-systemic-narrative approach. In: M. Andolfi (Ed.), *Immigrant Families and Transcultural Psychotherapy.* Milan: Angeli.

Losi, N., & Papadopoulos, R. (2004). Post-conflict constellations of violence and the psychosocial approach of the International Organization for Migration. In: F. R. Mollica et al. (Eds,), *Books of Best Practices: Trauma and the Role of Mental Health in Post-conflict Recovery.* Rome: Caritas.

Lützenkirchen, G. (1981). Il "Male" di San Donato. In: G. Lützenkirchen et al., *Mal di Luna* (pp. 28–56). Rome: Newton Compton.

Magris, C. (1991). *Itaca e oltre*. Milan: Garzanti.

Mauss, M. (1965). Effetto fisico nell'individuo dell'idea di morte suggerita dalla collettività. In: *Teoria generale della magia e altri saggi* (pp. 330–347). Turin: Einaudi.

Memel-Fotê, H. (Ed.) (1998). *Les représentations de la santé et de la maladie chez les Ivoiriens.* Paris: L'Harmattan.

Moro, M. R. (1994). *Parents en exil, psychopatologies et migration.* Paris: PUF.

Moro, M. R., & Nathan, T. (1989). Le bébé migrateur. Spécificités et psychopathologies des interaction précoces en situation migratoire. In: S. Lebovici & F. Weil-Halpern (Eds.), *Psychopatologie du bébé.* Paris: PUF.

Morokvasic, M. (1981). The invisible ones: A double role of women in the current European immigration. In: L. Eitinger & D. Schwartz (Eds.), *Stranger in the World* (pp. 70–83). Bern: Hans Huber.

Nathan, T. (1986). La folie des autres. *Traité d'ethnopsychiatrie clinique.* Paris: Dunod.

Nathan, T. (1988). *Le Sperme du diable.* Paris: PUF.

Nathan, T. (1993). *Fier de n'avoir ni pays ni amis, quelle sottise c'était . . . Principes d'ethnopsychanalyse.* Grenoble: La Pensée sauvage.

Nathan, T. (1994). *L'influence qui guérit.* Paris: Odile Jacob.

Nathan, T., Blanchet, A., Ionescu, S., & Zajde, N. (1998). *Psychothérapies.* Paris: Odile Jacob.

Nathan, T., & Stengers I. (1995). *Médecins et sorciers.* Paris: Ed. Les empêcheurs de penser en rond.

Ortigues, O. C., & Ortigues, E. (1973). *Oedipe Africain.* Paris: Plon.

Overbeck Ottino, S. von (1998a). Bébés en exil: à quel sein se vouer? *Petite Enfance, 66*: 46–52.

Overbeck Ottino, S. von (1998b). Familles victimes de violences collectives et en exil: quelle urgence, quel modèle de soins? Le point de vue d'une pédopsychiatre. *Revue Française de Psychiatrie et de Psychologie Médicale, 14.*

Overbeck Ottino, S. von (1999c). Migration, exil et intervention de crise. In: N. de Coulon, *La crise, stratégies d'intervention thérapeutique en psychiatrie.* Paris: Gaëtan Morin Editeur.

Pandolfi, M. (1993). Il corpo, I corpi: per un'etnografia dell'esperienza migrativa. In: V. De Micco & P Martelli (Eds.), *Passaggi di confine. Etnopsichiatria e migrazioni* (pp. 97–105). Napoli: Liguori.

Pichot, P., & Nathan, T. (1998). *Quel avenir pour la psychiatrie et la psychothérapie?* Paris: Les empêcheurs de penser en rond.

Pierre, D. (1993). Zohra, le mauvais oeil et la citrouille. Clivage du Moi che les enfants de migrants. *Nouvelle Revue d'Ethnopsychiatrie, 20*: 201–229.

Propp, V. Ja. (1958). *Morphology of the Folktale.* Bloomington, IN: Research Center, Indiana University.

Propp, V. Ja. (1971). *Fairy Tale Transformations.* In: *Readings in Russian Poetics: Formalist and Structuralist Views*, ed. L. Matejka & K. Pomorska. Cambridge, MA: MIT Press.

Propp, V. Ja. (1986). *Istoricheskie korni volshebnoi skazki* [The historical roots of fairy tales]. Leningrad: Izd-vo Leningradskogo universiteta.

Pynoos, R. S., & Eth, S. (1986). Witness to violence: The child interview. *Journal of the American Academy of Child and Adolescent Psychiatry, 25*: 306–319.

Radin, P. (Ed.) (1955). *Fiabe africane.* Turin: Einaudi.

Reyneri, E. (1979). *La catena migratoria.* Bologna: il Mulino.

Risso, M., & Boker, W. (1992). *Sortilegio e delirio. Psicopatologia dell'emigrazione in prospettiva transculturale.* Naples: Liguori.

Rodari, G. (1979). *La grammatica della fantasia.* Turin: Einaudi.

Rubin, G. (1996). Fonctions structurantes et contenantes des rituels de deuil. *Revue Française de Psychanalyse, 1*: 211–218.

Sacks, O. (1973). *Awakenings.* New York: Vintage Books.

Sayad, A. (1990). *L'immigration ou le paradoxe de l'altérité.* Brussells: De Boeck.

Selvini Palazzoli, M., Cirillo, S., Selvini, M., & Sorrentino, A. M. (1988). *I giochi psicotici nella famiglia.* Milan: Cortina.

Selvini Palazzoli, M., et al. (1975). *Paradosso e controparadosso, un nuovo modello nella terapia della famiglia a transazione schizofrenica.* Milan: Feltrinelli.

Simon, G. (1995). *Géodynamique des migrations internationales dans le monde.* Paris: PUF.

Sironi, F. (1989). Approche ethnopsychiatrique des victimes de torture. *Nouvelle Revue d'Ethnopsychiatrie, 13*: 67–68.

Sironi, F. (1995). "On torture un enfant" ou les avatars de l'ethnocentrisme psychologique. *Sud nord, folies et cultures, 4* (*Enfances*): 217–228.

Sluzki, C. E. (1979). Migration and family conflict. *Family Process, 18*: 379–390.

Stanfield, J. H., & Dennis, R. M. (Eds.) (1993). *Race and Ethnicity in Research Methods.* London: Sage.

Stern, D. (1987). *Il mondo interpersonale del bambino.* Turin: Boringhieri.

Sundquist, J. (1994). *Migration and Health.* Lund: Lund University Press.

Szatan, M. (1995). Le jeu dans les situation de violence. *Sud nord, folies et cultures, 4 (Enfances).*

Tabboni, S. (Ed.) (1984). *Vicinanza e lontananza. Modelli e figure dello straniero come categoria sociologica.* Milan: Angeli.

Tayeb Salih (1992). *La stagione della migrazione a Nord.* Palermo: Sellerio.

Tchetche, G. D. (1998). *Psychiatrie en Afrique Noire et contexte socioculturel.* Paris: L'Harmattan.

Teitelbaum, M. S. (1993). *Les effects du développement économique sur les pressions à l'émigration dans les pays d'origine*. Paris: Osce.

Terr, L. C. (1991). Childhood traumas: An outline and overview. *American Journal of Psychiatry, 148* (1): 10–20.

Thomas, L. V. (1975). *Anthropologie de la mort*. Paris: Payot.

Ticho, G. (1971). Cultural aspects of transference and countertransference. *Bulletin of Menninger Clinic, 35*.

Turner, V. (1972). *Il processo rituale. Struttura e antistruttura*. Brescia: Morcelliana.

van der Veer, G. (1992). *Counseling and Therapy with Refugees: Psychological Problems of Victims of War, Torture, and Repression*. Chichester: Wiley.

Zajde, N. (1998). Le traumatisme. In: T. Nathan, A. Blanchet, S. Ionescu, & N. Zajde, *Psychothérapies* (pp. 225–279). Paris: Odile Jacob.

Zivcic, I. (1993). Emotional reactions of children to war stress in Croatia. *Journal of American Academy of Child and Adolescent Psychiatry, 32* (4).

SELECTED BIBLIOGRAPHY

AA.VV. *La salute straniera. Epidemiologia Culture Diritti.* Naples: Edizioni Scientifiche Italiane, 1994.

AA.VV. *Mal di luna.* Rome: Newton Compton, 1981.

AA.VV. "Panseurs de secrets et de douleurs." *Autrement* (Special Issue, 1978).

AA.VV. *Psychothérapies.* Paris: Odile Jacob, 1998.

AA.VV. *Saggi di medicina e scienze umane.* Milan: Istituto Scientifico H. S. Raffaele, 1984.

AA.VV. *Trasmissione della vita psichica tra generazioni.* Rome: Borla, 1995.

Andolfi, M. *La famiglia trigenerazionale.* Rome: Bulzoni, 1988.

Anger, I. *Theory and Practice: Psychological Projects under War Conditions in Bosnia-Herzegovinia and Croatia.* Brussels: Echo/Ectf, 1995.

Arendt, H. *L'impérialisme.* Paris: Fayard, 1982.

Augé, M., & Herzlich, C. (Eds.). *In senso del male, antropologia, storia e sociologia della malattia.* Milan: il Saggiatore, 1983.

Barret, R. "Cultural formulation of psychiatric diagnosis. Death on a horse's back: Adjustment disorder with panic attacks." *Culture, Medicine and Psychiatry, 21* (1997): 481–496.

Barret, R. *La traite des fous, la construction sociale de la schizophrénie.* Paris: Les empêcheurs de penser en rond, 1998.

Barret, R., & Lucas, R. H. "Hot and cold in transformation: Is Iban medicine humoral?" *Social Science and Medicine, 38* (No. 2, 1994): 383–393.

Barret, R., Lucas, R. H. "The skulls are cold, the house is hot: Interpreting depths of meaning in Iban therapy." *Man, 28* (No. 3, 1993): 573–596.

Bateson, G. *Naven* (2nd. edition). Stanford, CA: Stanford University Press, 1958 (first published, 1936).

Bateson, G. *Steps to an Ecology of Mind.* New York: Ballantine Books, 1972.

Beneduce, R. (Ed.). *Linguaggi, saperi e tecniche nei sistemi di cura tradizionali.* Turin: L'Harmattan Italia, 1997 .

Beneduce, R., & Collignon, R. (Eds.). *Il sorriso della volpe.* Naples: Liguori, 1995 .

Bibeau, G. "Antropologi nel campo della salute mentale. Un programma finalizzato alla ricerca qualitative." *AM—Rivista della Società italiana di antropologia medica, 1–2* (October 1996): 23–55.

Bibeau, G. "Cultural psychiatry in a creolizing world: Questions for a new research agenda." *Transcultural Psychiatry, 34* (No. 1, 1997): 9–41.

Bibeau, G. "L'étranger dans le théâtre de la guérison. À propos de la dramaturgie Yoruba selon Wole Soyinka." *Nouvelle Revue d'Ethnopsychiatrie, 29* (1996): 8–46.

Bibeau, G. "Préalables à une épidémiologie anthropologique de la dépression." *Psycholopathologie Africaine, 17* (Nos. 1–3, 1981): 96–116.

Bibeau, G., & Charland, C. "Sur la piste des errances du renard pâle. Les recherches d'une équipe italo-malienne sur le haut-plateau dogon." *Psychologie Africaine, 26* (No. 3, 1994): 341–386.

Blanchet, A. "Le principe d'influence." *Nouvelle Revue d'Ethnopsychiatrie,* 27 (1994): 55–64.

Bonnie, L., et al. "Children and disaster: Age, gender and parental effects on PTSD symptoms." *Journal American Academy of Child and Adolescent Psychiatry, 30* (No. 6, 1991): 945–951.

Booth, H. *The Migration Process in Britain and West Germany: Two Demographic Studies of Migrant Populations.* Research in Ethnic Relations Series. Avebury: Ashgate Publishing, 1992.

Braun de Dunajevich, J., & Pelento, M. L. "Les vicissitudes de la pulsion de savoir dans certains deuils spéciaux." In: J. Puget & R. Kaës (Eds.), *Violence d'État et psychoanalyse* (pp. 86–105). Paris: Dunod, 1989.

Bruner, J. "Two modes of thought." In: *Actual Minds, Possible Worlds* (pp. 11–43). Cambridge, MA: Harvard University Press, 1986.

Buakasa, T. K. M. *L'impensé du discours*. Kinshasa & Brussels: UNAZA-CEDAF, Université Nationale du Zaïre, 1973.

Calvino, I. (Ed.). *Fiabe Italiane*. Turin: Einaudi, 1971.

Cardona, G. *I sei lati del mondo. Linguaggio ed esperienza*. Bari: Laterza, 1985.

Chauvenet, A., Despret, V., & Lemaire, J. M. *Clinique de la reconstruction. Une expérience avec des réfugiés en ex-Yougoslavie*. Paris: L'Harmattan, 1996.

Chraïbi, D. *Les boucs*. Paris: Denoël, 1955.

CIDIS. *La nostra Africa, l'avventura di crescere nel continente nero*. Rome/Perugia: Palombi Editori, 1989.

Collomb, H. "Rencontre de deux systèmes de soins. À propos de thérapeutique des maladies mentales en Afrique." *Social Science and Medicine* (1973).

Coppo P. *Etnopsichiatria*. Milan: Il Saggiatore, 1996.

Coppo, P. *Guaritori di follia. Storie dell'altopiano Dogon*. Turin: Bollati Boringhieri, 1994.

Corin, E., & Bibeau, G. "Psychiatric perspectives in Africa, Part II: The traditional viewpoint." *Transcultural Psychiatric Research Review, 17* (1980): 205–233.

Corin, E., & Murphy, H. B. M. "Psychiatric perspectives in Africa, Part I: The Western viewpoint." *Transcultural Psychiatric Research Review, 16* (1979): 147–178.

Davidson, J. R. "The shadow of the life: Psychological explanations for placenta rituals." *Culture, Medicine and Psychiatry, 9* (1985): 75–92.

de Coulon, N., & von Overbeck, S. "Migration et crise: les mécanismes d'inversion." *L'Évolution psychiatrique, 57* (No. 3, 1992): 439–454.

de Martino, E. *Il mondo magico*. Turin: Bollati Boringhieri, 1973.

de Martino, E. *La terra del rimorso*. Milan: il Saggiatore, 1961.

De Micco, V., & Martelli, P. (Eds.). *Passaggi di confine. Etnopsichiatria e migrazioni*. Naples: Liguori, 1993 .

De Pury, S. *Traité du malentendu*. Paris: Les empêcheurs de penser en rond, 1998.

Desjarlais, R., Eisenberg, L., Good, B., & Kleinman, A. *World Mental Health. Problems and Priorities in Low-Income Countries*. New York: Oxford University Press, 1995.

Devereux, G. *Dall'angoscia al metodo nelle scienze del comportamento*. Rome: Istituto dell'Enciclopedia Treccani, 1984.

Devereux, G. *Saggi di etnopsichiatria generale*. Paris: Gallimard, 1970.

Di Nicola, V. *A Stranger in the Family. Culture, Families and Therapy*. New York: W. W. Norton, 1997.

Di Nola, A. "Introduzione." In: G. Lützenkirchen et al., *Mal di Luna*. Rome: Newton Compton, 1981.

Doray, B., & Louzoun, C. (Eds.). *Les traumatismes dans le psychisme et la culture*. Paris: érès, 1997 .

Douglas, M. *Purezza e pericolo. Un'analisi dei concetti di contaminazione e tabù*. Bologna: il Mulino, 1998.

Durkheim, E. *Le forme elementari della vita religiosa*. Milan: Comunità, 1971.

Durkheim, E., Hubert, H., & Mauss, M. *Le origini dei poteri magici*. Turin: Boringhieri, 1977.

Eibl-Eibesfeldt, I. *Etologia Umana. Le basi biologiche e culturali del comportamento*. Turin: Bollati Boringhieri, 1993.

Faïk-Nzuji C. *La puissance du sacré. L'homme, la nature et l'art en Afrique noire*. Paris: Maissoneuve & Larose, 1993.

Favret-Saada, J. *Deadly Words: Witchcraft in the Bocage*. Cambridge: Cambridge University Press, 1980.

Fiore B. "Medicina Dogon tra Islam e tradizione." In: V. Lanternari & M. L. Ciminelli (Eds.), *Medicina, Magia, Religione, Valori* (pp. 367–390). Naples: Liguori, 1998.

Flick, U. *La perception quotidienne de la santé et de la maladie*. Paris: L'Harmattan, 1992.

Fodzo, L. *Psychiatrie en Afrique, l'expérience camerounaise*. Paris: L'Harmattan, 1997.

Forster, G. M. "Disease etiologies in non-Western medical systems." *American Anthropologist, 78* (1976): 773–782.

Frigessi Castelnuovo, D., & Risso, M. *A mezza parete. Emigrazione, nostalgia, malattia mentale*. Turin: Einaudi, 1982.

Furnham, A., & Malik, R. "Cross-cultural beliefs about "depression." *International Journal of Social Psychiatry, 40* (No. 2, 1994): 106–123.

Gargani, A. (Ed.). *Crisi della ragione*. Turin: Einaudi, 1979 .

Garza- Guerrero, A .C. "Culture shock: Its mourning and the vicissitudes of identity." *Journal of the American Psycho-Analytical Association, 22* (No. 2, 1974).

Gbaka Zady, R. *La nostra Africa, l'avventura di crescere nel continente nero*, ed. CIDIS. Rome/Perugia: Palombi Editore, 1989.

Ginzburg, C. *Occhiacci di legno*. Milan: Feltrinelli, 1998.

Goffman, E. *Asylums. Le istituzioni totali: I meccanismi dell'esclusione e della violenza*. Turin: Einaudi, 1968.

Grappe, M. "L'action humanitaire et les camps de réfugiés." In: V. Nahoum & M. Grappe (Eds.), *Vukovar, Sarajevo . . . La guerre en ex-Yougoslavie* (pp. 243–260). Paris: Esprit, 1993.

Grinberg, L., & Grinberg, R. *Psicoanalisi dell'emigrazione e dell'esilio*. Milan: Angeli, 1990.

Gupta, S. *The Mental Health Problems of Migrants: Report from Six European Countries*. Copenhagen. WHO, 1991.

Hampâté Bâ, A. (). *Amkoullel l'enfant Peul*. Paris: Actes Sud, 1991.

Hein Alocco, E. M. (Ed.). *La moglie di Lot. Vivere in esilio*, Rome: Edizioni del lavoro, 1996 .

Held, T. "La psychanalyse allemande et la question du traumatisme réel." *Revue Française de Psychanalyse, 6* (1988): 1422.

Helman, C. G. "Psyche, soma, and society: The social construction of psychosomatic disorders." *Culture, Medicine and Psychiatry, 9* (1985): 1–26.

Hertz, D. G. "The stress of migration." In: L. Eitinger & P. Schwarz (Eds.), *Strangers in the World* (pp. 70–83). Bern: Hans Huber, 1981.

Hertz, R. *Étude sur la représentation de la mort. Sociologie religieuse et folklore*. Paris: PUF, 1928.

Hiegel, J. P., & Hiegel-Landrac, C. *Vivre et revivre au camp de Khao I Dang. Une psychiatrie humanitaire*. Paris: Fayard, 1996a.

Houseman, M. Notes sur quelques propriétés générals de la transformation initiatique. *Nouvelle Revue d'Ethnopsychiatrie, 6* (1986): 31–40.

Janigro, N. *Dizionario di un paese che scompare*. Rome: Manifestolibri, 1994.

Janovic, C. S. "Introduzione." In: V. Ja. Propp, *Edipo alla luce del folklore* (pp. vii-xviii). Turin: Einaudi, 1975.

Jarvis, C. "Schizophrenia in British immigrants: Recent findings, issues and implications." *Transcultural Psychiatry, 35* (No. 1, 1998): 85–98.

Käes, R., Faimberg, H., Enriquez, M., & Baranes, J. J. *Trasmissione della vita psichica tra generazioni.* Rome: Borla, 1995.

Katamu, M. "Approche anthropo-psychologique des maladies mentales chez les Ntomba de Bikoro." *Revue d'Ethnopsychologie, 36* (No. 213, 1981): 119–128.

Kleinman, A. *Patients and Healers in the Context of Culture: An Exploration of the Borderland between Anthropology, Medicine, and Psychiatry.* Berkeley, CA: University of California Press, 1981.

Koss, J. D. , "Somatization and somatic complaint syndromes among Hispanics: Overview and ethnopsychological perspectives." *Transcultural Psychiatric Researc Review, 27* (1990): 5–29.

Lanternari, V. (Ed.), *Medicina, magia, religione, valori, Vol. 1.* Naples: Liguori, 1994.

Lanternari, V., & Ciminelli, M. L. (Eds.). *Medicina, magia, religione, valori, Vol. 2.* Naples: Liguori, 1998 .

Latour, B. "Note sur certains objets chevelus." *Nouvelle Revue d'Ethnopsychiatrie, 27* (1994): 21–36.

La-Vaka, L. "La dynamique de la psychothérapie traditionnelle Lobala." *Revue d'Ethnopsychologie, 36* (No. 213, 1981): 105–118.

Lebovici, S. "Fantasmatic and interaction intergenerational trasmission." *Infant Mental Health, 6* (No. 1, 1988): 10–19.

Leff, J. *Psichiatria e Cultura,* ed. A. Ancora. Turin/Milan: Ed. Sonda, 1992.

Leiris, M. *La possessione e I suoi aspetti teatrali tra gli Etiopi di Gondar.* Milan: Ubulibri, 1988.

Leman, J., & Gailly, A. (Eds.). *L'interaction soignant-soigné dans un contexte multiculturel et interdisciplinaire.* Brussels: De Boeck, 1991.

Lesne C. *Cinq essais d'ethnopsychiatrie antillaise.* Paris: L'Harmattan, 1990.

Lévi-Strauss, C. *Antropologia strutturale.* Milan: il Saggiatore, 1998a.

Lévy-Strauss, C. *Totemismo oggi.* Milan: Feltrinelli, 1964.

Littlewood, R. , "Against pathology. The new psychiatry and its critics." *British Journal of Psychiatry, 159* (1991): 696–702.

Littlewood, R. "La migration des syndromes liés à la culture." *Psychopathologie Africaine, 20* (No. 1, 1984–85): 5–16.

Littlewood, R., & Lipsedge, M. *Aliens and Alienists. Ethnic Minorities in Psychiatry.* Harmondsworth: Penguin, 1982.

Lombardo, M. G. "Metafore della vita. Analisi per un progetto d'intersezione tra medicina e scienze umane del simbolismo." In:

AA.VV., *Saggi di medicina e scienze umane.* Milan: Scientific Institute of S. Raffaele Hospital, 1984.

Losi, N. "Doppio, riscatto, imbroglio: categorie per la comprensione della follia degli altri." *Rivista Italiana di Gruppoanalisi, 11* (No. 2, 1996): 129–151.

Losi, N. *Gli amici dell'acqua. Medici, pazienti e medicine alternative.* Milan: Angeli, 1990.

Losi, N. *I progetti per il futuro dei profughi della ex Jugoslavia ospiti nei centri di accoglienza in Italia.* Rome: International Organization for Migration, 1995.

Lucas, R. H., & Barret, R. "Interpreting culture and psychopathology: Primitivist themes in cross-cultural debate." *Culture, Medicine and Psychiatry, 19* (1995): 287–326.

Magris, C. *Itaca e oltre.* Milan: Garzanti, 1991.

Mauss, M. *Teoria generale della magia ed altri saggi.* Turin: Einaudi, 1965.

McGoldrick, M., Giordano J., & Pearce J. K. (Eds.). *Ethnicity and Family Therapy.* New York: Guilford Press, 1996 .

Mellina, S. *Medici e Sciamani, fratelli separati.* Rome: Lombardo Editore, 1997.

Mellor, D. H. *La comunicazione.* Bari: Dedalo, 1992.

Memel-Fotê, H. (Ed.). *Les représentations de la santé et de la maladie chez les Ivoiriens.* Paris: L'Harmattan, 1998.

Migliore, S. "Gender, emotion, and physical distress: The Sicilian–Canadian 'nerves' complex." *Culture, Medicine and Psychiatry,* 18 (1994): 271–297.

Minas, H. I., Lambert, T., Kostov, S., & Boranga, G. *Mental Health Services for Non English Speaking Background Immigrants.* Canberra: Australian Government Publishing Service, 1996.

Mirdal, G. M. "The condition of tightness: The somatic complaints of Turkish migrant women." *Acta Psychiatrica Scandinavica, 71* (1985): 287–296.

Mondella, F. "Gregory Bateson: la mente fuori dal corpo." *Sanità Scienza e Storia, 2* (1987): 35–61.

Moro, M. R. *Parents en exil, psychopatologies et migration.* Paris: PUF, 1994.

Nathan T. "Les bienfaits des thérapies sauvages. Thérapie scientifique et thérapie sauvage." *Nouvelle Revue d'Ethnopsychiatrie, 27* (1994): 37–54.

Nathan, T. *Fier de n'avoir ni pays ni amis, quelle sottise c'était . . . Principes d'ethnopsychanalyse*. Grenoble: La Pensée sauvage, 1993.

Nathan, T. La folie des autres. *Traité d'ethnopsychiatrie clinique*. Paris: Dunod, 1986.

Nathan, T. *L'influence qui guérit*. Paris: Odile Jacob, 1994.

Nathan, T. *Le Sperme du diable*. Paris: PUF, 1988.

Nathan, T., & Stengers, I. *Médecins et sorciers*. Paris: Ed. Les empêcheurs de penser en rond, 1995.

Paniagua F.A. *Assessing and Treating Culturally Diverse Clients*. London: Sage, 1998.

Pichot, P., & Nathan, T. *Quel avenir pour la psychiatrie et la psychothérapie?* Paris: Les empêcheurs de penser en rond, 1998.

Propp, V. Ja. *Edipo alla luce del folclore*. Turin: Einaudi, 1975.

Propp, V. Ja. *Morphology of the Folktale*. Bloomington, IN: Research Center, Indiana University, 1958.

Puget, J., & Käes. R. (Eds.). *Violence d'Etat et psychanalyse*. Paris: Dunod, 1989.

Racamier, P. C. *Il genio delle origini. Psicoanalisi e psicosi*. Milan: Cortina, 1993.

Rack, P. H. "Psychiatric and social problems among immigrants." *Acta Psychiatrica Scandinavica, 344* (1988): 167–173.

Radin, P. (Ed.). *Fiabe africane*. Turin: Einaudi, 1955.

Reyneri, E. *La catena migratoria*. Bologna: il Mulino, 1979.

Risso, M., & Boker, W. *Sortilegio e delirio. Psicopatologia dell'emigrazione in prospettiva transculturale*. Naples: Liguori, 1992.

Rodari, G. *La grammatica della fantasia*. Turin: Einaudi, 1979.

Rubin, G. "Fonctions structurantes et contenantes des rituels de deuil." *Revue Française de Psychanalyse, 1* (1996): 211–218.

Rwangabo, P. C. *La médicine traditionnelle au Rwanda*. Paris: ACCT-Karthala, 1993.

Sacks, W. H. "Multiple forms of stress in refugee and immigrant children." *Child and Adolescent Psychiatric Clincs of North America, 7*, (No. 1, 1998): 153–167.

Sacks, O. *Awakenings*. New York: Vintage Books, 1973.

Sayad, A. *L'immigration ou le paradoxe de l'altérité*. Brussells: De Boeck, 1990.

Schreiber, S. "Migration, traumatic bereavement and transcultural aspects of psychological healing: Loss and grief of a refugee woman from Begameder County in Ethiopia." *British Journal of Medical Psychology*, 68 (1995): 135–142.

Selvini Palazzoli, M., Cirillo, S., Selvini, M., & Sorrentino, A. M. *I giochi psicotici nella famiglia*. Milan: Cortina, 1988.

Simon, G. *Géodynamique des migrations internationales dans le monde.* Paris: PUF, 1995.

Sluzki, C. E. "Migration and family conflict." *Family Process, 18* (1979): 379–390.

Stanfield, J. H., & Dennis, R. M. (Eds.). *Race and Ethnicity in Research Methods.* London: Sage, 1993.

Stern, D. *Il mondo interpersonale del bambino.* Turin: Boringhieri, 1987.

Strehlow, T. G. H. *I sentieri del sogno*. Milan: Mimesis, 1997.

Sundquist, J. *Migration and Health.* Lund: Lund University Press, 1994.

Tabboni, S. (Ed.). *Vicinanza e lontananza. Modelli e figure dello straniero come categoria sociologica*. Milan: Angeli, 1984.

Tayeb Salih. *La stagione della migrazione a Nord.* Palermo: Sellerio, 1992.

Tchetche, G. D. *Psychiatrie en Afrique Noire et contexte socioculturel.* Paris: L'Harmattan, 1998.

Tchetche, G. D. *Thérapie familiale et contextes socioculturels en Afrique noire.* Paris: L'Harmattan, 1996.

Teitelbaum, M. S. *Les effects du développement économique sur les pressions à l'émigration dans les pays d'origine*. Paris: Osce, 1993.

Tella, A. "Les pratiques médicales traditionnelles en Afrique." *Ethnomedizine, 4* (No. 3–4, 1976–77): 229–240.

Turner, V. *Il processo rituale. Struttura e antistruttura.* Brescia: Morcelliana, 1972.

van der Veer, G. *Counseling and Therapy with Refugees: Psychological Problems of Victims of War, Torture, and Repression.* Chichester: Wiley, 1992.

Vermeulen, H., & Govers C. *The Anthropology of Ethnicity. Beyond "Ethnic Groups and Bounderies."* Amsterdam: Het Spinhuis Publishers, 1994.

Von Franz, M. L. *Le fiabe del lieto fine, psicologia delle storie di redenzione.* Como: Red, 1987.

Von Franz, M. L. *L'individuazione nella fiaba*. Turin: Boringhieri, 1987.

Watters, C. "Representations of Asians' mental health in British psychiatry." In: C. Samsan & N. South (Eds.), *The Social Construction of Social Policy* (pp. 88–105). London: MacMillan, 1996.

Winnicott, D. W. *Playing and Reality*. London: Tavistock, 1971.

Wood, M. "Revue de la littérature sur la santé mentale des migrants." *Santé, Culture, Health, 5* (No. 1, 1988): 37–92.

World Federation for Mental Health. *Uprooting and Resettlement*. London/New York, 1968.

World Health Organization. *Depressive Disorders in Different Cultures*. Geneva, 1983.

Zalokar, J. *Psychological and Psychopathological Problems of Immigrants and Refugees*. Radovljica (Slovenia): Didakta, 1994.

Zempleni, A. "Deuil et interdit dans une société 'totémique'. Un cas gouro." *Psychopathologie Africaine, 11* (No. 3, 1975): 375–394.

The following are the main journals that publish articles on ethnopsychiatry:

Culture, Medicine and Psychiatry
Nouvelle Revue d'Ethnopsychiatrie
Psychopathologie africaine
Santé, Culture, Health
Transcultural Psychiatry

INDEX